Design Concepts with Code:

A Developer Approach

Kelly Carey and Stanko Blatnik

APress Media, LLC

Design Concepts with Code: A Developer Approach
Copyright ©2003 by Kelly Carey and Stanko Blatnik
Originally published by Apress in 2003

ISBN 978-1-59059-111-6   ISBN 978-1-4302-0790-0 (eBook)
DOI 10.1007/978-1-4302-0790-0

Trademarked names may appear in this book. Rather than use a trademark symbol with every occurrence of a trademarked name, we use the names only in an editorial fashion and to the benefit of the trademark owner, with no intention of infringement of the trademark.

Technical Reviewer: Ken Oda

Assistant Publisher: Grace Wong

Project Manager: Nate McFadden

Copy Editor: Kim Wimpsett

Production Manager: Kari Brooks

Compositor and Proofreader: Kinetic Publishing Services, LLC

Indexer: Bill Johncocks

Cover and Interior Designer: Kurt Krames

Manufacturing Manager: Tom Debolski

In the United States: phone 1-800-SPRINGER, email orders@springer-ny.com, or visit http://www.springer-ny.com. Outside the United States: fax +49 6221 345229, email orders@springer.de, or visit http://www.springer.de.

For information on translations, please contact Apress directly at 2560 Ninth Street, Suite 219, Berkeley, CA 94710. Phone 510-549-5930, fax 510-549-5939, email info@apress.com, or visit http://www.apress.com.

To Donette Dake
Friend, mentor, innovative teacher, and retiring dean of
career education and workforce development at West
Valley College in Saratoga, California.
                                        —Kelly Carey

To Emil Coffou, who taught me code and debugging.
And to Ismet Mujezinović, Bosnian painter, who
introduced me to the world of art.
                                        —Stanko Blatnik

Contents at a Glance

Contents

About the Authors

 **Kelly Carey** teaches Internet services courses at West Valley College, a community college in California. Code-related topics Kelly teaches include XML technologies, SVG, XHTML/CSS, PHP/mySQL, and graphics topics including how to create and review a digital portfolio and how to build a commercial Web site project. Kelly has a doctorate degree in education from the University of San Francisco, and her dissertation topic involved the language, space, and ontology of the Internet. Her understanding of code, design, and critical hermeneutics has led to speaking at several international conferences.

 **Stanko Blatnik** teaches online courses for the University of Sarajevo on XML technologies, SVG, and process control. He also directs a nonprofit institute in Velenje, Slovenia: the Institute for Symbolic Analysis and Development of Information Technologies. In addition, Stanko writes about topics such as Balkan and European beaurocracy, patents and new technologies, and the hydrogen economy for journals in Slovenia. A physicist by trade, Stanko spent 15 years teaching and administering at the University of Tuzla, in Tuzla, Bosnia-Herzegovina. Stanko has a doctorate degree in theoretical particle physics from the University of Zagreb in the former Yugoslavia. Above all, however, Stanko is a swimmer.

About the Technical Reviewer

Ken Oda began his digital persona with a 12MHz Intel 80286 and a DOS command line. He lives and works in Silicon Valley and, in his spare time, enjoys working with Flash animation and teaching his four-year-old nephew the finer points of life.

Acknowledgments

```
<acknowledgments>
  <apress>
```
Simon Hayes, marketing director and assistant editorial director

Jim Sumser, editorial director

Nate McFadden, project manager

Ken Oda, technical reviewer

Kim Wimpsett, copy editor

Kari Brooks, production manager

Beth Christmas, editorial coordinator

Hollie Fischer, product manager

Doris Wong, product manager

Wanshun Tam, system administrator and Webmaster

Kurt Krames, designer

Kinetic Publishing Services, LLC, compositor

Thistle Hill Publishing Services, proofreader
```
  </apress>
  <clients class="alphabetical">
```
Enver Budnjo, Jure Lodrant, and Damijan Onižak, Air Quality Monitoring System, Artes

Greg Mainis, Simplified Software (www.simplifiedsoftware.net)

Jean McIntosh, SItalk (www.sitalk.info)

Praxis Development, Open-Source Portal (www.praxis.ws)

Anna Quirk, IPSE

Jeff Rascov, EyeStockArt

West Valley College, Converging Technologies Center (www.convergingtech.org)
```
  </clients>
  <designers class="alphabetical">
```
Steve Contreras (www.contreras.tv)

Jean McIntosh (www.jrmacks.com)

Hye Park (www.hyeparkdesign.com)
```
  </designers>
  <developer id="thankYou">
```
Rouslan Kadyrov, visiting scientist at the Institute for Symbolic Analysis and Development of Information Technologies, for double-checking code and developing the code for the Chapter 8 Web-safe color palette. And for working with Stanko on several other projects.

Davor Dolenčič for SVG ideas.
```
  </developer>
```

ACKNOWLEDGMENTS

```
<familyFriends>
```
John Focht and Manuel Jimenez for letting us use your computers, connection,
   house, food, and money

Olga Blatnik for workspace, a sleeping place, food, and your company

Rudi Leskošek for beer, BBQ, and important conversation
```
</familyFriends>
</acknowledgments>
```

Introduction

```
<preface>
  <purpose>
```
Good design sells products. Good design invites users to return. *Design Concepts with Code: A Developer Approach* understands that developers aren't particularly interested in learning graphics applications or reading a treatise on design. The book offers clear and concise design concepts, examples, and projects to support developer proficiency with design in a short time.
```
  </purpose>
  <targetAudience>
```
The target audience is Web developers looking to improve the design and navigation of Web sites and Web-based applications using code. Product managers and project managers who want to understand what works and what doesn't work when developing project prototypes and final site designs will also find this book useful. Finally, this book will help freelance Web designers/producers/developers transitioning from application-based sites to code-based projects.
```
  </targetAudience>
  <bookOrganization>
```
Each chapter begins with a design concept, offers examples graphically and with code, and ends with a set of design axioms to consider on your next project. Chapters 3, 6, 9, and 10 present the graphics and code from projects developed as a result of the ideas presented in the concept chapters.

The order of the chapters follows the design process of typical projects. The text, read from beginning to end, provides a good overview of project design. Read out of order, the text provides a focused approach to specific design issues in which you're interested. Design fundamentals and axioms don't change over time. The book is a resource for later questions and ideas you may have.
```
  </bookOrganization>
  </bookCode>
```
If you want to follow along with the book's examples, you can find all the source code in the Downloads section of the Apress Web site (www.apress.com). Additionally, you can find a continuation of the book's ideas and projects at www.praxis.ws/design.

 NOTE In some cases, one line of code has been split into two lines of text because of the layout of the book. Should you return an object error, it is because Enter (a line break) is keyed where it shouldn't be for the code to run correctly. Please visit www.apress.com or www.praxis.ws/design for access to the actual code.

```
  </bookCode>
</preface>
```

Introducing Interface Design

What is ultimately important in the text and in the work of art in general is not the object which it depicts but the world that it generates.

—Paul Ricoeur in an interview to Charles E. Reagan[1]

The way we have traditionally communicated for thousands of years, through spoken and written text, is changing. In spoken and written text, communicative roles usually follow the pattern of speaker and hearer or of author and reader. The Internet provides a living, interactive text where interaction between the author and the reader transforms communication from the physical sending and receiving of data to the building of relationships and expanding of new horizons. Online, meaning and understanding take place in a model not pre-determined by the speaker or author.

Your role as a developer is to combine the design of style and the functionality of code to enable a relationship to build between the client and the user. A *client* is the company or organization you work for or contract with to build the Web site or Web-based application. A *user* is the current, past, and potential users of the client's product. Web-based products that look good but don't work well bring in users once to look and a second time to explore, get lost, and then give up. Products that work well but look bad never capture the audience their functionality supports.

The best interface is so simple and clear that the user isn't aware of its existence. When you make a phone call, do you think of the keypad design or are you intent on the conversation? When reading email, can you almost "hear" the voice of the person who sent the mail? Whether you're talking on the phone or working in email, your primary area of interest is the relationship.

---

1.   *Paul Ricoeur: His Life and Work* by Charles E. Reagan (University of Chicago Press, 1996)

Most likely, you're already knowledgeable in the areas of user analysis, human-computer interaction, and requirements specifications. This chapter describes how to utilize the data available in user analysis reports and requirements documents for designing and implementing visual products that meet client and user expectations.

Users don't want to look at a Web site; they want to do something with it. The days of Web pages are over; Web-based products and applications that allow users to interact and control meet current user expectations. Web sites that are more complex require markup languages with data manipulation capabilities such as Extensible Markup Language (XML) and, in some cases, Extensible Hypertext Markup Language (XHTML). However, these complex sites create style issues with browsers for several reasons:

- Sliced images from Photoshop/ImageReady can vary in positioning between browser versions, resulting in small gaps in the layout.

- Sliced graphics combined with XHTML and HTML (from editors such as Dreamweaver and GoLive) aren't always well-formed and are rarely validated, thus limiting data modification possibilities.

- Incorporated layouts and graphics that were not, at the outset, modelled to output with Extensible Stylesheet Language Transformation (XSLT) or even Cascading Style Sheets (CSS) create several debugging problems.

- Validation tools seem to vary from month to month in determining which CSS properties are supported.

- Learning and keeping current with various graphics applications is typically not of interest to developers.

These and other issues—including the wait for Extensible Stylesheet Language: Formatting Objects (XSL-FO) to be uniformly supported (outside of creating Portable Document Format, or PDF, files)—bring developers more and more into the design process.

Because a bad interface can't communicate the benefits of a product to the user, a better interface must be created. If a product is more complex than a typical Web site, developers may need to code both the design and the functionality; few designers code beyond CSS. Good designers remain a critical part of the process; their layouts are always a little better. Design decisions related to how a product works, however, move closer to the developer's responsibility as the implementation of design becomes more complex in Web-based applications.

User Analysis: On the Way to Design

Making the most of user analysis clarifies and simplifies interface design. User analysis typically begins with the following:

- The purpose of the product
- The audience for the product
- The user goals

The first rule of transforming user analysis data to good interface design is to forget about the computer. Don't start by thinking about which tools to use, what your color choice is, which graphics to select, or how many buttons to create until you or your team talk with the client and with potential product users.

User expectations of a Web-based product aren't much different from their expectations of traditional products. Your job is to discern, from the data, what the user priorities are and to apply those priorities to modelling, designing, and developing a product. Follow these guidelines:

Do ask the client if you should incorporate an existing logo, concept, or color scheme into the Web-based product.

Do ask the client if there's an existing product or site they like. This site shouldn't guide your design; however, it can give you an idea of the client's preference of conceptual ideas such as the use of space.

Don't ask the client what they want the site to look like, how many buttons they want, what the buttons should say, or how they want the navigation set up. You're inviting delays if the client gets too involved in the design in the same way that you probably hesitate to give a client your code, schema, or Document Type Definition (DTD) to review.

Do ask for stakeholder feedback at the prototype stage. Redesign can be as expensive and time consuming as recoding. A *stakeholder* is all the people working for or associated with the client who have a stake (a vote) in the decision-making process. Stakeholders on some projects have different goals. For example, a director of sales may see the purpose of the project differently than a director of technical support. All stakeholders need to sign off on the design to reduce the risk of time-consuming redesign and recoding.

Do adjust the selected prototype to better serve the user.

At the beginning of the design process, clients like to talk about layout, type, and color ideas given to them from a relative, a magazine article, or a popular Web site. A "too-many-cooks-in-the-kitchen" approach to design muddles things up even more than it does with code. Clients feel more comfortable talking about how they think something should look rather than how its code should function.

Clients like to have conversations about who they are and what they offer. Be open to discussing how the company and project got started—many people want to share their stories with you. Watch for what's important to the speaker. Listen for priorities, hopes, and disappointments. These verbal cues signal how the client views the world, what the story will be, and what you shouldn't pursue. Trust yourself. Language is critical at this stage; determining shapes and space is more of a matching process than you may think. Getting the words right sets the context for self-driven design. The following seven questions offer ideas for talking with clients:

- How would you describe the strengths of the company?

- What are some great things about your product(s)?

- What are your hopes for how customers understand and appreciate your company and your product(s)?

- If your company and product(s) revolutionize the market, what will people understand about what you offer?

- When in conversation within your company, do you compare yourselves or your products with other great inventions, innovations, or accomplishments?

- If you could sit down, for five minutes, with each of your customers, what would you say that helps them get to know and appreciate you, your company, and your product(s)?

- What three or four words would you use to describe how you want your family, friends, and the community to view your company and your product(s)?

 TIP Keep in mind that these aren't interview questions. You won't get a good response with written or spoken surveys. In other words, engage in conversation.

As people, it seems we're always in conversation about films, sports, politics, art, technology, or the weather. We have opinions, ideas, and complaints, and we love to share them. Think of conversations you recently participated in regarding the economy, the media, or a recent event. It's likely that much of what you said includes what you think, hear, know, wonder, hope, hate, or don't understand at all. This respectful, yet casual, approach to conversation with users works well in user analysis and interface design. You're not selling anything; you simply want to know what they think, what they need, and what they hope to accomplish in the relationship with your client. Although we all tend to think of ourselves as individuals, you'll find there is a pattern to user responses. Out of 10 users, seven are so similar that descriptive words are easy to capture and categorize. The following are a few questions to help you get started:

- What kinds of things do you want to know about our product or company?

- What could we do well to keep you coming back to our company to make you a loyal customer?

- What do we do well now? What do we do poorly now?

- Describe an ideal purchase or project with our company.

- How would you describe our company and products, as you currently understand us?

- What two or three things can we offer you that would really help you to succeed or to save time? What do we offer that has value for you?

 TIP Be ready for good and bad news about your client. Both help you prepare to visually present the client's identity the way users anticipate.

Moving from Language to Initial Sketches

The words you hear in conversation translate from client and user expectations to initial sketches. In conversation with users, note the priorities of the purpose, audience, and goals of the product. In addition, note the specific language used to describe the "look and feel" of the site. If possible, record conversations with potential users and play them back as you begin the design process. If there's no available transcript, locate five or six potential users for the product. People you know who fit the user profile can help in this capacity if actual or potential users aren't available. Conversations centered on how users want to access information, what their priorities are for the product, and how they use the product produce adjectives that reduce design time.

No one outside of the development team sees the initial sketches you develop as a result of interpreting and understanding the needs and expectations of the client and users. As such, don't spend time making them anything other than shapes and notes to yourself. You can lose too much time in concern, frustration, or embarrassment over how the drawings look.

Do not skip the sketch step in the design process; moving directly to the keyboard and screen results in an important missed element of the communication process. Probably more than most people in this industry, you know that the simple things created with a pencil and paper can be the most complex to implement with code. Sketches can help you identify and play with shapes that directly connect the client and the user.

If you pass the sketch process and go directly to the computer, it's tempting to design a slightly different version of the standard top and left bar design (see Figure 1-1).

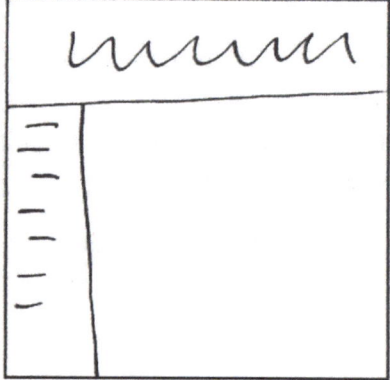

FIGURE 1-1 *A sketch of a standard design*

If, however, you take the time to sketch, how often does your best idea of shape look like Figure 1-1? Imagine you're talking with a client excited about their company or product. The purpose of the site is to communicate the story of their organization and the benefits of their products. They have poured their ideas, time, and money into the project. Is this the best design? It may be in some cases, but it's probably not for the millions of sites where you see it now.

There are times when the traditional layout of Figure 1-1 works best. For example, say you build a page for a poison control center. Users at this site are, many times, in a hurry to find a specific piece of information. A site that needs a plug-in or that requires two or three clicks to find out what to do in the event of a poisoning has no place here. A traditional layout is perfect when the client needs "familiar, comfortable, safe, secure, fast access to data."

Your experience with code enhances your ability to deliver good design. Listening to user language, creating initial sketches, and building small examples of the sketches in code allows you to maneuver between concept and implementation. Your approach should be to gather the language, complete a few sketches, key the code, and then look back to the language for code adjustments that better clarify your intent. This three-step process allows you to access the ideas you envision and the browser issues you'll encounter. Imagine spending a week on sketches only to have positioning problems with CSS. Imagine creating an image in an application only to have it display poorly on the screen. Your willingness to work back and forth between language, sketches, and code supports quick variations, multiple versions, and better design.

Getting Initial Sketch Ideas

In this book, you'll see several sketches accompanying suggested Scalable Vector Graphics (SVG) code. This process saves time and frustration. The drawing process accesses one part of the brain, and keying code to represent that sketch accesses another. Ideas evolve in coding that fine-tune the original sketch. Simple sketches, simple code, and an understanding of how the two can result in a design that meets client and user needs always works.

For example, which of the adjectives in Figure 1-2 best "fit" with its sketch?

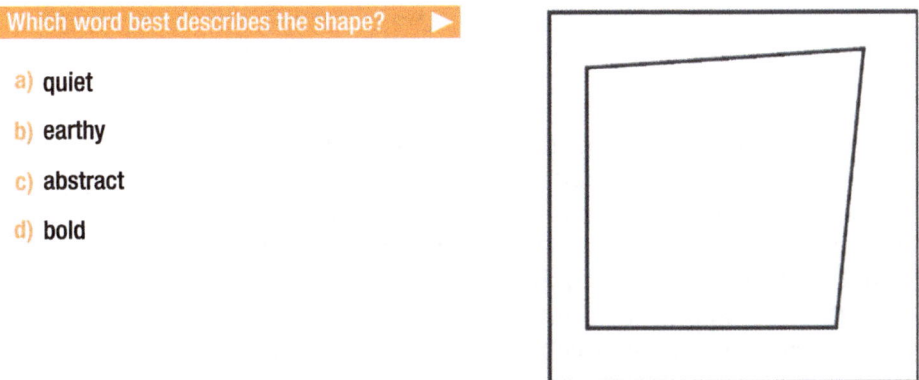

Which word best describes the shape? ▶

a) quiet

b) earthy

c) abstract

d) bold

FIGURE 1-2 *Adjectives and shapes*

Your first impression of the shape in Figure 1-2 was probably more *abstract* or *bold* than *quiet* or *earthy*. Your first impressions of a shape don't come from studying design; they connect your mind, eyes, and memory to familiar objects for an immediate interpretation. (Chapter 4 describes how simple shapes reflect the personality of a company or a product.) Listing 1-1 generates the Figure 1-2 shape.

LISTING 1-1 *An Abstract, Bold Shape*

```
<?xml version='1.0'?>
<svg width="250" height="250">
<rect x="50" y="50" width="200" height="200"
style="fill:none; stroke:black; stroke-width:2;" />
<polygon points="70 80,70 220,205 220,220 70"
style="fill:none; stroke:black; stroke-width:2" />
</svg>
```

The shape in Figure 1-3 more closely resembles available Web pages. How does your impression change with this shape?

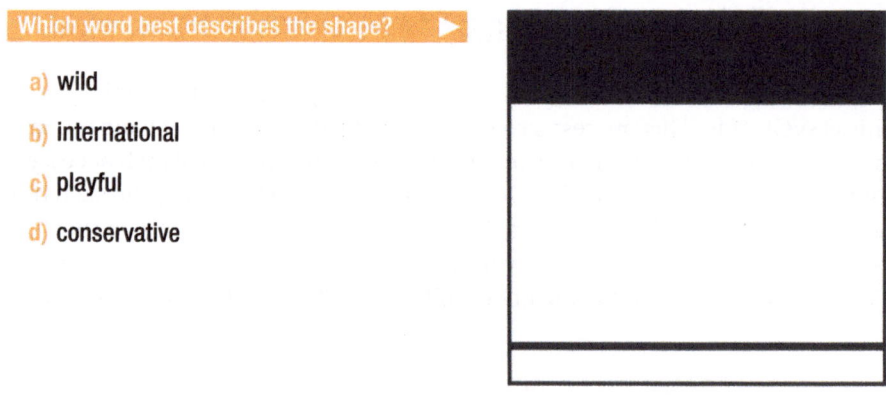

Which word best describes the shape? ▶

a) **wild**

b) **international**

c) **playful**

d) **conservative**

FIGURE 1-3 *A familiar shape*

Conservative best describes the Figure 1-3 shape yet millions of sites use this approach for products that want to be viewed as *wild, international,* or *playful.* The shapes seem so solid they look cemented in place. It's difficult to begin with this layout and make it interesting. Some have tried to throw in color or lighten the look with good graphics. If you're absolutely stuck with this as the only design option the client wants, either run in the opposite direction or focus all of your energy on creating interesting content. Listing 1-2 generates the Figure 1-3 shape.

LISTING 1-2 *A Conservative Shape*

```
<?xml version='1.0'?>
<svg width="300" height="300">
<rect x="50" y="50" width="200" height="200"
style="fill:none; stroke:black; stroke-width:2;" />
<line x1="50" y1="230" x2="250" y2="230" style="stroke:black; stroke-width:4;" />
<rect x="50" y="50" width="200" height="50" style="fill:black;" />
</svg>
```

The shape of Figure 1-4 starts taking risks. Does your impression of this shape vary slightly or significantly in comparison with Figure 1-3?

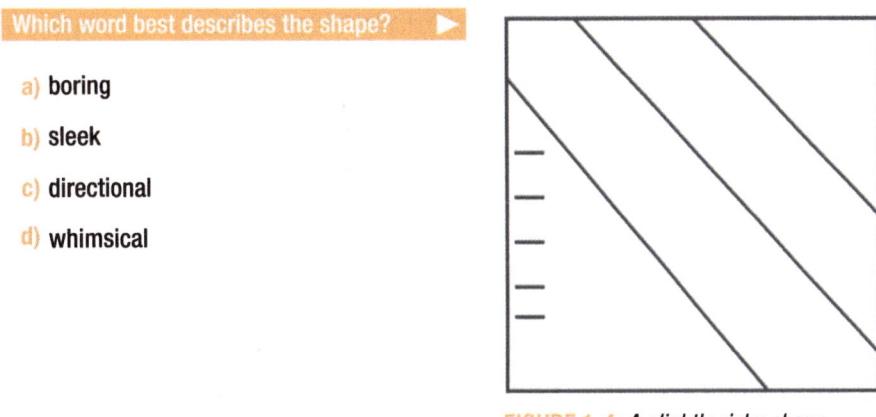

Which word best describes the shape? ▶

a) boring

b) sleek

c) directional

d) whimsical

FIGURE 1-4 *A slightly risky shape*

The angled lines of Figure 1-4 imply the word *directional.* With color and texture, the site may present the word *sleek,* as well. Variations of the code include stroke-width or line placement. Changes in button shape or position convey an organized or *whimsical* approach to its *directional* nature. Listing 1-3 generates the Figure 1-4 shape.

LISTING 1-3 *A Directional Shape*

```
<?xml version='1.0'?>
<svg width="300" height="300">
<rect x="50" y="50" width="200" height="200"
style="fill:none; stroke:black; stroke-width:2;" />
<line x1="50" y1="82" x2="190" y2="250" style="stroke:black; stroke-width:2;" />
<line x1="86" y1="50" x2="250" y2="230" style="stroke:black; stroke-width:2;" />
<line x1="150" y1="50" x2="250" y2="156" style="stroke:black; stroke-width:2;" />
<line x1="54" y1="122" x2="70" y2="122" style="stroke:black; stroke-width:2;" />
<line x1="54" y1="146" x2="70" y2="146" style="stroke:black; stroke-width:2;" />
<line x1="54" y1="170" x2="70" y2="170" style="stroke:black; stroke-width:2;" />
<line x1="54" y1="194" x2="70" y2="194" style="stroke:black; stroke-width:2;" />
<line x1="54" y1="210" x2="70" y2="210" style="stroke:black; stroke-width:2;" />
</svg>
```

The shape of Figure 1-5 moves away from most developers' understanding of Web design and starts to become a shape that conveys something other than simply "this is a Web page." Do you see how this may evolve into a Web layout?

Which word best describes the shape? ▶

a) geometric

b) avant-garde

c) quiet

d) humorous

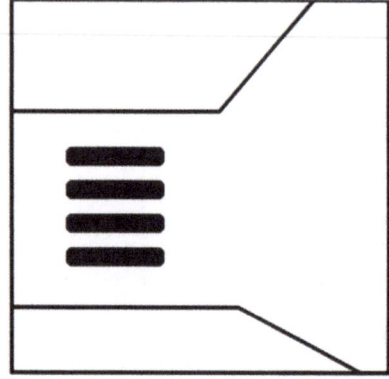

FIGURE 1-5 *An unusual shape*

Avant-garde best describes the Figure 1-5 shape. The shape can easily transform to *geometric*, especially if the angular lines are reduced to a slightly more conservative approach with repetitive rectangles. Interestingly, at the outset of a job, many clients use words such as *unique* and *avant-garde* to describe how they envision their site. Typically, unless the client is a conceptual artist or haute couture designer, what they really want is something different from the typical sites that blanket the Web. Listing 1-4 generates the Figure 1-5 shape.

LISTING 1-4 *An Avant-Garde Shape*

```
<?xml version='1.0'?>
<svg width="300" height="300">
<rect x="50" y="50" width="200" height="200"
style="fill:none; stroke:black; stroke-width:2;" />
<rect x="80" y="130" width="50" height="8" rx="2" ry="2"
style="fill:black; stroke:black; stroke-width:2;" />
<rect x="80" y="148" width="50" height="8" rx="2" ry="2"
style="fill:black; stroke:black; stroke-width:2;" />
<rect x="80" y="166" width="50" height="8" rx="2" ry="2"
style="fill:black; stroke:black; stroke-width:2;" />
<rect x="80" y="184" width="50" height="8" rx="2" ry="2"
style="fill:black; stroke:black; stroke-width:2;" />
<polyline points="50 110,160 110,210 50"
style="fill:none; stroke:black; stroke-width:2;" />
<polyline points="50 215,170 215,235 250"
style="fill:none; stroke:black; stroke-width:2;" />
</svg>
```

Listing 1-4 contains rectangular shapes and a couple of lines. Changing the buttons to circles or changing the positioning and degrees of the angles completely alters the design. Adjustments to the stroke-width either emphasize or downplay the background shape.

The shape in Figure 1-6 looks nothing like a typical Web layout. Sometimes a company product or logo demands a completely different approach to Web site design. Figure 1-5's *geometric* adjective has no relevance to Figure 1-6. A different shape completely changes the perspective and interaction of the user with the product.

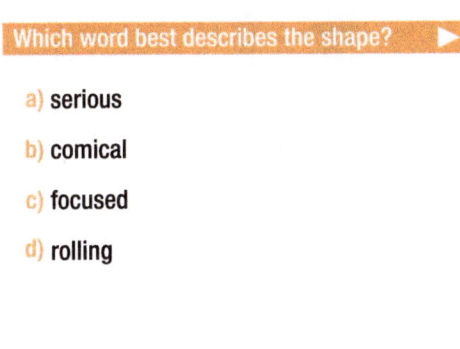

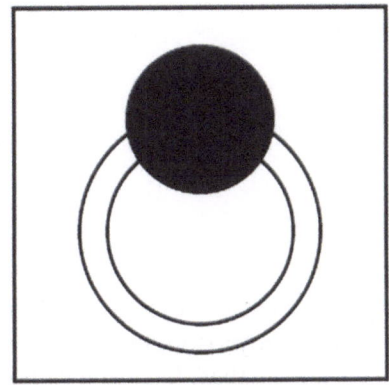

FIGURE 1-6 *A product-driven shape*

Comical or *rolling* describes the Figure 1-6 shape, depending on the color and tilt balance of the two circles. Listing 1-5 generates the Figure 1-6 shape. Try moving the circle around or changing its size. Try enlarging the diameter of the circle and lightening its weight. This design can work as an icon, as a background element, or in a set of shapes with different angles.

LISTING 1-5 *A Comical or Rolling Shape*

```
<?xml version='1.0'?>
<svg width="300" height="300">
<rect x="50" y="50" width="200" height="200"
style="fill:none; stroke:black; stroke-width:2;" />
<circle cx="150" cy="110" r="40" style="fill:black;" />
<circle cx="150" cy="170" r="65" style="fill:none; stroke:black;
stroke-width:2;" />
<circle cx="150" cy="170" r="50" style="fill:none; stroke:black;
stroke-width:2;" />
</svg>
```

The shape in Figure 1-7 utilizes rectangles in a less conservative manner. At first glance, does it appear the shape is stable, or do you think it's about to tip over?

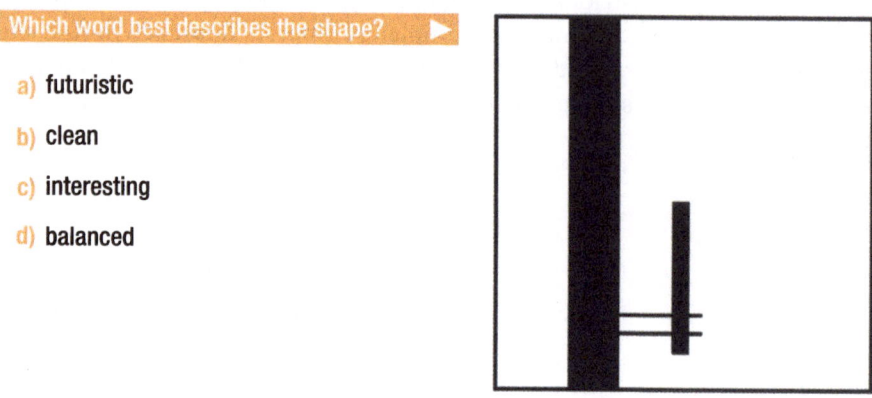

Which word best describes the shape? ▶

a) futuristic

b) clean

c) interesting

d) balanced

FIGURE 1-7 *Using rectangles as lines*

Figure 1-7 can be described as *futuristic, clean,* and *interesting.* If the shapes don't appear ready to topple to one side, then your impression is that the shapes are balanced. Design that's balanced without being glued in place is interesting. If the column on the left was duplicated on the right, no one would notice what you're trying to say. Designs that are so balanced they don't catch the eye are boring, and users tend to gloss over them. Listing 1-6 generates the Figure 1-7 shape.

LISTING 1-6 *A Futuristic, Clean, and Interesting Shape*

```
<?xml version='1.0'?>
<svg width="300" height="300">
<rect x="50" y="50" width="200" height="200"
style="fill:none; stroke:black; stroke-width:2;" />
<rect x="90" y="50" width="25" height="200"
style="fill:black; stroke:black; stroke-width:2;" />
<rect x="145" y="150" width="7" height="80"
style="fill:black; stroke:black; stroke-width:2;" />
<line x1="115" y1="220" x2="160" y2="220" style="stroke:black; stroke-width:2;" />
<line x1="115" y1="210" x2="160" y2="210" style="stroke:black; stroke-width:2;" />
</svg>
```

Playing with line density, line placement, and the small bridge between the shapes results in a different perspective for this design. The most interesting element in the sketch, however, is the space. Do you see how well it supports the shapes?

Interpreting Initial Sketch Shapes

Creating sketches takes a little practice. After a few minutes, however, you realize it's interesting and fun to design with such a simple, quick approach. You may draw 30 or more sketches before you select two with which you can work. Each sketch takes only one or two minutes to draw. Furthermore, design doesn't necessarily have to take place in an art studio. The edge of a computer desk, a little paper, a ruler, a pencil, and a felt pen results in several ideas in a short time. Of course, that's not to say sitting in a park with a portable easel and looking at a pond of ducks is a bad thing for design. The point is that drawing shapes and lines that represent words somehow directly connects your presentation to the user. The interaction that results has been studied for years. How do people interpret design? What do they think of, experience, remember, and bring to an exploration of your product?

Start with a sketch as though it's a personal letter to your client's customer. Which sketch in Figure 1-8 conveys a conceptual layout for the words *earthly, natural,* and *holistic*?

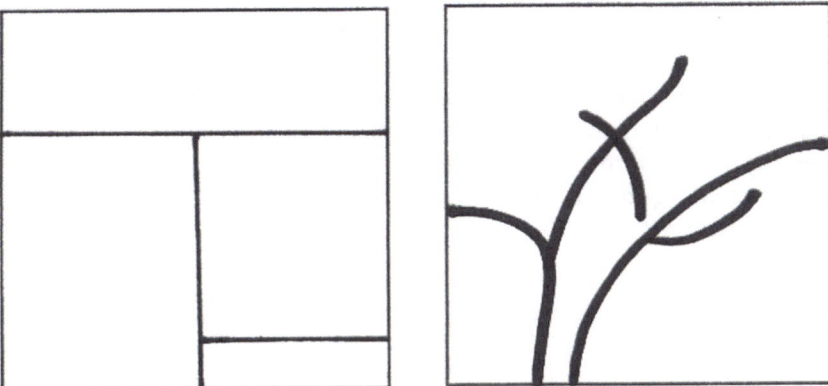

FIGURE 1-8 *Which sketch conveys the words* earthly, natural, *and* holistic?

The sketch on the left is a simple division of space with a top bar. Splitting a screen in half typically results in a static design. This attempt to change the height of the top bar and to split one side demonstrates a slight variation of a traditional layout. On the other hand, the sketch on the right is reminiscent of a tree. Curvilinear lines often represent the natural world.

Which sketch in Figure 1-9 conveys a conceptual layout for the words *familiar, modern,* and *smooth*?

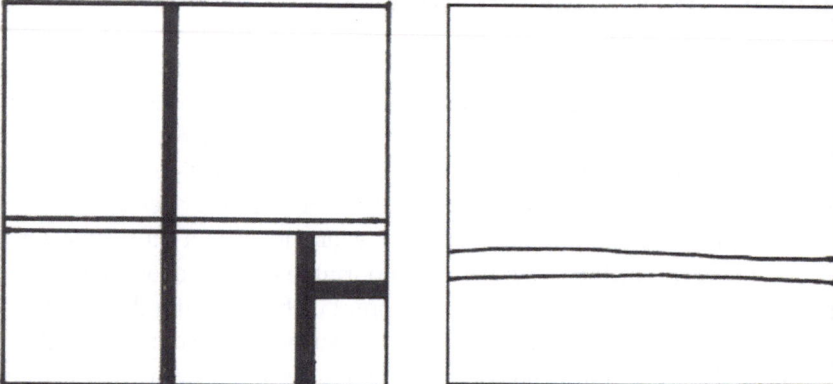

FIGURE 1-9 *Which sketch conveys the words* familiar, modern, *and* smooth*?*

The left sketch in Figure 1-9 is reminiscent of artist Piet Mondrian's *Composition with Blue and Yellow* (1932). The right sketch in Figure 1-9 is reminiscent of a simple horizon sketch from any beginning drawing class. Either one may or may not be *familiar*; however, one is more *modern*. What about *smooth*? Some words have multiple meanings. Is the word *smooth*, in this context, smooth to the touch or smooth as in sophisticated, classy, and unique? The sketch on the left is a better fit for the combination of words *familiar*, *modern*, and *smooth*. Be careful to not base your sketch on only one word that can be interpreted in multiple ways, especially by an international audience.

Which sketch in Figure 1-10 conveys a conceptual layout for the words *fast, changing,* and *technical*?

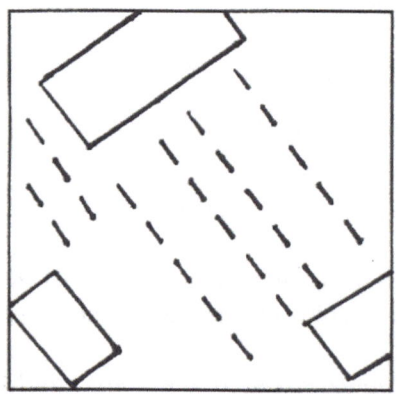 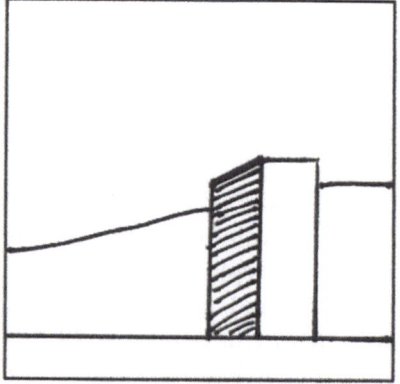

FIGURE 1-10 *Which sketch conveys the words* fast, changing, *and* technical*?*

The sketch on the left of Figure 1-10 intends to remind you of traffic moving between buildings. In contrast, the sketch on the right represents an office building that stands in one place for a long time. The hill in the background has been there even longer. Both sketches speak of technology, but the sketch on the left better communicates *fast* and *changing*.

Which sketch in Figure 1-11 conveys a conceptual layout for the words *global*, *cultural*, and *flexible*?

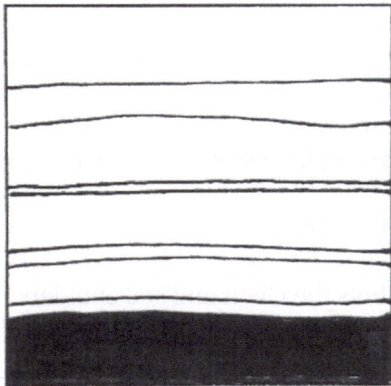

FIGURE 1-11   *Which sketch conveys the words* global, cultural, *and* flexible*?*

The sketch on the left of Figure 1-11 is a variation of horizon lines with a possibly of the sea on the bottom. Sketches such as this typically don't end up looking like the sea and the sky; these shapes often quietly convey a horizon with final colors and use density or the placement of lines to communicate an environmental metaphor. The sketch on the right could be a close-up of a tree. A cross-like figure often represents something inner or spiritual. Here, the curvilinear shape also conveys a natural simplicity. Both may work to communicate the words *global*, *cultural*, and *flexible*, but the one on the right probably conveys the client's story better. It's common to have more than one design to work with at this stage. As you move closer to layout, a final decision may hinge on which design works best with the addition of site content.

Transitioning Initial Sketches to Layout Sketches

Capturing the language of the client and user and then translating the meaning of their words into shapes also allows you to build conceptual diagrams for eventual layouts. In other words, start with language and create a shape. When the shapes evolve to a visual representation of the client and user language, start thinking about how the shapes can combine, with space, to form a layout for your site. You can use shapes as icons or as background. The term *layout* implies the design of the page including shapes, lines, space, and content.

It's interesting how people tend to understand themselves differently from the way others view them and how they believe a design layout does or does not tell their story. For example, you may assume that members of a technical organization want their site designed with red, black, and chrome colors and linear, geometric shapes. In conversation, however, you learn that the members realize outsiders may stereotype them as linear thinkers, but within the organization they see themselves differently and, as such, want the site to promote their association's self-image of warm, welcoming, and inviting.

Do red, black, and chrome colors and linear, geometric shapes translate to the words *warm*, *welcoming*, and *inviting*? No.

Once you understand how the client hopes to build a relationship with the user and what the user expects in return, you can begin to sketch your shapes as the theme for your layout.

Flexible steps of this process include the following:

1. Select four or five words that best describe how the client and stakeholders see themselves and how they want to communicate their story, mission, and plans to users. These four or five words are a little different from the language you collected for your initial sketch shapes. At this point, you're determining how you can meet the stakeholders' goals with your layout. Examples include an *aggressive law firm*, a *fun kids' center*, or a *sexy lingerie shop*.

2. Select four or five words from users who communicate what their expectations are from the client. Again, this is different from the words you used to create your initial shapes. In this case, words help in developing the navigation portion of a site layout. For example, clients often like to see an About Us button as a primary navigation option. Users, however, typically want to access products and at some point later they may want to know more about the company. The About Us button may be primary for the stakeholder, but it's of secondary importance for the user.

3. Remember to not limit these words to an online environment. Typically, client and user needs and expectations are the same in an online relationship as they are in a face-to-face relationship. Users often describe their interaction with products and the client using geographic terms such as *department*, *aisle*, *section*, *home*, and *area*. These words help you determine how to structure the layout and navigation of a site.

4. Often, it can be constructive to have the client tell you a couple of stories about their most significant accomplishments. Truer words seem to come out of this type of conversation.

5. Look for a pattern in the words. Some may be similar. Some may convey ideas that remind you of something such as the sea, a mountain, a quiet place, a festive occasion, and so on. These metaphors can help you to later determine layout details such as space and color (explained in Chapters 4 and 8).

Evolving Layout Sketches

These ideas then allow you to transition from your initial sketches toward layout. The next group of sketches begins to look more like the conceptual idea of a Web page. Keep in mind that you need space for content. At the outset, however, think about what you want to communicate. Find one or two potential concepts that support your language and then think about how you might begin to incorporate content and space. This process results in working toward a layout that supports your entire process up to this point.

Does Figure 1-12 communicate *warm*, *welcoming*, and *inviting* for the technical organization?

FIGURE 1-12 *A shape and language match?*

If Figure 1-12 doesn't communicate *warm*, *welcoming*, and *inviting*, why does it represent the majority of available pages on the Web? Listing 1-7 generates the Figure 1-12 shape.

LISTING 1-7 *Same Ol' Shape*

```
<?xml version='1.0'?>
<svg width="300" height="300">
<rect x="50" y="50" width="200" height="200" style="fill:none; stroke:black;
stroke-width:2;" />
<rect x="50" y="50" width="200" height="40" style="fill:black;" />
<rect x="50" y="90" width="40" height="160" style="fill:black;" />
</svg>
```

Getting rid of one of the rectangles in this code begins to open things up. Replacing the block with simple shapes and lines lightens things up even more.

Basic shapes can communicate interesting layout ideas. Figure 1-13 speaks of an international flag-like shape. The shapes begin a concept that may be realized as an overall layout, as a small logo, or as visual cues throughout the site. The audience for this shape can range from a governmental travel advisory site to a Ché Guevara manifesto.

FIGURE 1-13 *A flag-like shape*

Layout sketches represent possible concepts to be incorporated at varying levels of size and significance. A final decision isn't made until later in the process. It's important to try any kind of sketch that helps you to see how the story may or may not be effectively told to users. The total work involved in 20 layout sketches you throw away is only an hour. The purpose of 20 unusable sketches is to clear uncertainty from your mind and help you begin to see the possibilities in the sketches you choose to keep.

Listing 1-8 generates the Figure 1-13 shape. Try moving the shapes around to suggest different layout options.

LISTING 1-8 *An International Shape*

```
<?xml version='1.0'?>
<svg width="300" height="300">
<rect x="50" y="50" width="200" height="200" style="fill:none; stroke:black;
stroke-width:2;" />
<rect x="130" y="130" width="40" height="120" style="fill:black; stroke:black;
stroke-width:2;" />
<rect x="50" y="90" width="200" height="40" style="fill:black; stroke:black;
stroke-width:2;" />
</svg>
```

A simple use of a line can take a concept from words such as *flag-like* or *bal-anced* to completely different words such as *sexy* or *voluptuous* with two strokes of a pen, as in Figure 1-14.

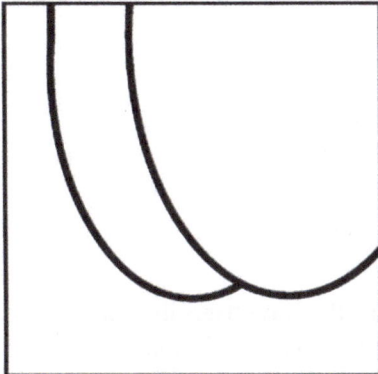

FIGURE 1-14 *Natural, full shapes*

How does Figure 1-14 communicate differently with curved lines than with geometric rectangles? Listing 1-9 generates the Figure 1-14 shape.

LISTING 1-9 *A Voluptuous Shape*

```
<?xml version='1.0'?>
<svg width="300" height="300">
<rect x="50" y="50" width="200" height="200" style="fill:none; stroke:black;
stroke-width:2;" />
<path d="M 75,50 L75,70 A 75,125 0  0 0 177,200" style="stroke:black; fill:none;
stroke-width:4;" />
<path d="M 117,50 A 85,140 0  0 0 250,182" style="stroke:black; fill:none;
stroke-width:4;" />
</svg>
```

Patterns of curved lines communicate differently than single or paired lines. Repetition adds depth, density, and an awareness of space. Moving the paths of the Figure 1-14 code or increasing the stroke-width changes the volume of the design. The repetitive lines of Figure 1-15, with less of an angular curve, convey volume but at a different level than those in Figure 1-14. Figure 1-15 creates space and bars that seem tangible and yet not as full as in Figure 1-14.

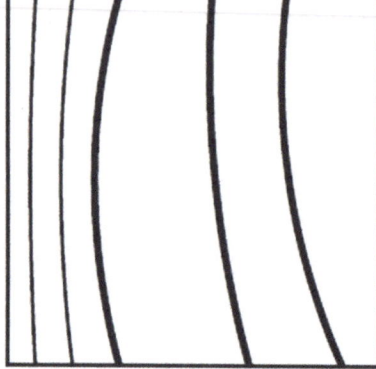

FIGURE 1-15 *Patterns of lines*

Repetition and repetition with variation change the ways users interpret shape, line, and space. Placement contributes to words such as *crowded, motion, open,* or *still.* Try changing the stroke-width and line placement in Figure 1-15. Does your impression of the space change? Listing 1-10 generates the Figure 1-15 shape.

LISTING 1-10 *Repetition and Shape*

```
<?xml version='1.0'?>
<svg width="300" height="300">
<rect x="50" y="50" width="200" height="200" style="fill:none; stroke:black;
stroke-width:2;" />
<path d="M 65,50  A 400,825 0  0 0 65,250" style="stroke:black; fill:none;
stroke-width:2;" />
<path d="M 85,50  A 500,625 0  0 0 85,250" style="stroke:black; fill:none;
stroke-width:2;" />
<path d="M 110,50  A 350,365 0  0 0 110,250" style="stroke:black; fill:none;
stroke-width:4;" />
<path d="M 160,50  A 350,465 0  0 0 180,250" style="stroke:black; fill:none;
stroke-width:4;" />
<path d="M 200,50  A 350,365 0  0 0 230,250" style="stroke:black; fill:none;
stroke-width:4;" />
</svg>
```

Moving from Layout Sketches to Layout Examples

Layout sketches don't have to be complicated to convey purpose and interest users. A simple focal point and block area of interest resulted in the Figure 1-16 sketch. This particular site is for a digital portfolio. The designer, Jean McIntosh, wanted to convey *strong, abstract, interesting,* and *clean.* The entry page changes a couple of times a year when Jean gets tired of it, but the concept remains the same because her intent doesn't shift. This simple design allows for minor modifications in content even as the theme remains intact.

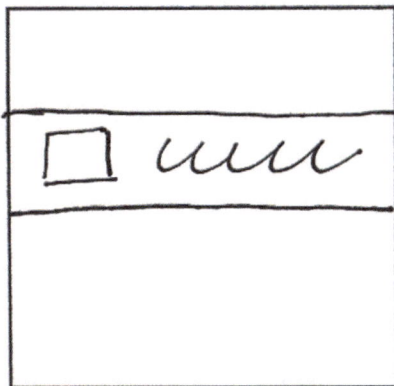

FIGURE 1-16 *The sketch for* `jrmacks.com`

One version of the `jrmacks.com` entry page, as shown in Figure 1-17, incorporates Figure 1-16's simple sketch into a layout that meets Jean's intent.

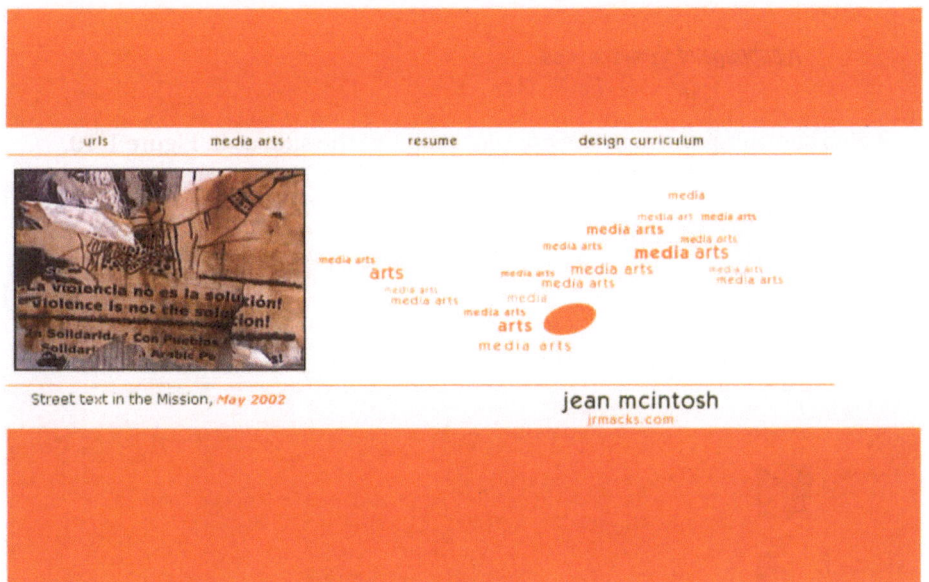

FIGURE 1-17 *The splash page from* `jrmacks.com`

The design concept continues through the subpages of the site, as in Figure 1-18.

FIGURE 1-18 *A subpage of* jrmacks.com

It also continues through the content pages of the site, as in Figure 1-19.

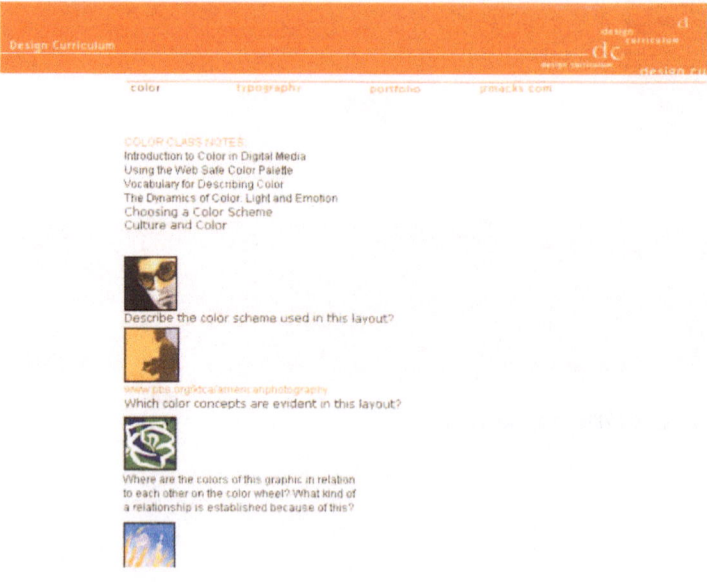

FIGURE 1-19 *A content page from* jrmacks.com

Beginning the development process with a sketch prevents you from designing only to your current design level of interest and ability with code. In other words, a sketch changes your perspective from "I'll use this code and fit the content in" to "I'll find a way to make the code work to this design." There are always browser issues, and, in some cases, design concepts will need revision to run on the Web. However, the hours spent trying to make CSS or XSL work to the design can result in a product that does a much better job of telling the client's story.

As an example, Steve Contreras is a freelance Web mechanic. Steve has a knack for getting things to run. He doesn't want to market himself as a designer or a developer, but he sometimes works as both. He's great at identifying problems and finding ways around the limitations of applications and the Internet. Steve wanted to create a simple marketing site that shows his work and his personality. At a glance, which of the shapes shown in Figure 1-20 best conveys Steve?

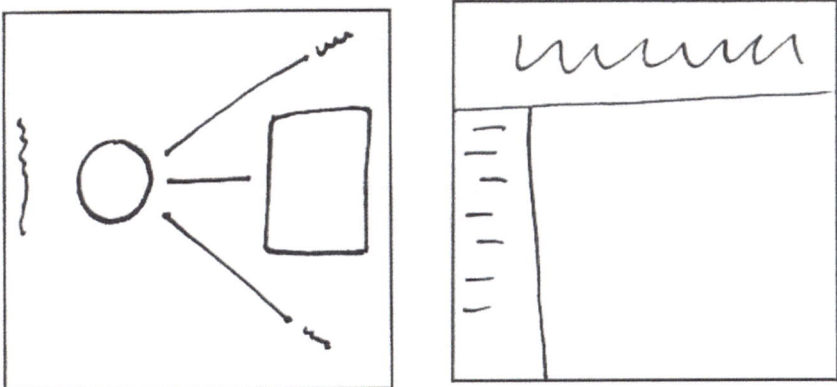

FIGURE 1-20 *Sketches for* contreras.tv

Figure 1-21 shows one version of Steve's entry page.

FIGURE 1-21 *The splash page for* contreras.tv

The design concept continues through the subpages of the site, as in Figure 1-22, which is an example of Steve's portfolio work.

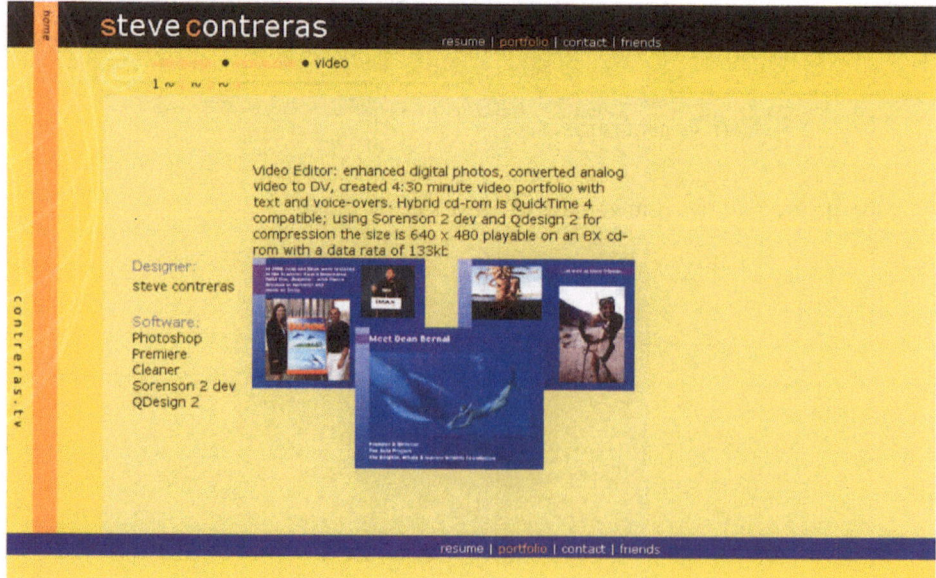

FIGURE 1-22 *A subpage of* contreras.tv

It also continues through the content pages of the site, as in Figure 1-23, Steve's résumé.

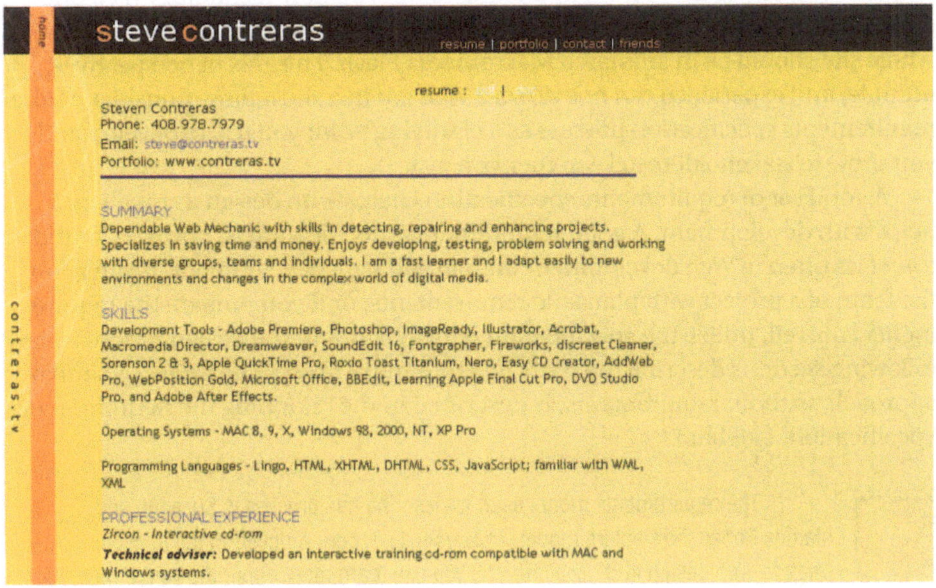

FIGURE 1-23 *The résumé page of* contreras.tv

The steps from language to layout also incorporate design principles (Chapter 2) and design elements (Chapters 4 and 5). As you work with clients and users, consider creating a mini-requirements specification to clarify design and technical criteria for the job. The combination of creating and organizing pulls ideas and information together toward innovative design and a well-run, profitable project.

A Parallel Design Consideration: Requirements Specifications

Web design and development jobs succeed more often and with fewer problems with a requirements specification. Although much has been written about requirements specifications in the context of software development, many developers either avoid requirements whenever possible or ignore them for the Web. Differences between software and the Web include development time and client expertise. With software, not tracking requirements or not taking the time to develop use case scenarios slows a project down with recoding. However, most of the stakeholders in a software product are project, system, or development professionals. With the Web, you may work with one developer, one nephew studying Web design on the weekends, one contact person representing the company who hopes eventually to move from marketing to Information Technology (IT), one director of sales who wants the site yesterday, and one intern who thinks the whole site should be in animated Macromedia Flash. This mix of perspectives, attitude, and experience can bog down a Web job in a short time. Consider a mini-requirements specification process as a clarifying point you use to develop and you show to stakeholders to keep them on task.

A good set of requirements specifications helps with design as much as it helps with development. A good requirements specification is, however, found even less often in Web development than in software development. If you're on the team of a project with plausible requirements, or if you prepare the requirements yourself, utilize the specification data to shortcut the design process. The following sections describe the parts of a requirements specification. (A similar approach, without requirements, is described in the "Skipping the Requirements Specification" sidebar.)

NOTE The requirements model used to describe this process is Suzanne and James Robertson's Volere model (atlsysguild.com) reduced to the sections common to Web design and development. You can learn more about the Volere model in *Mastering the Requirements Process* by Suzanne and James Robertson (Addison-Wesley, 1999).

The Purpose of the Product

The purpose section covers the user problem or background to the project and the goals of the project. The narrative of the purpose section may follow the data of the user analysis. Look for keywords that describe what problems were associated with previous products/projects, what worked, and which goals/ideas need to be developed in the new project. The wording of this section is typically for all stakeholders, not only developers, and offers language that helps to transition goals to visual elements. For example, the document may state the new design should be "simple and clean" or it should "reflect the company's history and long-term commitment to the community." These two phrases transition toward different conceptual ideas of a Web site. The narrative may say the product introduces "change and motion" or that it "maintains tradition." Translating these words into visual communication results in clients who say, "That's exactly what I wanted to convey."

Which sketch in Figure 1-24 conveys the words *change* and *motion*?

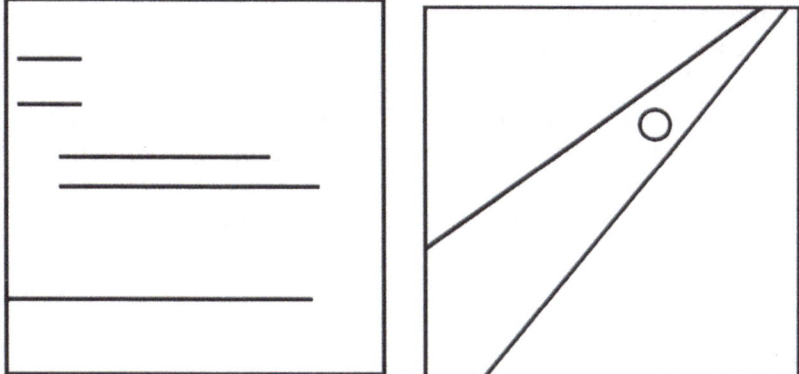

FIGURE 1-24 *Which sketch best conveys the words* change *and* motion?

Listing 1-11 generates the shape on the left in Figure 1-24.

LISTING 1-11 *A Simple, Calming Shape*

```
<?xml version='1.0'?>
<svg width="300" height="300">
<rect x="50" y="50" width="200" height="200"
style="fill:none; stroke:black; stroke-width:2;" />
<line x1="56" y1="82" x2="90" y2="82" style="stroke:black; stroke-width:2;" />
<line x1="56" y1="106" x2="90" y2="106" style="stroke:black; stroke-width:2;" />
<line x1="78" y1="134" x2="190" y2="134" style="stroke:black; stroke-width:2;" />
<line x1="78" y1="150" x2="216" y2="150" style="stroke:black; stroke-width:2;" />
<line x1="50" y1="210" x2="212" y2="210" style="stroke:black; stroke-width:2;" />
</svg>
```

Listing 1-12 generates the shape on the right in Figure 1-24.

LISTING 1-12 *Change and Motion*

```
<?xml version='1.0'?>
<svg width="300" height="300">
<rect x="50" y="50" width="200" height="200"
style="fill:none; stroke:black; stroke-width:2;" />
<line x1="50" y1="180" x2="230" y2="50" style="stroke:black; stroke-width:2;" />
<line x1="50" y1="180" x2="230" y2="50" style="stroke:black; stroke-width:2;" />
<line x1="80" y1="250" x2="244" y2="50" style="stroke:black; stroke-width:2;" />
<circle cx="172" cy="113" r="8" style="fill:none; stroke:black; stroke-width:2;" />
</svg>
```

Both sketches in Figure 1-24 consist of simple lines. The sketch on the right includes a small circle. Change and motion, however, are related primarily to line placement. Diagonal lines convey direction or motion. Horizontal lines convey stability. The circle acts as a focal point; change and motion are emphasized by the circle's ability to draw eyes and move them toward the top-right corner. The lines, however, determine the majority of the change and motion interpretation.

Which of the following two concepts in Figure 1-25 conveys *maintains traditions*?

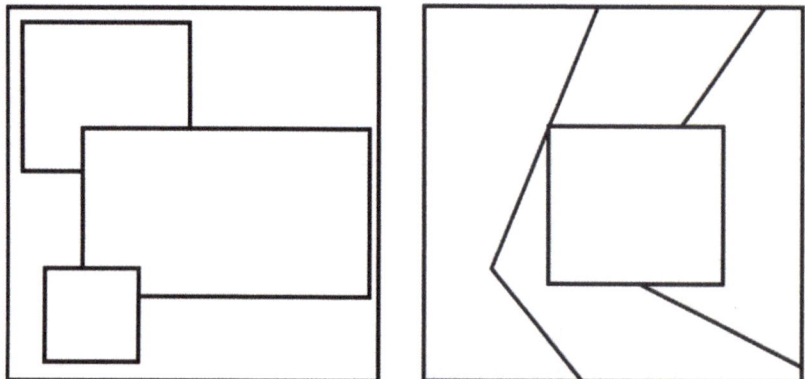

FIGURE 1-25 *Which sketch conveys the phrase* maintains traditions*?*

Listing 1-13 generates the shape on the left in Figure 1-25.

LISTING 1-13 *Maintains Tradition*

```
<?xml version='1.0'?>
<svg width="300" height="300">
<rect x="50" y="50" width="200" height="200"
style="fill:none; stroke:black; stroke-width:2;" />
<polyline
points="90 190,90 115,245 115,245 205,120 205"
style="fill:none; stroke:black; stroke-width:2;" />
<polyline
points="90 138,58 138,58 58,148 58,148 115"
style="fill:none; stroke:black; stroke-width:2;" />
<rect x="70" y="190" width="50" height="50"
style="fill:none; stroke:black; stroke-width:2;" />
</svg>
```

Listing 1-14 generates the shape on the right in Figure 1-25.

LISTING 1-14 *Strays from Static Rectangles*

```
<?xml version='1.0'?>
<svg width="300" height="300">
<rect x="50" y="50" width="200" height="200"
style="fill:none; stroke:black; stroke-width:2;" />
<rect x="116" y="114" width="92" height="84"
style="fill:none; stroke:black; stroke-width:2;" />
<path d="M 142 50, 86 190,134 250" style="fill:none; stroke:black;
stroke-width:2;" />
<path d="M 230 50, 186 114" style="fill:none; stroke:black; stroke-width:2;" />
<path d="M 164 198, 250 242" style="fill:none; stroke:black; stroke-width:2;" />
</svg>
```

The shape on the left in Figure 1-25 is conservative and suggests tradition. Rectangles convey traditionalism although their placement can vary to make the design a little more interesting. The shape on the right keeps a rectangle/square; however, its overall presentation with diagonal lines conveys a less traditional approach. Content often requires the use of rectangles or squares although placement and support shapes can help to convey a more modern approach.

Client, Customer, and Other Stakeholders

This section includes all the people who have a vote or influence in the design and development approval process:

- The client is the person(s) paying for the development and is the owner of the delivered system.

- The customer is the person/s who buys the product from the client.

- Other stakeholders.

The stakeholder section is critical to the design process. Imagine this scenario: You have a contact person, say, from marketing. You talk on the phone a few times and meet. When you meet, a second person attends, the director of marketing. You're comfortable because the director seems to have approval responsibility. You make a couple of sketch prototypes, create a digital prototype of your best two designs, and schedule to meet for design approval. At the meeting, however, two more people show up: the director of Information Systems (IS) and someone from finance. The director of IS is "concerned" that a product that the marketing department likes can't be supported. The finance person wants to talk about all of the costs involved. During the meeting, the director of sales drops in and says, "We're the ones who sell the product, we know what people want, and marketing knows what the company wants to sell."

This story can grow to include customer service, human resources, and various other stakeholders who can snag the approval process. Understanding this section of the document speeds up the design process by allowing you to understand who needs to see the prototypes. Delivery dates for code and testing cycles are based on the design approval date, rather than on a contract date. Stakeholders are sometimes hesitant to slow the code process because they don't completely understand it; however, they love to talk about what can happen to make something "look better." The key is to design to the user and the relationship. Everyone involved has an opinion such as "I like this one" or "I don't like it." If you're in the position to say, "This prototype best supports what the company wants to communicate and it meets the users' expectations," then the discussion moves away from personal taste and toward accomplishing a goal.

Users of the Product

This section includes information about the following:

- The users of the product
- The priorities assigned to users
- User participation

Address the user needs clearly and you're not in the position of participating in conversations centered on artist name-dropping or comparing college degrees to prove your design is worthy. Simple is better. Shapes can convey a theme, a feel for a site. Space (addressed in the next chapter) is critical. Other considerations such as color and type can come a little later. For now, the priority is your understanding of the user and translating the client and user ideas into words that transition into shapes.

A young, teenage audience, for example, has a different viewpoint of itself and different priorities than does a group of adult clients who remember being a teenager. An older-than-65 audience sees itself differently than does other people's sometimes stereotyped assumptions of "senior" interests and needs. Furthermore, audiences don't follow generic international design criteria for Asians, Hispanics, or Europeans. If you design a site for an audience of Mexican American professionals, don't design for the broad Hispanic market; talk with professional Mexican Americans to identify and prioritize their expectations. Do this well, and the designs will always work because the link between the client and the audience is established.

Will the shapes shown in Figure 1-26 draw a young, teenage audience (13–15 years old) for a product that teaches algebra? Do you know, or are you guessing? How can either shape evolve to accept content?

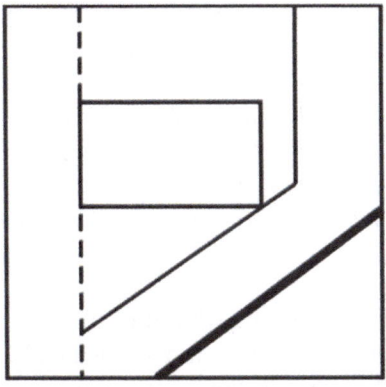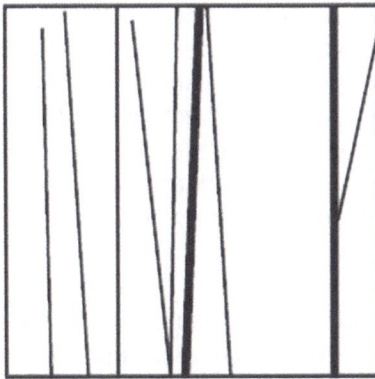

FIGURE 1-26 *Target audience perspective*

Listing 1-15 generates the shape on the left of Figure 1-26.

LISTING 1-15 *Offbeat, a Little Out of Balance*

```
<?xml version='1.0'?>
<svg width="300" height="300">
<rect style="fill:none; stroke:black; stroke-width:2;"
x="50" y="50" width="200" height="200" />
<rect style="fill:none; stroke:black; stroke-width:2;"
x="90" y="102" width="96" height="56" />
<line x1="90" y1="50" x2="90" y2="250" style="stroke:black; stroke-width:2;
stroke-dasharray: 9, 5;" />
<line x1="204" y1="146" x2="90" y2="226" style="stroke:black; stroke-width:2;" />
<line x1="130" y1="250" x2="250" y2="160" style="stroke:black; stroke-width:5;" />
<line x1="204" y1="50" x2="204" y2="146" style="stroke:black; stroke-width:2;" />
</svg>
```

Listing 1-16 generates the shape on the right of Figure 1-26.

LISTING 1-16 *Vertical Lines in Alternative Combinations*

```
<?xml version='1.0'?>
<svg width="300" height="300">
<rect style="fill:none; stroke:black; stroke-width:2;"
x="50" y="50" width="200" height="200" />
<line x1="70" y1="62" x2="74" y2="250"
style="stroke:black; stroke-width:2;" />
<line x1="82" y1="53" x2="94" y2="250"
style="stroke:black; stroke-width:2;" />
```

```
<line x1="110" y1="50" x2="110" y2="250" style="stroke:black; stroke-width:2;" />
<line x1="118" y1="58" x2="138" y2="250" style="stroke:black; stroke-width:2;" />
<line x1="142" y1="50" x2="138" y2="250" style="stroke:black; stroke-width:2;" />
<line x1="158" y1="50" x2="170" y2="250" style="stroke:black; stroke-width:2;" />
<line x1="154" y1="50" x2="146" y2="250" style="stroke:black; stroke-width:5;" />
<line x1="226" y1="50" x2="226" y2="250" style="stroke:black; stroke-width:5;" />
<line x1="250" y1="66" x2="228" y2="166" style="stroke:black; stroke-width:2;" />
</svg>
```

Talking with a young, teenage audience and determining what they like, use, buy, and enjoy suggests language that translates to shape, line, and space. Don't make assumptions; instead, ask and explore so that your designs emerge from a confident perspective rather than a hopeful supposition.

Mandated Constraints

Design and development converge at mandated constraints. For some reason, clients always seem to think a Web-based application needs an "innovative design" and a database. Maybe there's truth in their assumption, but what they're really looking for is a product that visually communicates their purpose and offers data manipulation capabilities. Your experience as a developer (knowing which components or tools to use and knowing which languages to model and how) is an important part of this process. How you incorporate the design element is also a critical decision. Browsers remain weak in the combination of code and positioning. Existing client materials such as printed matter and intranet data often don't translate well to commercial projects. Months of archived press releases about a company are of little interest to the user. Streaming media and full-screen video continue to have issues with download time.

How can you as the designer and developer of the site translate all of this information into a viable product? Include elements in the project that add significant value; leave the rest out. If a pet project of the client needs incorporating, simple solutions that focus on the major priorities look good, work well, and can grow later. Constraints are everywhere. Think "clean, simple, and focused on the user." It's not always possible, but in most cases, it works.

Naming Conventions and Definitions

Never skip over this section until you're sure stakeholders understand what you mean by *user analysis, prototype, test cycle, mirror site, go live,* and other terminologies that can slow the project down or result in extra meetings.

Relevant Facts and Assumptions

Watch out for assumptions about browsers, platforms, plug-ins, language, and documentation in addition to your typical developer concerns. Remember, the largest consumer audience uses America Online. These assumptions affect design and need clarification.

Look and Feel Requirements

The look and feel of the site link back to the language issues discussed earlier in the chapter. You also need to incorporate existing client assets, especially those that establish branding of a product or of the client organization. The style of the product reflects the personality of the product and client. The interface reflects the relationship between the client and the user. Chapter 5 discusses navigation and layout. In the meantime, understand that navigation doesn't have to be unique for a product to be innovative. If buttons on the left meet the needs of the user, then use them; it's important not to overload the user with too many options. Users tell you the categories of content because they want to access them. Ironically, companies typically think an About Us button that tells of the company's history and management should be a priority button; users always view it as a secondary interest. Users who go to a site want to be in a relationship with the people and the product of the company. They logically understand the ratio of the relationship may be 1 to 500,000. However, they still want to "feel" like it's 1 to 1. For example:

- Users at Oprah Winfrey's site want to visit with Oprah, even though the site may draw more than a million visitors a day. They don't want to feel they're in a huge money-making Oprah factory site.

- Users at eBay want to find a great product or a great bargain. Their expectations are the same as in a physical store: good information, easy-to-find merchandise, plenty of products on hand, and a quick checkout.

- Users playing WarCraft or StarCraft quickly move in and out of groups. Their expectations are to play individually or in small groups with fast response times regardless if there are more than 100,000 players.

Usability Requirements

This section is the simplest and most obvious requirement. Somehow, though, it often misses inclusion in the design. Profitable products are purchased, used, and reused. Take the time to create a usability requirement that defines user needs. A simple use of icons for a multilanguage site can mean the difference between success and failure.

> ## Skipping the Requirements Specification
>
> If you work on a project/product design with no requirements specification, utilize user analysis data and talk to six additional potential users who fit the target group portfolio. If there's no user analysis, you must make the time to do some on your own. People are fickle about design. You can easily lose your profit margin trying to satisfy design ideas that were never the best fit for the product. Talking to users and clarifying their priorities creates a map for design. Translating the data to language and again to visual representation tells their story. Determining shapes in simple conceptual drawings begins the transformation from user analysis and requirements data to a visual interface.

Performance Requirements

What is the project's priority, speed, or accuracy? Is the bold, new design with plug-ins or graphics supposed to run on a Commodore (just kidding)? Is there a large amount of content, simple navigation, or both? How can the design be incorporated throughout the project and support the requirements?

The Volere model includes several other important sections. This text offers examples directly related to a product's conceptual design.

You must address several functional requirements from the Volere model or your own model for the purpose of a complete build. This chapter presented a small sampling for design purposes only.

Interface Design Axioms

Determine a product's design concept by understanding client and target audience expectations.

Clients and users can help in the design process by communicating their purpose, goals, and expectations of a site. Don't have clients and users tell you how to design the product. Do have clients and users tell you how they like to interact with each other. Have a conversation with the client about the story they want to communicate and about how they like to do business with the user. Have conversations with potential users (or friends who meet the target group profile) to evaluate how they want to interact with the client. Listen for keywords that describe the priorities and expectations of both parties. Adjectives do a great job of expressing ideas that can transition to shapes and themes for a site.

Initial sketches tap your imagination for concepts and shapes that can become eventual layouts. Don't skip the sketch step in the design process. Moving directly to the keyboard and screen misses an important element of the communication process. Furthermore, beginning development with a sketch stops you from designing to your current level of interest and ability with code.

A good set of requirements specifications helps with design as much as it helps with development. Look through a requirements document for priorities and keywords that help in the creation and delivery of the design. Think about code in the back of your mind, but design to needs and expectations. There's time in the process to adjust for functional requirements.

The next step is to consider a set of basic design principles that help to solidify the balance, emphasis, rhythm, unity, and contrast of your conceptual shapes.

Introducing Design Principles

Delay always breeds danger; and to protract a great design is often to ruin it.
—The character Don Quixote in the book of the same name[1]

In Chapter 1, you began with conversation narratives, user analysis data, and requirements specifications. You then transformed the resulting information into descriptive words that led to basic conceptual shapes and initial sketches. In this chapter, you'll analyze the initial sketches and incorporate design principles for bringing the sketch one step closer to a prototype.

Incorporating basic design principles into an interface design enhances the user experience. The design principles common to most, if not all, design books and design courses include balance, emphasis, rhythm, unity, and contrast. For you, the developer, taking the time to analyze a concept in relationship to these five principles builds confidence in your work and, in return, client satisfaction in your design.

Design principles apply to design elements. Design principles help you to understand how to apply design elements in such a way as to visually communicate your intent. Design elements include line, type, shape, texture, space, size, and value (covered in Chapter 4). The principles, then, are the concepts that you apply, together and separately, to each design element.

Understanding Balance

Symmetrical balance implies organization. Similar elements evenly distributed to the right and to the left of the center have symmetry, as in Figure 2-1.

---

1. *Don Quixote* by Miguel de Cervantes, Spanish author (1547–1616).

Asymmetrical balance implies that the design wants to influence the interaction or interpretation away from the expected. Dissimilar elements distributed to the right and left that nonetheless appear balanced are asymmetrical, as in Figure 2-2. Radial balance, not often used in Web-based applications, implies a circular, orbital perspective of balance.

FIGURE 2-1 *Symmetrical balance*

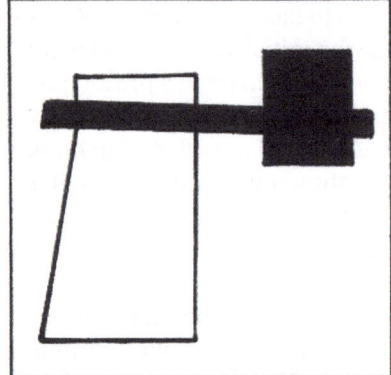

FIGURE 2-2 *Asymmetrical balance*

Dark areas appear heavier than light areas. Shapes of different sizes, colors, and textures unite to present asymmetrical balance. Unbalanced shapes tend to disorient the user.

Symmetrical design represents stability and familiarity. Asymmetry represents uniqueness, informality, entertainment, and even adventure.

Techniques of symmetry can include repetition of shapes and equal amounts of space. Techniques of asymmetry can include combinations of shapes and space that don't match as individual elements and yet appear balanced as a whole.

As an initial sketch toward a potential layout, Figure 2-3 might be suitable for what kind of client?

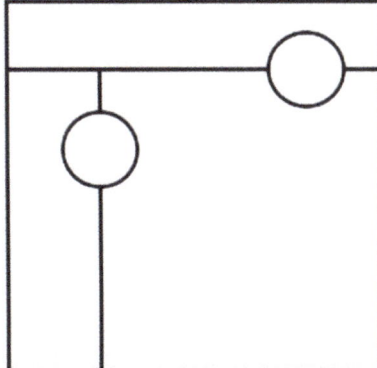

FIGURE 2-3 *Balance and shape*

The circles in this asymmetrical layout create strong focal points that might draw a user's eye to a logo, icon, or product. There's a familiar aspect to the top and left space and enough open area for significant content. Varied use of color, line, or circle placement conveys different voices. Listing 2-1 generates the Figure 2-3 shape.

LISTING 2-1 *Circles and Lines*

```xml
<?xml version="1.0"?>
<svg width="300" height="300">
<rect x="50" y="50" width="200" height="200" style=" fill:none;
stroke:black; stroke-width:2;" />
<line x1="100" y1="87" x2="100" y2="110" style="stroke:black; stroke-width:2;" />
<line x1="100" y1="150" x2="100" y2="250" style="stroke:black; stroke-width:2;" />
<line x1="50" y1="87" x2="190" y2="87" style="stroke:black; stroke-width:2;" />
<line x1="230" y1="87" x2="250" y2="87" style="stroke:black; stroke-width:2;" />
<circle cx="210" cy="87" r="20" style="fill:none; stroke:black; stroke-width:2;" />
<circle cx="100" cy="130" r="20" style="fill:none;
stroke:black; stroke-width:2;" />
</svg>
```

What does Figure 2-4 make you think of?

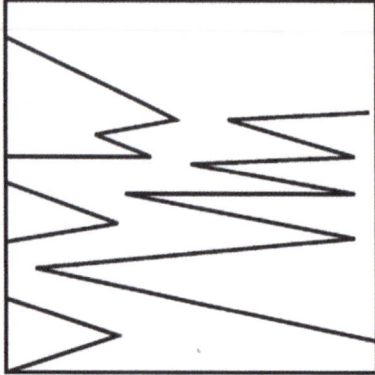

FIGURE 2-4 *Asymmetrical lines*

The lines in this asymmetrical layout create balance and yet tension. It probably makes you think of California earthquakes. Listing 2-2 generates the Figure 2-4 shape.

LISTING 2-2 *Lines and Space*

```
<?xml version="1.0"?>
<svg width="300" height="300">
<rect x="50" y="50" width="200" height="200"
style=" fill:none; stroke:black;
stroke-width:2;" />
<path d="M246 110, 170 114,238 134, 150 138,238
154, 114 154,238 178, 66 194, 250 233"
style="fill:none; stroke:black; stroke-width:2;" />
<path d="M 50 250, 110 230, 50 210"
style="fill:none; stroke:black; stroke-width:2;" />
<path d="M 50 180, 110 170, 50 148"
style="fill:none; stroke:black; stroke-width:2;" />
<path d="M 50 70, 142 114, 98 122,128 134,
50 134" style="fill:none; stroke:black;
stroke-width:2;" />
</svg>
```

Figure 2-5 offers a symmetrical design that expresses stability and yet offers something different. The lines and rectangles in the symmetrical layout model a window, viewed either from the inside or from the outside.

FIGURE 2-5 *Symmetrical lines*

The solid feeling of the design comes from the symmetry between the right and left sides of the graphic. Listing 2-3 generates the Figure 2-5 shape.

LISTING 2-3 *Lines as Object*

```
<?xml version="1.0"?>
<svg width="300" height="300">
<rect x="50" y="50" width="200" height="200"
style=" fill:none; stroke:black; stroke-width:2;" />
<rect style="fill:none; stroke:black;
stroke-width:2;" x="86" y="50"
width="136" height="156" />
<rect style="fill:none; stroke:black;
stroke-width:2;" x="102" y="50"
width="100" height="136" />
<line x1="102" y1="98" x2="202" y2="98"
style="stroke:black;stroke-width:2;" />
<line x1="102" y1="130" x2="202" y2="130"
style="stroke:black; stroke-width:2;" />
<line x1="152" y1="50" x2="152" y2="186"
style="stroke:black; stroke-width:2;" />
<line x1="102" y1="186" x2="86" y2="206"
style="stroke:black; stroke-width:2;" />
<line x1="202" y1="186" x2="222" y2="206"
style="stroke:black; stroke-width:2;" />
</svg>
```

Figure 2-6's asymmetry remains somewhat in balance because of the combination of space and shape. Designs can be unusual and innovative but still have balance

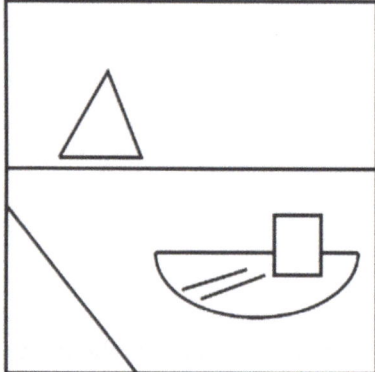

FIGURE 2-6 *Asymmetrical, nearly out of balance*

Shapes and space that convey the same weight or depth convey balance, whether they're identical or dissimilar. Balance doesn't have to convey flat and boring. Listing 2-4 generates the Figure 2-6 shape.

LISTING 2-4 *Lines and Shape*

```
<?xml version="1.0"?>
<svg width="300" height="300">
<rect x="50" y="50" width="200" height="200"
style="fill:none; stroke:black; stroke-width:2;" />
<rect style="fill:none; stroke:black; stroke-width:2;"
x="195" y="165" width="25" height="32" />
<line x1="50" y1="140" x2="250" y2="140"
style="stroke:black; stroke-width:2;" />
<path d="M78 134, 122 134,104 88, 78 134"
style="fill:none; stroke:black; stroke-width:2;" />
<line x1="50" y1="160" x2="120" y2="250"
style="stroke:black; stroke-width:2;" />
<line x1="130" y1="185" x2="195" y2="185"
style="stroke:black; stroke-width:2;" />
<line x1="220" y1="185" x2="240" y2="185"
style="stroke:black; stroke-width:2;" />
<line x1="190" y1="197" x2="155" y2="210"
style="stroke:black; stroke-width:2;" />
```

```
<line x1="180" y1="194" x2="145" y2="205"
style="stroke:black; stroke-width:2;" />
<path d="M130,185 A 55,35 0 1,0 240,185"
style="fill:none; stroke:black; stroke-width:2;" />
</svg>
```

Occasionally, a client may want a design that's so modern or different it appears unbalanced. Unbalanced work breaks down in interpretation and typically comes across as unfinished or choppy rather than avant-garde or postmodern. A better approach is to push the asymmetrical limits by incorporating shape, color, texture, and other design elements in such a way that they tell a unique, asymmetrical story.

Figure 2-7 shows an asymmetrical design. Figure 2-8 is based on Figure 2-7 and is unbalanced.

FIGURE 2-7 *Within balance*

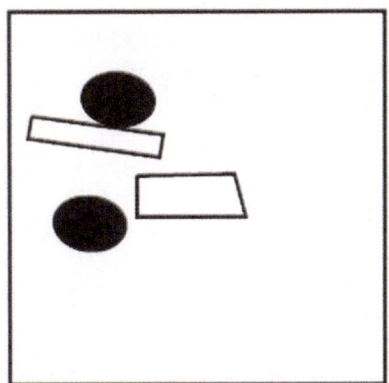

FIGURE 2-8 *Out of balance*

The asymmetrical design in Figure 2-7 is different and yet balanced enough that the user may view it as fun or unusual. The unbalanced Figure 2-8 design is unbalanced to the degree that users notice that something is wrong, even if they're not exactly clear what isn't working.

Listing 2-5 generates the Figure 2-7 shape.

LISTING 2-5 *Shapes with Supporting Space*

```xml
<?xml version="1.0"?>
<svg width="300" height="300">
<rect x="50" y="50" width="200" height="200"
style=" fill:none;
stroke:black; stroke-width:2;" />
<ellipse cx="108" cy="97" rx="20" ry="15" transform="rotate(7,108,97)"
style="fill:black;" />
<path d="M62 106 ,60 118,130 128,132 116,62 106" style="fill:none;
stroke:black; stroke-width:2;" />
<path d="M118 128 ,170 127,176 150,118 150,118 128" style="fill:none;
stroke:black; stroke-width:2;" />
<path d="M150 170 ,166 194,240 151,223 126,150 170" style="fill:none;
stroke:black; stroke-width:2;" />
</svg>
```

Listing 2-6 generates the Figure 2-8 shape.

LISTING 2-6 *Shapes Without Supporting Space*

```xml
<?xml version="1.0"?>
<svg width="300" height="300">
<rect x="50" y="50" width="200" height="200"
style=" fill:none;
stroke:black; stroke-width:2;" />
<ellipse cx="108" cy="97" rx="20" ry="15" transform="rotate(7,108,97)"
style="fill:black;" />
<ellipse cx="101" cy="165" rx="20" ry="15" transform="rotate(7,108,97)"
style="fill:black;" />
<path d="M62 106 ,60 118,130 128,132 116,62 106" style="fill:none;
stroke:black; stroke-width:2;" />
<path d="M118 138 ,170 137,176 160,118 160,118 138"
style="fill:none;
stroke:black; stroke-width:2;" />
</svg>
```

Understanding Emphasis

All layouts need a focal point. You determine where you want the user to look first. With Web-based applications, the client may think the focal point should be the corporate logo. In some cases, a clear purpose of the product becomes the focal point of the layout. For example, if your client is a travel agent promoting sailboat cruises, the focal point that communicates the most is a sailboat on a quiet sea rather than a large logo for Sun and Sail Tours, for example. The focal point supports the priorities you gleaned from conversations with the client and users. Focal points represent the key priority of the visual story. Sometimes that priority is a product, and sometimes it's how you convey the words such as *trust, emergency, fun, party,* or *important.*

Another important element of a focal point is that it directs users to what you want them to see and how you want them to interpret what they see. Too much information, with no clear focal point, results in the user moving on without paying particular attention to what you intended.

Often, you create a focal point by identifying a priority and then visually communicating it with shape, color, or other design elements that vary from the rest of the design. In Figure 2-9, attention is drawn from the top bar and four possible buttons or items on the left to the sweeping curve on the right/center.

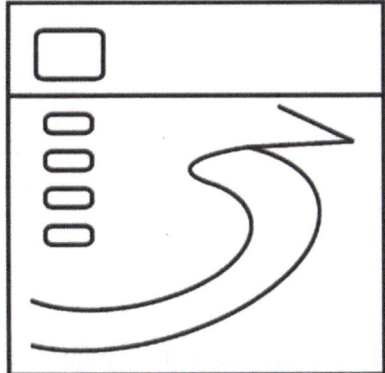

FIGURE 2-9 *A focal point with a varied shape or texture*

Listing 2-7 generates the Figure 2-9 shape.

LISTING 2-7 *Shape and Focal Point*

```xml
<?xml version="1.0"?>
<svg width="300" height="300">
<rect x="50" y="50" width="200" height="200"
style=" fill:none;
stroke:black; stroke-width:2;" />
<rect style="fill:none; stroke:black;
stroke-width:2;" x="65" y="65" width="36"
height="26" rx="5" ry="3" />
<g id="button">
<rect style="fill:none; stroke:black;
stroke-width:2;" x="70" y="110" width="25"
height="10" rx="4" ry="3" />
</g>
<use xlink:href="#button" transform="translate(0,20)" />
<use xlink:href="#button" transform="translate(0,40)" />
<use xlink:href="#button" transform="translate(0,60)" />
<line x1="50" y1="100" x2="250" y2="100"
style="stroke:black; stroke-width:2;" />
<path d="M 178,128 A95,50 -15 1,1 62 234"
style="fill:none;
stroke:black; stroke-width:2;" />
<line x1="178" y1="128" x2="234" y2="125"
style="stroke:black; stroke-width:2;" />
<line x1="194" y1="106" x2="234" y2="125"
style="stroke:black; stroke-width:2;" />
<path d="M 178,128 A80,15 0 0,0 160 148"
style="fill:none; stroke:black;stroke-width:2;" />
<path d="M 160 148 A50,25 -10 1,1 62 210"
style="fill:none; stroke:black; stroke-width:2;" />
</svg>
```

You can create a focal point by placing text or another design element at a curve or angle that draws attention from the balance of straight text, as in Figure 2-10.

The basic question that determines focal point is "What do your eyes see first?" When you look through an art book or go to a gallery, it's great practice to ask yourself the following questions each time: Where is the focal point? What draws your eyes? What is the significance of that particular aspect of the drawing, painting, or photograph?

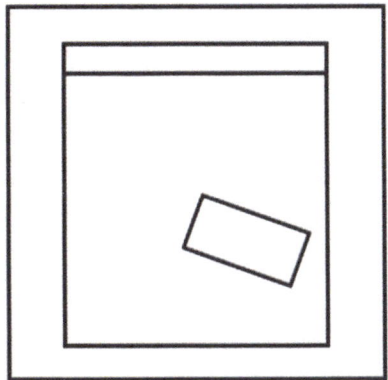

FIGURE 2-10 *A focal point supported by space*

Listing 2-8 generates the Figure 2-10 shape.

LISTING 2-8 *Space and Focal Point*

```
<?xml version='1.0'?>
<svg width="300" height="300">
<rect x="50" y="50" width="200" height="200"
style="fill:none; stroke:black; stroke-width:2;" />
<rect x="80" y="70" width="140" height="16"
style="fill:none; stroke:black; stroke-width:2;" />
<rect x="80" y="86" width="140" height="146"
style="fill:none;stroke:black; stroke-width:2;" />
<rect x="200" y="200" width="60" height="30"
transform="rotate(200,200,200)"
style="fill:none;stroke:black; stroke-width:2;" />
</svg>
```

The focal point of a Web site or any other piece of visual media exhibits the essence of your subject. The focal point is where the client first meets the user. Artists advise against placing the focal point too close to the edges or corners of the work. One approach is to take the actual size of the piece or window, draw an X from corner to corner, and then create a square that resides halfway between the edges and the center point. This exercise defines four positions where a focal point works well, as shown in Figure 2-11.

Listing 2-9 generates the Figure 2-11 shape.

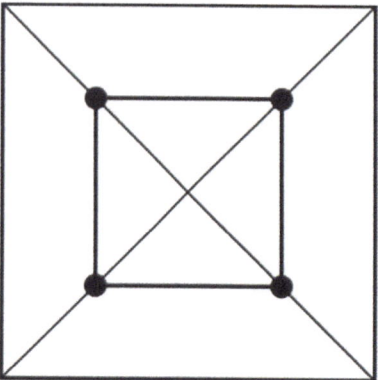

FIGURE 2-11 *Potential focal points*

LISTING 2-9 *Traditional Focal Point*

```
<?xml version='1.0'?>
<svg width="300" height="300">
<rect x="50" y="50" width="200" height="200"
style="fill:none; stroke:black; stroke-width:2;" />
<line x1="50" y1="50" x2="250" y2="250"
style="stroke:black; stroke-width=1;" />
<line x1="50" y1="250" x2="250" y2="50"
style="stroke:black; stroke-width=1;" />
<rect x="100" y="100" width="100" height="100"
style="fill:none; stroke:black; stroke-width:2;" />
<circle cx="100" cy="100" r="6" style="fill:black;" />
<circle cx="100" cy="200" r="6" style="fill:black;" />
<circle cx="200" cy="100" r="6" style="fill:black;" />
<circle cx="200" cy="200" r="6" style="fill:black;" />
</svg>
```

Try not to divide the window in half or place the focal point exactly in the center, as shown in Figures 2-12 and 2-13.

FIGURE 2-12 *A center focal point*

FIGURE 2-13 *A halved screen*

Halves and exact-center focal points tend to result in static interfaces. Shapes placed in perfect order and evenly distributed can result in interesting geometrics in some instances, but they typically result in flat designs of minimal excitement.

You can create focal points with positives or negatives of shapes or space. Shapes create the focal point in Figure 2-14.

FIGURE 2-14 *A focal point with shape*

Listing 2-10 generates the Figure 2-14 shape.

LISTING 2-10 *Nontraditional Focal Point*

```
<?xml version='1.0'?>
<svg width="300" height="300">
<rect x="50" y="50" width="200" height="200"
style="fill:none; stroke:black; stroke-width:2;" />
<rect x="50" y="98" width="124" height="80" rx="3" ry="3"
style="fill:black; stroke:black; stroke-width:2;" />
<path d="M 50 238, 250 230, 250 250, 50 250" style="stroke:black;" />
</svg>
```

Space creates the focal point in Figure 2-15.

FIGURE 2-15 *A focal point with space*

Listing 2-11 generates the Figure 2-15 shape.

LISTING 2-11 *Focal Space*

```
<?xml version='1.0'?>
<svg width="300" height="300">
<rect x="50" y="50" width="200" height="200"
style="fill:none; stroke:black; stroke-width:2;" />
<polygon points="50 50,250 50,250 110,50 70"
style="fill:black;" />
<polygon points="50 230,50 220,250 190,250 205"
style="fill:black;" />
</svg>
```

The decision of whether to add emphasis with shape or with space always refers to the main goal of the design. How do you want the user to interact with the interface? Create a focal point that first draws attention and then interests the user to look at the broader design. A too-demanding focal point draws a user's attention and then never invites exploration of the rest of the screen. A weak focal point doesn't guide the user. Your goal is to invite, focus, and interest the user in the purpose of the site and the relationships it may create.

Understanding Rhythm

Rhythm adds tempo to a design. Shapes or text are typically placed and repeated to convey a sense of motion. This repetition is accompanied by changes in form and/or by changes in position. Simple repetition with equal amounts of space and similar shapes conveys a smooth rhythm. Too much sameness can become boring. Experiment with less and with more to find the moment when the rhythm is clear and then stop. Repetition with varied amounts of space and changes in size and density communicates more of a tense or exciting rhythm.

Vertical Rhythm

Vertical rhythm conveys words such as the following:

- Elevate, upraise, heighten
- Growth, development, maturation
- Soar above, command, transcend

The shapes shown in Figure 2-16 can represent vertical rhythm.

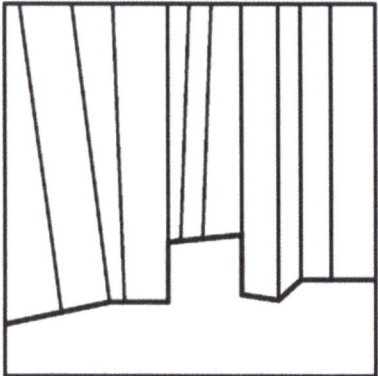

FIGURE 2-16 *Vertical rhythm*

Clients communicating growth, goal attainment, and metaphors tied to words such *skyscrapers*, *stars*, or *limitless heights*, for example, relate well to vertical rhythm. There are subtle differences in language you need to consider. For example, the word *expansion*, as in a product or company expanding, implies a more horizontal or rounded growth than it implies a vertical growth. What kinds of things in the physical world expand? What kinds of things grow? What kinds of things reach? The language of your response implies a potential shape.

Listing 2-12 generates the Figure 2-16 shape.

LISTING 2-12 *Vertical Rhythm*

```
<?xml version="1.0"?>
<svg width="300" height="300">
<rect x="50" y="50" width="200" height="200"
style=" fill:none;
stroke:black; stroke-width:2;" />
<path d="M 50 222, 106 210, 138 210,138 178, 178 174,
178 206,198 209, 210 198, 250 198" style="fill:none;
stroke:black; stroke-width:3;" />
<line x1="58" y1="50" x2="80" y2="214"
style="stroke:black;stroke-width:2;" />
<line x1="86" y1="50" x2="106" y2="211"
style="stroke:black; stroke-width:2;" />
<line x1="108" y1="50" x2="114" y2="210"
style="stroke:black; stroke-width:2;" />
```

```
<line x1="138" y1="50" x2="138" y2="210"
style="stroke:black; stroke-width:2;" />
<line x1="150" y1="50" x2="145" y2="178"
style="stroke:black; stroke-width:2;" />
<line x1="162" y1="50" x2="157" y2="177"
style="stroke:black; stroke-width:2;" />
<line x1="178" y1="50" x2="178" y2="180"
style="stroke:black; stroke-width:2;" />
<line x1="198" y1="50" x2="198" y2="209"
style="stroke:black; stroke-width:2;" />
<line x1="210" y1="50" x2="210" y2="198"
style="stroke:black; stroke-width:2;" />
<line x1="226" y1="50" x2="226" y2="198"
style="stroke:black; stroke-width:2;" />
</svg>
```

Rectangular Rhythm

Rectangular rhythm conveys words such as the following:

- Tradition, comfort, solace
- Steady, firm, stable
- Simple, uniform, easy

The shapes shown in Figure 2-17 can represent rectangular rhythm.

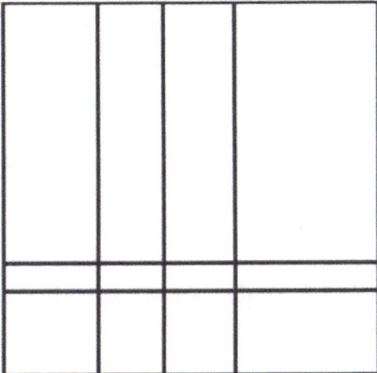

FIGURE 2-17 *Rectangular rhythm*

Rectangular rhythm conveys a solid, somewhat traditional meshing of information. Rectangles with a unique sense of space free themselves, somewhat, from the traditionalist mode. Financial, governmental, and law professions make good use of rectangles. Music, art, entertainment, adventure, and dance sites seem flat with collections of rectangles of information. In some cases, content demands rectangles. If so, bring in interesting elements of line, space, and color to liven things up.

Listing 2-13 generates the Figure 2-17 shape.

LISTING 2-13 *Rectangular Rhythm*

```xml
<?xml version="1.0"?>
<svg width="300" height="300">
<rect x="50" y="50" width="200" height="200"
style=" fill:none;
stroke:black; stroke-width:2;" />
<line x1="173" y1="50" x2="173" y2="250"
style="stroke:black; stroke-width:2;" />
<line x1="100" y1="50" x2="100" y2="250"
style="stroke:black; stroke-width:2;" />
<line x1="135" y1="50" x2="135" y2="250"
style="stroke:black; stroke-width:2;" />
<line x1="50" y1="190" x2="250" y2="190"
style="stroke:black; stroke-width:2;" />
<line x1="50" y1="205" x2="250" y2="205"
style="stroke:black; stroke-width:2;" />
</svg>
```

Triangular Rhythm

Triangular rhythm often reminds users of Cubist art or religious symbols and conveys words such as the following:

- Dramatic, theatrical, starring

- Ascend, tower, escalate

- Redemption, divinity, religion

Figure 2-18 portrays triangular rhythm. The same triangles, shown upside down, create a sense of imbalance because the stability communicated from the triangle's base is disrupted, as shown in Figure 2-19.

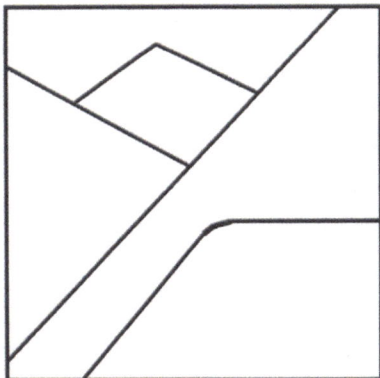

FIGURE 2-18   *Triangular rhythm*

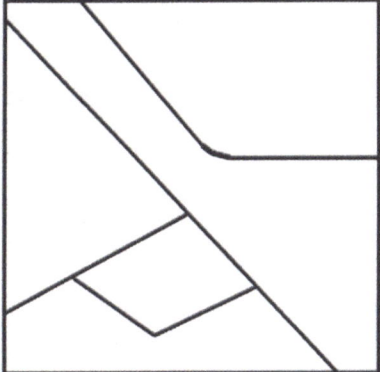

FIGURE 2-19   *Triangular rhythm, upside down*

Listing 2-14 generates the Figure 2-18 shape. The Figure 2-19 shape is inverted.

Triangular rhythm—and angular lines in general—convey more of a freestyle story. Triangular rhythm doesn't exist solely as a group of triangles, and there are inherent problems placing Web copy in the corners. Remember, you don't need to go to extremes in communicating any shape; subtle changes in angles and rhythm can coexist with content space.

LISTING 2-14 *Triangular Rhythm*

```xml
<?xml version="1.0"?>
<svg width="300" height="300">
<rect x="50" y="50" width="200" height="200"
style=" fill:none; stroke:black;
stroke-width:2;" />
<path d="M 155 172, 160 168,163 167,169 165.5, 170 165"
style="fill:none; stroke:black; stroke-width:3;" />
<line x1="50" y1="240" x2="228" y2="50"
style="stroke:black; stroke-width:2;" />
<line x1="147" y1="135" x2="50" y2="82"
style="stroke:black; stroke-width:2;" />
<line x1="87" y1="101" x2="130" y2="70"
style="stroke:black; stroke-width:2;" />
<line x1="130" y1="70" x2="184" y2="96"
style="stroke:black; stroke-width:2;" />
<line x1="90" y1="250" x2="155" y2="172"
style="stroke:black; stroke-width:2;" />
<line x1="170" y1="165" x2="250" y2="165"
style="stroke:black; stroke-width:2;" />
</svg>
```

Circular Rhythm

Circular rhythm conveys, among other things, a motion or target and additional words such as the following:

- Cycle, orbit, zone

- Aim, goal, sport

- Revolve, rotate, roll

One question to ask yourself with circular rhythm is "Are you pulling the focal point into the center of the circle only?" Does the user look to the center and then back out to the balance of your design? Figure 2-20 offers an example of circular rhythm.

Circular rhythm is interesting in that it can tell macro and micro stories. From a metaphor perspective, circles convey everything including atoms, bubbles, footballs/soccer balls, planets, and galaxies. Circular rhythm can roll, expand, explode, shrink, bounce, and zoom, among other things. The key to effective circular rhythm is in controlling how a user's eyes move through the story's priorities. Circular rhythm can be effective when planned as part of an overall concept but fails when utilized casually without an underlying rationale.

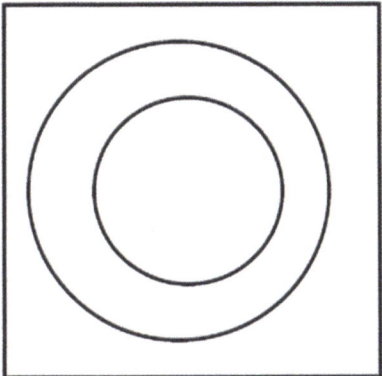

FIGURE 2-20 *Circular rhythm*

Listing 2-15 generates the Figure 2-20 shape.

LISTING 2-15 *Circular Rhythm*

```
<?xml version="1.0"?>
<svg width="300" height="300">
<rect x="50" y="50" width="200" height="200"
style=" fill:none;
stroke:black; stroke-width:2;" />
<circle cx="148" cy="150" r="50" style="fill:none;
stroke:black; stroke-width:2;" />
<circle cx="143" cy="150" r="80" style="fill:none;
stroke:black; stroke-width:2;" />
</svg>
```

Diagonal Rhythm

Diagonal rhythm conveys an offbeat approach and adds action or excitement to a design as it communicates words such as the following:

- Offset, unusual, topsy-turvy
- Bias, transverse, oblique
- Excite, provoke, stimulate

Figure 2-21 shows an example of diagonal rhythm.

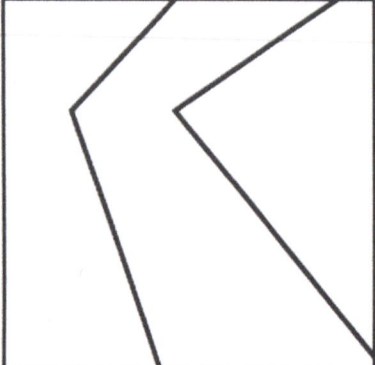

FIGURE 2-21 *Diagonal rhythm*

Diagonal rhythm works well as both a primary and secondary focal point. Sites that need significant content space may have more squares or rectangles than the design ideally needs. In these cases, diagonal rhythm can provide a more engaging alternative. Developers who want to create a different look and yet aren't comfortable going wild and crazy can utilize a subtle diagonal rhythm effectively. Think geometry with a little offbeat space or shape, either as a primary or as a supporting player.

Listing 2-16 generates the Figure 2-21 shape.

LISTING 2-16 *Diagonal Rhythm*

```
<?xml version='1.0'?>
<svg width="300" height="300">
<rect x="50" y="50" width="200" height="200"
style="fill:none; stroke:black; stroke-width:2;" />
<path d="M 134 250, 86 110,142 50" style="fill:none;
stroke:black; stroke-width:3;" />
<path d="M 230 50, 142 110,250 242" style="fill:none;
stroke:black; stroke-width:3;" />
</svg>
```

Curvilinear Rhythm

Curvilinear rhythm conveys natural shapes and a sense of calmness with words such as the following:

- Resting bodies, reclining animals

- Falling leaves, sand dunes, rolling hills

- Serenity, at ease, soothing

The shapes shown in Figure 2-22 can convey curvilinear rhythm.

FIGURE 2-22 *Curvilinear rhythm*

Listing 2-17 generates the Figure 2-22 shape.

LISTING 2-17 *Curvilinear Rhythm*

```
<?xml version='1.0'?>
<svg width="300" height="300">
<g id="leaf">
<ellipse cx="210" cy="150" rx="4" ry="10"
style="fill:none; stroke:black;
stroke-width:2;" transform="rotate(40,210,160)" />
</g>
<use xlink:href="#leaf" transform="rotate(290,210,160)" />
<use xlink:href="#leaf" transform="translate(0,70) rotate(20,210,160)" />
<use xlink:href="#leaf" transform="translate(-80,60) rotate(270,210,160)" />
<use xlink:href="#leaf" transform="translate(-80,60) rotate(135,210,160)" />
<use xlink:href="#leaf" transform="translate(-40,58) rotate(180,210,160)" />
<use xlink:href="#leaf" transform="translate(0,70) rotate(320,210,160)" />
<use xlink:href="#leaf" transform="translate(4,-35) rotate(330,210,160)" />
<rect x="50" y="50" width="200" height="200"
style="fill:none; stroke:black; stroke-width:2;" />
<path d="M 50,230 A100 95, 0 0, 1 170 175"
style="fill:none; stroke:black;
stroke-width:3;" />
<path d="M 60,250 A100 95, 0 0, 1 190 195"
style="fill:none; stroke:black;
stroke-width:3;" />
```

```
<path d="M 170,175 A100 95, 0 0, 1 250 50"
style="fill:none; stroke:black;
stroke-width:3;" />
<path d="M 190,195 A100 95, 0 0, 1 250 70"
style="fill:none; stroke:black;
stroke-width:3;" />
<path d="M 110,230 A100 95, 0 0, 1 210 230"
style="fill:none; stroke:black;
stroke-width:2;" />
<path d="M 90,230 A30 195, 0 0, 0 110 230"
style="fill:none; stroke:black;
stroke-width:2;" />
<path d="M 210,230 A100 95, 0 0, 1 210 160"
style="fill:none; stroke:black;
stroke-width:2;" />
<path d="M 210,160 A100 95, 0 0, 0 214 125"
style="fill:none; stroke:black;
stroke-width:2;" />
</svg>
```

Understanding Unity

Users need unity in design to allow them to see a unified product or project. Unity is disrupted when, for example, multiple fonts are used in a project or too many combinations of shapes or color palettes interrupt a single vision of the product. If one portion of a project looks conservative and another portion looks modern, the project seems disjointed and never satisfies.

Three approaches to unity include grouping, repeating, and developing a grid. Grouping implies the obvious; elements grouped together often look as though they belong together. Figure 2-23 shows an example of grouped elements.

These shapes meet the criteria of similar elements, grouped closely, and yet they don't imply unity.

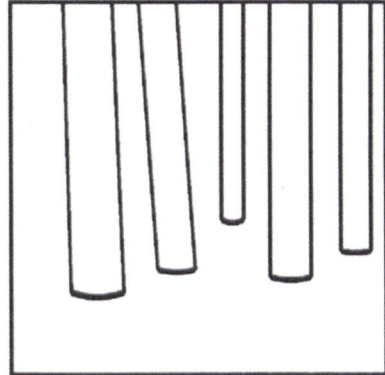

FIGURE 2-23 *Grouped elements*

Listing 2-18 generates the Figure 2-23 shape.

LISTING 2-18 *Shapes Separated*

```
<?xml version="1.0"?>
<svg width="300" height="300">
<rect x="50" y="50" width="200" height="200"
style="fill:none; stroke:black;stroke-width:2;" />
<path d="M 82,206 A 60,90 0 0,0 110,206"
style="fill:none; stroke:black; stroke-width:3;" />
<path d="M 188,198 A 60,90 0 0,0 210,198"
style="fill:none; stroke:black; stroke-width:3;" />
<path d="M 226,184 A 60,90 0 0,0 242,184"
style="fill:none; stroke:black; stroke-width:3;" />
<path d="M 82,206 A 60,90 0 0,0 110,206"
style="fill:none; stroke:black; stroke-width:3;" />
<path d="M 128,194 A 60,90 0 0,0 148,194"
style="fill:none; stroke:black; stroke-width:3;" />
<path d="M 162,167 A 30,90 0 0,0 174,167"
style="fill:none; stroke:black; stroke-width:3;" />
<line x1="78" y1="50" x2="82" y2="206"
style="stroke:black; stroke-width:2;" />
<line x1="104" y1="50" x2="110" y2="206"
style="stroke:black; stroke-width:2;" />
<line x1="118" y1="50" x2="128" y2="194"
style="stroke:black; stroke-width:2;" />
<line x1="138" y1="50" x2="148" y2="194"
style="stroke:black; stroke-width:2;" />
<line x1="174" y1="50" x2="174" y2="167"
style="stroke:black; stroke-width:2;" />
```

```
<line x1="162" y1="50" x2="162" y2="167"
style="stroke:black; stroke-width:2;" />
<line x1="188" y1="50" x2="188" y2="198"
style="stroke:black; stroke-width:2;" />
<line x1="242" y1="50" x2="242" y2="184"
style="stroke:black; stroke-width:2;" />
<line x1="210" y1="50" x2="210" y2="198"
style="stroke:black; stroke-width:2;" />
<line x1="226" y1="50" x2="226" y2="184"
style="stroke:black; stroke-width:2;" />
</svg>
```

One possible remedy to achieve unity is to change the number, spacing, or density of the shapes, and another is to unify the design as one, as shown in Figure 2-24.

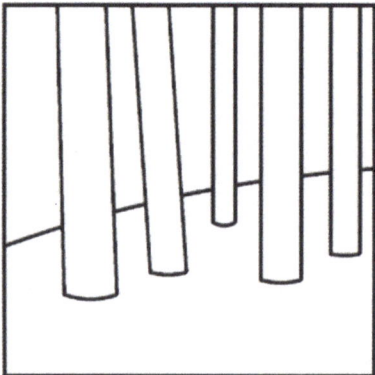

FIGURE 2-24 *Grouped elements, unified*

Listing 2-19 generates the Figure 2-24 shape.

LISTING 2-19 *Shapes Unified*

```
<?xml version="1.0"?>
<svg width="300" height="300">
<rect style="fill:none;stroke:black;stroke-width:2;"
x="50" y="50" width="200" height="200" />
<path d="M 50,180 A 500,300 0 0,1 250 138"
style="fill:none; stroke:black; stroke-width:2;" />
<path d="M 78,50 82,206 A 60,90 0 0,0 110,206 M110,206 104,50 78,50"
style="fill:white; stroke:black; stroke-width:2;" />
<path d="M 188,50 188,198 A 60,90 0 0,0 210,198 M210,198 210,50,188,50"
style="fill:white; stroke:black; stroke-width:2;" />
```

```
<path d="M 226 50 226,184 A 60,90 0 0,0 242,184 M242,184 242,50 226,50"
style="fill:white; stroke:black; stroke-width:2;" />
<path d="M 118,50 128,194 A 60,90 0 0,0 148,194 M 148,194, 138,50 118,50"
style="fill:white; stroke:black; stroke-width:2;" />
<path d="M 162,50 162,167 A 30,90 0 0,0 174,167 M174,167 174,50 162,50"
style="fill:white; stroke:black; stroke-width:2;" />
</svg>
```

Figure 2-24 is unified with a connecting line. You can also achieve unity by incorporating color and texture. A shape or color from a logo can repeat in other aspects of the site such as buttons or a background. Elements can repeat thematically as well as identically. A texture from a product can double as a section title or a graphic border. Repeated elements don't need to be so exactly organized that the design becomes dull. Figure 2-25 shows an example of different lines or shapes as repeated elements in a unified design.

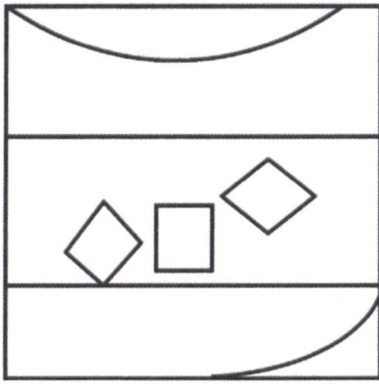

FIGURE 2-25 *Repeated elements*

Listing 2-20 generates the Figure 2-25 shape.

LISTING 2-20 *Shapes Repeated*

```
<?xml version="1.0"?>
<svg width="300" height="300">
<rect x="50" y="50" width="200" height="200"
style=" fill:none; stroke:black; stroke-width:2;" />
<rect style="fill:none; stroke:black;
stroke-width:2;" x="130" y="157" width="30" height="35" />
<line x1="50" y1="120" x2="250" y2="120"
style="stroke:black; stroke-width:2;" />
<path d="M102 200,122 177,102 155,82 182,102 200"
style="fill:none; stroke:black; stroke-width:2;" />
```

```
<path d="M190 132, 165 152, 190 172, 215 152, 190 132"
style="fill:none; stroke:black; stroke-width:2;" />
<line x1="50" y1="200" x2="250" y2="200" style="stroke:black;
stroke-width:2;" />
<path d="M50,50 A 186,235 0 0,0 230,50" style="fill:none;
stroke:black; stroke-width:2;" />
<path d="M160,249 A 100,55 0 0,0 250,205" style="fill:none;
stroke:black; stroke-width:2;" />
</svg>
```

Repeated elements may be simple shapes to categorize content or unified objects, as in Figure 2-26.

FIGURE 2-26 *Repeated elements*

Listing 2-21 generates the Figure 2-26 shape.

LISTING 2-21 *Shapes as Objects or Metaphors*

```
<?xml version='1.0'?>
<svg width="300" height="300">
<g id="leaf">
<ellipse cx="90" cy="220" rx="4" ry="10"
style="fill:none; stroke:black;stroke-width:2;" transform="rotate(40,105,220)" />
</g>
<use xlink:href="#leaf" transform="translate(50,-38) rotate(60,105,220)" />
<use xlink:href="#leaf" transform="translate(75,-9) rotate(100,105,220)" />
<use xlink:href="#leaf" transform="translate(64,-26) rotate(60,105,220)" />
<use xlink:href="#leaf" transform="translate(2,10) rotate(80,105,220)" />
<use xlink:href="#leaf" transform="translate(-2,-40) rotate(90,105,220)" />
<use xlink:href="#leaf" transform="translate(2,-65) rotate(105,105,220)" />
```

```
<use xlink:href="#leaf" transform="translate(-14,-80) rotate(210,105,220)" />
<use xlink:href="#leaf" transform="translate(-17,-60) rotate(210,105,220)" />
<use xlink:href="#leaf" transform="translate(41,-38)" />
<use xlink:href="#leaf" transform="translate(102,-26)" />
<use xlink:href="#leaf" transform="translate(59,-24)" />
<rect x="50" y="50" width="200" height="200"
style="fill:none; stroke:black; stroke-width:2;" />
<path d="M 50,130 A100 95, 0 0, 1 142 70" style="fill:none;
stroke:black; stroke-width:6;" />
<path d="M 120,105 A100 95, 0 0, 0 190 195" style="fill:none;
stroke:black; stroke-width:3;" />
<path d="M 50,50 A100 95, 0 0, 0 160 130" style="fill:none;
stroke:black; stroke-width:6;" />
<path d="M 148,105 A100 95, 0 0, 0 110 230" style="fill:none;
stroke:black; stroke-width:3;" />
</svg>
```

A grid implies a division of space for the purpose of placing graphics, images, or text. Grids don't have to consist of squares or rectangles. Grids are commonly found on news sites where a large amount of content is shown and the piece strives to remain unified and readable. Grids can vary in size and placement to keep the product from appearing too mechanical. In some cases, content almost demands a grid. If so, don't fight it by trying to make something bright, curvy, or distorted. Grids that are clean, simple, and set up their color as clear, crisp, and clean are a pleasure to read. Figure 2-27 uses a traditional grid; its near twin, Figure 2-28, removes some of the lines to add a modicum of variety.

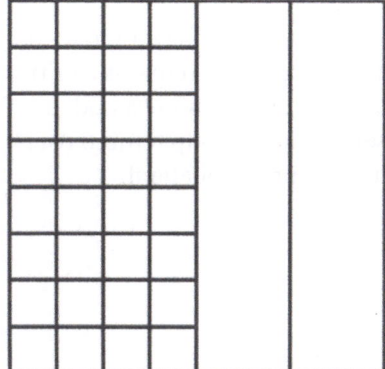

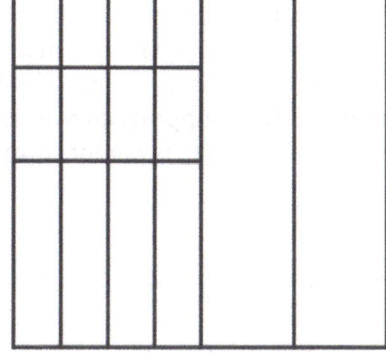

FIGURE 2-27 *Grid elements, crowded*   FIGURE 2-28 *Grid elements, light*

Listing 2-22 generates Figure 2-27. Figure 2-28 uses the same code, minus a few lines.

LISTING 2-22 *Shape, Grid, and Density*

```xml
<?xml version="1.0"?>
<svg width="300" height="300">
<rect x="50" y="50" width="200" height="200"
style="fill:none;
stroke:black; stroke-width:2;" />
<line x1="50" y1="50" x2="50" y2="250" style="stroke:black; stroke-width:2;" />
<line x1="125" y1="50" x2="125" y2="250" style="stroke:black; stroke-width:2;" />
<line x1="200" y1="50" x2="200" y2="250" style="stroke:black; stroke-width:2;" />
<line x1="200" y1="50" x2="250" y2="50" style="stroke:black; stroke-width:2;" />
<line x1="50" y1="50" x2="50" y2="250" style="stroke:black; stroke-width:2;" />
<line x1="75" y1="50" x2="75" y2="250" style="stroke:black; stroke-width:2;" />
<line x1="100" y1="50" x2="100" y2="250" style="stroke:black; stroke-width:2;" />
<line x1="150" y1="50" x2="150" y2="250" style="stroke:black; stroke-width:2;" />
<line x1="50" y1="75" x2="150" y2="75" style="stroke:black; stroke-width:2;" />
<line x1="50" y1="125" x2="150" y2="125" style="stroke:black; stroke-width:2;" />
<line x1="50" y1="75" x2="150" y2="75" style="stroke:black; stroke-width:2;" />
<line x1="50" y1="125" x2="150" y2="125" style="stroke:black; stroke-width:2;" />
<line x1="50" y1="175" x2="150" y2="175" style="stroke:black; stroke-width:2;" />
<line x1="50" y1="100" x2="150" y2="100" style="stroke:black; stroke-width:2;" />
<line x1="50" y1="150" x2="150" y2="150" style="stroke:black; stroke-width:2;" />
<line x1="50" y1="200" x2="150" y2="200" style="stroke:black; stroke-width:2;" />
<line x1="50" y1="225" x2="150" y2="225" style="stroke:black; stroke-width:2;" />
</svg>
```

The goal of unity is to understand which design elements you want to incorporate into a whole and then to tell its visual story. A focal point remains a critical element of the design; emphasis is placed both on the point of interest and on the unified product. Unity supports an overall theme and can help remind users of the link between a product, its parent company, and print collateral.

Understanding Contrast

Contrast can keep a design from becoming static. Contrast implies "let's mix it up" and allows some shapes to be bold and interesting. Contrast can also serve to help users understand the size or scope of an image in relationship to another. Contrast "wakes up" a design visually in the same way that words of different strengths can enliven a conversation.

Figure 2-29, as an example, shows a lot of activity but no contrast.

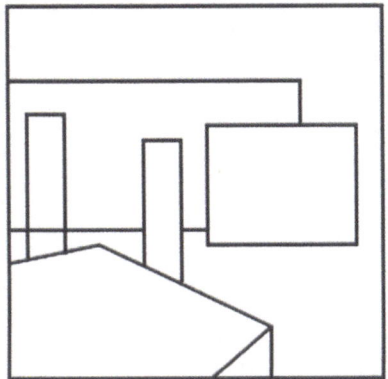

FIGURE 2-29 *Geometric shapes, no contrast*

Listing 2-23 generates the Figure 2-29 shape.

LISTING 2-23 *Shapes Without Contrast*

```
<?xml version="1.0"?>
<svg width="300" height="300">
<rect x="50" y="50" width="200" height="200"
style=" fill:none;
stroke:black; stroke-width:2;" />
<rect style="fill:none; stroke:black;
stroke-width:2;" x="156" y="114" width="80" height="64" />
<path d="M 50 90,206 90,206 114" style="fill:none; stroke:black;
stroke-width:2;" />
<path d="M 122 189,122 122,142 122,142 198" style="fill:none;
stroke:black; stroke-width:2;" />
<path d="M 50 188,98 178,190 222,158 250,190 250,190 222"
style="fill:none; stroke:black; stroke-width:2;" />
<line x1="50" y1="170" x2="122" y2="170" style="stroke:black;
stroke-width:2;" />
<line x1="142" y1="170" x2="156" y2="170" style="stroke:black;
stroke-width:2;" />
<path d="M 60 185,60 108,80 108,80 183" style="fill:none; stroke:black;
stroke-width:2;" />
</svg>
```

Adjusting line density can change the contrast of the design. You can add contrast by incorporating color or texture from the company logo or samples of company products. Background images, collage effects, and an interesting combination of space and shape significantly changes the design contrast.

Figure 2-30 conveys contrast.

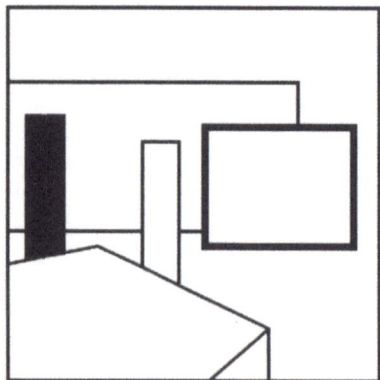

FIGURE 2-30 *Geometric shapes, line contrast*

Contrast changes the focal point and the order of where you want the user to look. Listing 2-24 generates the Figure 2-30 shape.

LISTING 2-24 *Shapes with Contrast*

```
<?xml version="1.0"?>
<svg width="300" height="300">
<rect style="fill:none;stroke:black;
stroke-width:2;" x="50" y="50"
width="200" height="200" />
<rect style="fill:none; stroke:black;
stroke-width:4;" x="156" y="114"
width="80" height="64" />
<path d="M 50 90,206 90,206 114"
style="fill:none; stroke:black;
stroke-width:2;" />
<path d="M 122 189,122 122,142 122,142 198" style="fill:none;
stroke:black; stroke-width:2;" />
<path d="M 50 188,98 178,190 222,158 250,190 250,190 222"
style="fill:none; stroke:black; stroke-width:2;" />
<line x1="50" y1="170" x2="122" y2="170" style="stroke:black; stroke-width:2;" />
<line x1="142" y1="170" x2="156" y2="170" style="stroke:black; stroke-width:2;" />
<path d="M 60 185,60 108,80 108,80 183" style="fill:black; stroke:black;
stroke-width:2;" />
</svg>
```

You can apply the design principles of balance, emphasis, rhythm, unity, and contrast to all design elements. Critiquing initial sketches and incorporating the design elements described in Chapter 4 ensures a simple transition to layout that meets client and user expectations.

Design Principle Axioms

Balance is an aesthetically pleasing integration of design elements and includes the following types:

- Symmetrical balance: Similar elements balanced to the right and left of center.

- Asymmetrical balance: Different positive and negative elements that, together, appear balanced.

- Unbalanced: Sometimes a viable but risky solution. Be careful because an unbalanced design often creates confusion or disorientation for the user.

- Radial balance: This is atypical for Web design; it balances a radial or orbital space.

Balance does not imply an exact set of shapes. Size, shape, color, and density can "weigh" shapes so that some elements are emphasized for the purpose of the story and others exist to support and unify.

Emphasis is the visual priority point of the design, often set by placement, isolation, or shape. The goal of a focal point is to direct the user to the key design element and invite interpretation and exploration of the balance of the work. Without a focal point, users glance at a design and find no "entry point" to inter-action. Content appears as too much information with no direction, and the user typically leaves.

Rhythm sets the tempo for the design. Typically a combination of repetition of shape or space, different rhythm styles set a mood of movement in the design. Simple, same-sized repetition of shape and space communicates a smooth rhythm. Interruptions in repetition and changes in space and shape speed up the tempo. Vertical, rectangular, triangular, diagonal, circular, and curvilinear rhythms act as metaphors for the theme of the project. Too much repetition becomes annoying to the user. Experiment with more and with less repetition to find the point where the addition confirms your intent and then stop at that point.

Unity unifies the multiple pieces of a project into a whole. Especially important for sites with a heavy content emphasis, unity helps to remind users of the theme and purpose of the site as they interact with one piece. Three approaches to unity include grouping, repeating, and developing a grid. If there are so many pieces to a project that unity seems impossible, keep the design elements (type, line, space, and color) as clean as possible and strive for clarity and readability.

Contrast supports emphasis on certain elements. This is different from the focal point. A focal point draws the user to your priority, and contrast breaks up the monotony and helps a site to be less static. Contrast and unity often take place with simple changes to color, line density, and space that affect the overall interpretation of the user.

Chapter 3 incorporates the concepts of Chapter 1 and this chapter into a commercial project.

In Chapter 4 you will see how design principles, applied to design elements, mesh to transition your ideas closer to the Chapter 5 focus of layout. This sounds like a lot of concept, but the following is how the design process model looks in summary:

1. Language (words) transitions to visual representation (shapes).

2. Shapes (concepts) transition to initial sketches.

3. The critique of initial sketches incorporates the principles of design.

4. The improvement of sketches takes place by identifying how the design elements apply, based on design principles.

5. The design elements, then, become a preliminary layout, typically in the form of a sketch prototype.

6. The preliminary layout is critiqued based on the layout principles and on how the layout looks and works with the addition of content. Style, functionality, and navigation are critiqued together.

7. Color is added or adjusted as a design element and is tested for browsers and for project output devices.

8. Typography is incorporated and critiqued as a design element and is tested for browsers and for project output devices.

9. The digital prototype is created and tested.

10. Upon prototype approval, the project build begins.

This process may take place over a day, a week, or a month, depending on the client and the magnitude of the project. It's important to note, however, that although it may appear to be 10 extra steps that you have little time to support, following all or part of this guideline directly affects client and user satisfaction and, as a result, your profit. In the same way that user analysis and documentation take time up front to save money and time over the long run, these steps result in a product design that all stakeholders are satisfied with and a confident client who steps away enough to allow you to complete the build.

Finally, the best designs happen with the fewest necessary elements. By the time you create your initial sketches, you have a good understanding of the client's needs and, often, the users' needs. Sketches allow you to stretch your imagination a bit and utilize the creative side of your brain to model expressive shapes. Transitioning from basic shapes to a layout or product design can get a little frustrating. On one hand, you understand generally where you want to go and yet, on the other hand, the ideas, product content, code, browser issues, and project deadlines begin to weigh on you. Rather than sitting at your keyboard waiting for a flash of inspiration, think about incorporating design principles as the natural next step in the design and development process.

Project 1:
Building an Open-Source Portal

Only when he no longer knows what he is doing does the painter do good things.

—Edgar Degas, painter (1834–1917)

This chapter's open-source portal offers a free e-learning portal for non-profit organizations around the world. We call the model *Dynamic Learning*. The concept for the Dynamic Learning model was the result of learning that e-learning portals cost about $5,000 Euro/USD in countries where the average monthly wage is less than $500 Euro/USD. These existing portals may well provide components worth their price; the point of this chapter isn't to criticize but to offer an alternative to individuals and groups with no budget money to spend. You can also modify the code for this project to create other types of portals.

The chapter starts by looking at a mini-requirements document for the project based on the first six sections of the Volere Requirements Specification Template, and then the chapter presents the underlying code.

Creating a Mini-Requirements Specification for the Open-Source Portal

As detailed in Chapter 2, a requirements specification contains several sections: the purpose of the product, the stakeholders, the users of the product, the mandated constraints, the naming conventions and definitions, and any relevant facts and assumptions. The following sections define the requirements specification for the open-source e-learning portal.

The Purpose of the Product

The purpose of the product is as follows:

The user problem or background to the project effort: Online curriculum has been severely limited because of the difficulty of providing well-constructed, easily navigated online course portals for organizations with limited financial resources. Educators without technical, financial, and/or time resources can't easily create structured online courses. Users of the delivered product will create an upload-ready online course from flexible, customizable templates.

The goal of the project: The goal of the product is to produce, at no cost to the customer, online course construction tools with sufficient capabilities to handle secondary and post-secondary educational coursework. Furthermore, it should be simple enough to be easily implemented and used by nontechnical customers.

Clients, Customers, and Other Stakeholders

The clients, customers, and other stakeholders are as follows:

The client (the people paying for the development and the owners of the delivered system): The clients are Kelly Carey and Stanko Blatnik.

The customer (the people who will buy the product from the client): The potential customer base is composed of secondary and/or post-secondary educators and nonprofit organizations wanting to offer coursework online. The portal will be free to educators and organizations.

Other stakeholders: Other stakeholders include online students and secondary/post-secondary educators. For online students, no direct knowledge is necessary for project completion. However, the student stakeholder as a tester/user is paramount in the project test phase and will determine, to a significant degree, the success or failure of the project.

It will be necessary to get input from the secondary/post-secondary online educators to create an interface that nontechnical users can easily use. The secondary/post-secondary online educator stakeholder as a tester/user is also paramount in the project test phase and will determine, to a significant degree, the success or failure of the project.

Users of the Product

The following sections detail the users of the product.

The Users of the Product

Potential users of the product are secondary and post-secondary students not defined by age or gender. The product must conform to Federal Regulations Section 508 of the Rehabilitation Act of 1973 (accessibility), and the minimum technological experience of the user is "novice." The product will be customizable to allow for a range of users.

All users will have basic computer skills including the ability to save files and the ability to point and select items in a graphical user interface. Users are expected to be able to use standard Internet browsers.

Users will be using freeware and shareware to set up their services that will host the product. The person(s) loading and maintaining the software on the server will need specialized knowledge.

The Priorities Assigned to Users

The key users are as follows:

- Teachers and support staff
- Students
- Information Technology (IT) support staff

  The secondary users are as follows:

- System designers
- Educational institutions
- Nonprofit institutions

User Participation

Feedback from the primary users (teachers and support staff, students, and IT support staff) is necessary to assess the viability of the product interface.

Teachers and/or support staff will be expected to input their own material. Teachers will need to convert existing material to online material and to create new online material. The product will provide the templates, instructions, and technical support to aid in the creation and conversion process.

Mandated Constraints

The following sections describe the mandated constraints of the product.

Solution Constraints

The solution constraints are as follows:

- The product must be accessible via a 56Kbps modem, a 15-inch monitor, Internet Explorer 5+/Netscape 4.76+ or Opera 5+/America Online 7+, and Windows 9.*x*, Windows NT, Windows 2000+, Windows ME, Windows XP, or Mac OS 8+.

- The solutions must be delivered with open-source code.

- The final product must be available for free.

- Faculty and students must use the same conceptual interface.

- It must be simple to use, edit, and update the Web-based application.

- Server-side code must include options for PHP, JavaServer Pages (JSP), and Active Server Pages (ASP).

- The underlying code will be based on or compatible with Extensible Markup Language (XML).

Implementation Environment of the Current System

The product will be "upload ready" to a server running an Apache or Windows 2000+ server.

Partner Applications

The partner applications are a Scalable Vector Graphics (SVG) viewer and Adobe Acrobat Reader 4+ if any materials are uploaded as Portable Document Format (PDF) file links.

Commercial Off-the-Shelf Packages

The portal must support browser software as described in the "Solution Constraints" section. Users will also need access to the Internet.

Anticipated Workplace Environment

A typical workplace will be in the home, educational institution, or job environment; this includes any suitable indoor environment for a personal computer (including such requirements as adequate power supply, telephone or other Internet access line, raised work surface, and proper seating).

Not all users will have immediate access to printers or more than occasional access to the Internet. Content will be delivered from the Internet, from a hard drive, or from a disk/CD-ROM/DVD.

Development Period

The beta is due in September 2003. Version 1 is due in January 2004. Version 2 is due in June 2004.

Financial Budget

There's no financial budget. Zip, nada, none.

Naming Conventions and Definitions

The product will use the following naming conventions and definitions:

- **Designer**: This person constructs the product interface.
- **Developer**: This person generates the source code to implement the product.
- **Technical writer**: This person generates the original copy for the documentation and technical support.
- **Interface**: This is the product/user online interface.
- **Prerelease product**: This is any form of the product that has not been beta tested.
- **Product**: This is the complete, user-ready, beta-tested e-learning portal.

Relevant Facts and Assumptions

The process includes the facts and assumptions in the following sections.

External Factors

External factors that affect the product but are not mandated constraints include but are not limited to unintentional copyright infringements, mandated use of pre-existing online course systems by educational institutions, future versions of operating systems, and advances in the availability and the cost of broadband connections. Initially, the product will be distributed in English. As the testing progresses in different countries, separate versions will be made available in different languages.

Assumptions

The team is making the following assumptions:

- Time will be allocated to meet production deadlines and provide continuing customer support.

- Online learning environments will continue to gain acceptance as a viable alternative to standard classroom delivery.

- Demand for the product will not be precluded by a similar, superior product, first to market.

- Open-source code will continue to be supported.

- Initial components may need to be delivered on a CD-ROM.

- Templates will need to be provided to assist in setting up different server configurations.

- Technical support and documentation will be a key part of the project's success and acceptance.

- Participating teachers, educational institutions, and nonprofit organizations will agree to the terms of the shareware agreement.

- The skill levels of users will vary widely.

Examining the Code

The descriptive language driving the interface design is as follows:

- Unique but familiar

- Simple

- Open and supportive with content as the focal point

Figure 3-1 shows one of four template designs. Listing 3-1 generates the Figure 3-1 layout.

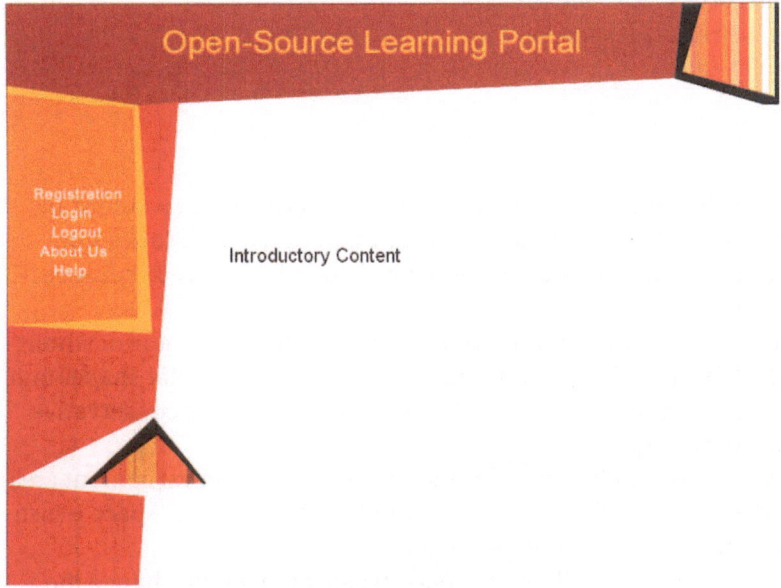

FIGURE 3-1 *Design of the index page*

LISTING 3-1 *Index Page Layout*

```
<?xml version="1.0" encoding="UTF-8"?>
<!DOCTYPE html PUBLIC "-//W3C//DTD XHTML 1.0 Strict//EN"
"http://www.w3.org/TR/xhtml1/DTD/xhtml1-strict.dtd">
<html xmlns="http://www.w3.org/1999/xhtml" xml:lang="en" lang="en">
<head>
<title>Open-Source Learning Portal</title>
<!--The style is defined in portal1.css-->
<link rel="stylesheet" type="text/css" href="portal1.css"/>
</head>
<body>
<!-- The graphics are saved in the documents templateA
and templateB and are called using the object element.-->
<p class="svg1"><object data="templateA.svg"
type="image/svg+xml" width="900" height="105">
<p>Sorry, your browser does not support SVG</p></object></p>
<p class="svg2"><object data="templateB.svg"
type="image/svg+xml" width="225" height="700">
<p>Sorry, your browser does not support SVG</p></object></p>
<!-- The data from the form are sent to document createTest.asp to process.-->
```

```
<form action="createTest.asp" method="post">
<p class="text1">Introductory Content</p>
</form>
</body>
</html>
```

The `<p>..</p>` element nests `<object>..</object>` because you wouldn't be able to validate without it. (Check this with your validation tool; it varies from time to time.) The code doesn't use the deprecated `<embed>..</embed>` because it doesn't validate either.

The design's top-and-side bar is for the benefit of educators, some of whom feel more comfortable working in a traditional design. The triangular shapes and a bit of a diagonal emphasis on the top-and-side bar break up the conservative feel and yet keep the design familiar.

Readability is important for any educational tool, so the central content area of the site is white for the addition of large amounts of content. The space is also large enough for faculty to include content graphics.

One design priority was to allow each person using the tool to change the labeling on the top bar and on the buttons. Historically, graphics as buttons have been problematic because you needed the original file and application it was created in to change the button content. Additionally, changing the word on a button from *Home* to *Course Offerings*, for example, could throw off an entire layout because of a change in the graphic size.

This layout uses two graphics to combine the graphical element with text because it's not possible to incorporate forms and SVG. If it were possible to build an active form with SVG, you could build the layout and form within one SVG file.

Figure 3-2 represents the first graphic.

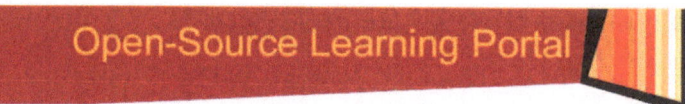

FIGURE 3-2 *The top bar*

Listing 3-2 generates the Figure 3-2 graphic.

LISTING 3-2 *The Top Bar*

```
<?xml version='1.0'?>
<svg width="800" height="105">
<!-- The graphics generate from several SVG polyline elements.
The color of the shape is defined by the value of attribute "fill"
using rgb mode.-->
<polyline points="0 0,690 0,690 78, 134 105,0 85, 0 0"
style="fill:rgb(166,0,0);" />
```

```
<polyline points="179 101, 134 105,177 105, 179 101"
style="fill:rgb(198,33,0);" />
<polyline points="0 101, 0 85,135 105,89 105, 0 101"
style="fill:rgb(255,168,0);" />
<polyline points="0 105, 91 105, 0 93,0 105"
style="fill:rgb(255,112,23);" />
<!--The title is generates from the SVG "text" element.-->
<text x="161" y="51" style="fill:rgb(255,168,0);
font-size:22pt;">Open-Source Learning Portal</text>
<g id="top" transform="translate(690,0)">
<polyline points="0 0,8 0, 0 78, 0 0"
style="fill:rgb(166,0,0);" />
<polyline points="17 40,17 74,7 71,16 40"
style="fill:rgb(250,175,70);" />
<polyline points="17 36,17 74,22 76,22 18,17 36"
style="fill:rgb(255,96,57);" />
<polyline points="22 76,22 23,28 0,35 0, 35 79,22 76"
style="fill:rgb(255,111,30);" />
<polyline points="35 0, 35 79, 50 84,50 0, 35 0"
style="fill:rgb(255,55,27);" />
<polyline points="50 84,50 0, 56 0, 56 85,50 84"
style="fill:rgb(251,114,18);" />
<polyline points="56 0, 56 85,59 86, 59 0,56 0"
style="fill:rgb(255,51,26);" />
<polyline points="59 86, 59 0,68 0, 68 88,59 86"
style="fill:rgb(255,173,93);" />
<polyline points="68 0, 68 88,78 91, 78 0,68 0"
style="fill:rgb(255,42,26);" />
<polyline points="78 91, 78 0,84 0, 84 92,78 91"
style="fill:rgb(252,222,123);" />
<polyline points="84 0, 84 93,92 95, 94 0,84 0"
style="fill:rgb(254,169,78);" />
<polyline points="92 95, 92 0,99 0, 99 97,92 95"
style="fill:rgb(255,255,255);" />
<polyline points="99 0, 99 97,101 98, 101 0,99 0"
style="fill:rgb(255,175,56);" />
<polyline points="101 98, 101 0,105 0, 105 99"
style="fill:rgb(251,226,123);" />
<polyline points="106 0, 110 0, 110 110, 0 78, 8 0, 29 0, 8 71, 105 97, 105 0"
style="fill:rgb(0,0,0);" />
</g>
</svg>
```

Figure 3-3 shows the second graphic.

FIGURE 3-3 *The side bar*

Listing 3-3 generates the Figure 3-3 graphic.

LISTING 3-3 *The Side Bar*

```
<?xml version='1.0'?>
<svg>
<g transform="translate(0,313)">
<!-- The graphics generate from several SVG "polyline"
elements using attribute "fill" for colors. -->
<polyline points="81 84, 152 15, 206 84, 203 84, 156 32, 87 84"
style="fill:rgb(0,0,0);" />
<polyline points="87 84, 91 78, 95 79, 95 84,87 84"
style="fill:rgb(194,52,10);" />
<polyline points="95 77, 100 74, 100 84, 95 84,95 77"
style="fill:rgb(195,57,13);" />
<polyline points="99 84, 99 74, 101 74, 101 84,99 84"
style="fill:rgb(147,40,13);" />
<polyline points="101 84, 101 74, 116 61, 116 84,101 84"
style="fill:rgb(253,72,5);" />
<polyline points="102 84, 102 71,103 71,103 84,102 84"
style="fill:rgb(0,0,0);" />
<polyline points="116 84, 116 62, 124 56,124 84,116 84"
```

```
style="fill:rgb(211,46,2);" />
<polyline points="124 84, 124 56, 127 52, 127 84"
style="fill:rgb(252,131,15);" />
<polyline points="127 84, 127 50, 129 52, 129 84,127 84"
style="fill:rgb(217, 124,41);" />
<polyline points="129 84, 129 52,155 33,155 84,129 84"
style="fill:rgb(217, 124,41);" />
<polyline points="132 84, 132 47, 134 46, 134 84, 132 84"
style="fill:rgb(173,85,36);" />
<polyline points="142 84, 142 41, 143 40, 143 84, 142 84"
style="fill:rgb(173,85,36);" />
<polyline points="155 84,155 31,166 44,166 84"
style="fill:rgb(204,48,3);" />
<polyline points="166 84,166 44,187 65,187 84,166 84"
style="fill:rgb(253,72,5);" />
<polyline points="186 84,186 64,194 73,194 84, 186 84"
style="fill:rgb(147,40,13);" />
<polyline points="194 84,194 75, 202 82,202 84, 192 84"
style="fill:rgb(238,72,6);" />
<polyline points="174 84,174 53,175 55,175 84,174 84"
style="fill:rgb(216,52,4);" />
<polyline points="179 84,179 58,181 61,181 84,179 84"
style="fill:rgb(203,52,8);" />
<polyline points="81 84, 152 15, 206 84, 203 84, 156 32, 87 84"
style="fill:rgb(0,0,0);" />
</g>

<polyline points="0 0, 177 0,153 322,0 398, 0 0"
style="fill:rgb(198,33,0);" />
<polyline points="89 0, 136 0,150 240,0 231, 0 0, 89 0"
style="fill:rgb(255,168,0);" />
<polyline points="0 0, 133 24,150 240,0 231, 0 0"
style="fill:rgb(255,168,0);" />
<polyline points="0 0, 89 0,91 0,131 5,135 224,0 231, 0 0"
style="fill:rgb(255,112,23);" />
<polyline points="0 398, 143 410,125 671,0 671, 0 398"
style="fill:rgb(198,33,0);" />
<!-- The menu generates from "text" and a xlink:href...
element. You can easily change link text. -->
<a xlink:href="RegTeacher.html">
<text x="27" y="100" style="fill:white; font-size:9pt;
letter-spacing:1;">Registration</text></a>
<a xlink:href="LogTeacher.html">
```

```
<text x="46" y="120" style="fill:white; font-size:9pt;
letter-spacing:1;">Login</text></a>
<a xlink:href="LogoutTeacher.html"><text x="46" y="140"
style="fill:white; font-size:9pt; letter-spacing:1;">Logout</text></a>
<a xlink:href="aboutUsTeacher.html">
<text x="34" y="160"
style="fill:white; font-size:9pt; letter-spacing:1;">About Us</text></a>
<a xlink:href="HelpTeacher.html">
<text x="48" y="180" style="fill:white; font-size:9pt;
letter-spacing:1;">Help</text></a>
</svg>
```

Listing 3-4 shows the Extensible Hypertext Markup Language (XHTML) and SVG combination used for the Cascading Style Sheet (CSS) code.

LISTING 3-4 *Style Information*

```
.svg1 {position: absolute; top: 0 px; left:0;}
.svg2 {position: absolute; top: 105px; left:0;}
.text1 {position: absolute; left: 230px; top: 180px;
font-family: arial, helvetica, sans-serif; font-size: 12pt;}
.text2{position: absolute; left: 230px; top: 210px;
font-family: arial, helvetica, sans-serif; font-size: 12pt;}
.text3{position: absolute; left: 240px; top: 240px;
font-family: arial, helvetica, sans-serif; font-size: 12pt;}
.text4{position: absolute; left: 230px; top: 270px;
font-family: arial, helvetica, sans-serif; font-size: 12pt;}
.text5{position: absolute; left: 230px; top: 300px;
font-family: arial, helvetica, sans-serif; font-size: 12pt;}
.text6{position: absolute; left: 240px; top: 330px;
font-family: arial, helvetica, sans-serif; font-size: 12pt;}
```

You could simplify this particular CSS file because there's repetition in the `font-family` properties and in the positioning. Although it's nice to write the code as compactly as possible, you have to make sure that it runs in multiple browsers. You should test any use of CSS attributes or substring selectors in browsers you anticipate your users to use.

The decision to use this much CSS was because of, in great part, the implementation problems associated with tables in pre-5.0 browsers and the inconsistent presentation output in post-5.0 browsers.

SVG allows for a quick change in color palette, as shown in Figure 3-4.

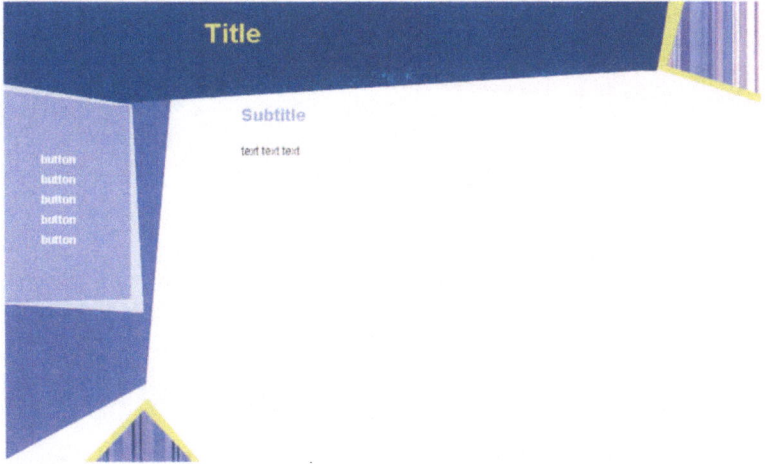

FIGURE 3-4 *Changing the color*

Addressing Implementation Issues

Regardless of how you nest the tables for this design, there's always whitespace between the SVG files and whitespace at the top-left corner of the screen. Additionally, we had trouble placing the form where we wanted it. The code was correct, but the browser output didn't work from a visual perspective. Debugging focused on how to keep the code as simple as possible and yet output the graphics as though they had been created and sliced in an illustration application. The focus of this process is to really do it right visually. It's easy to have just a little gap and decide to live with it. But don't shortcut visual presentation; it has to look perfect, and you must browser test it. Figure 3-5 shows the XHTML code for the table attempt (shown from the root element on).

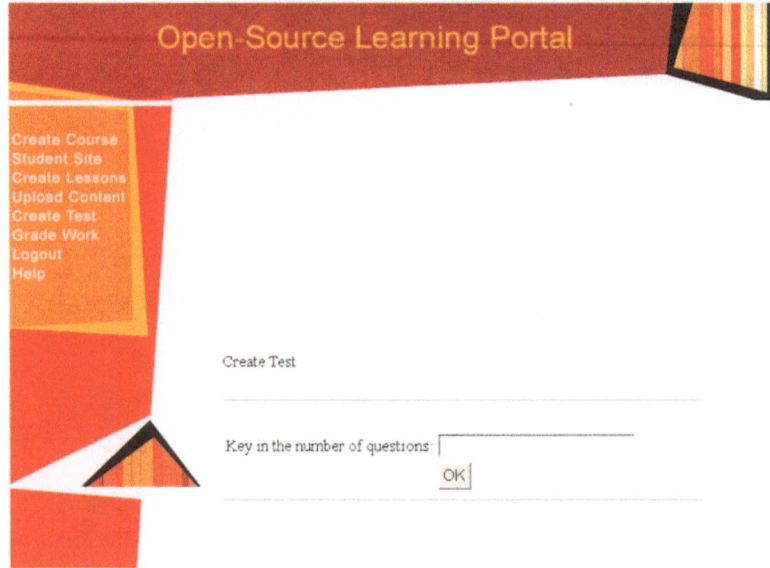

FIGURE 3-5 *Table implementation issues*

Listing 3-5 generates the Figure 3-5 graphic.

LISTING 3-5 *Using Tables*

```
<html>
<!-- The graphics are saved in the documents templateA and
templateB and are called using the object element-->
<table>
<tr>
<td><object data="templateA.svg" type="image/svg+xml" width="900" height="105">
<p>Sorry, your browser does not support SVG</p>
</object></td>
</tr>
</table>
<table>
<tr><td>
<object data="templateB1.svg" type="image/svg+xml" width="225" height="700">
<p>Sorry, your browser does not support SVG</p></object></td>
<td><table width="500" border="0" cellspacing="0" cellpadding="0" >
<tr>
<td>
<!--Start-->
<p>Create Test</p>
<hr />
```

```
<!--The form is used to input the number of questions,
data are processed with the createTest.asp document-->
<form action="createTest.asp" method="post">
<table border="0">
<tr>
<td>Key in the number of questions:</td>
<td><input type="text" name="countQ"></td>
</tr>
<tr>
<td> </td>
<td><input type="submit" name="B1" value="OK"></td>
</tr>
</table>
<hr />
</form>
<!--End-->
</p></td></tr></table></tr></table></html>
```

Once users enter the site, the left navigation links change. Figure 3-6 shows the secondary navigation graphic.

FIGURE 3-6 *The secondary navigation graphic*

Listing 3-6 generates the Figure 3-6 graphic.

LISTING 3-6 *The Secondary Navigation*

```
<?xml version='1.0'?>
<svg>
<g transform="translate(0,313)">
<polyline points="81 84, 152 15, 206 84, 203 84, 156 32, 87 84"
style="fill:rgb(0,0,0);" />
<polyline points="87 84, 91 78, 95 79, 95 84,87 84"
style="fill:rgb(194,52,10);" />
<polyline points="95 77, 100 74, 100 84, 95 84,95 77"
style="fill:rgb(195,57,13);" />
<polyline points="99 84, 99 74, 101 74, 101 84,99 84"
style="fill:rgb(147,40,13);" />
<polyline points="101 84, 101 74, 116 61, 116 84,101 84"
style="fill:rgb(253,72,5);" />
<polyline points="102 84, 102 71,103 71,103 84,102 84"
style="fill:rgb(0,0,0);" />
<polyline points="116 84, 116 62, 124 56,124 84,116 84"
style="fill:rgb(211,46,2);" />
<polyline points="124 84, 124 56, 127 52, 127 84"
style="fill:rgb(252,131,15);" />
<polyline points="127 84, 127 50, 129 52, 129 84,127 84"
style="fill:rgb(217, 124,41);" />
<polyline points="129 84, 129 52,155 33,155 84,129 84"
style="fill:rgb(217, 124,41);" />
<polyline points="132 84, 132 47, 134 46, 134 84, 132 84"
style="fill:rgb(173,85,36);" />
<polyline points="142 84, 142 41, 143 40, 143 84, 142 84"
style="fill:rgb(173,85,36);" />
<polyline points="155 84,155 31,166 44,166 84"
style="fill:rgb(204,48,3);" />
<polyline points="166 84,166 44,187 65,187 84,166 84"
style="fill:rgb(253,72,5);" />
<polyline points="186 84,186 64,194 73,194 84, 186 84"
style="fill:rgb(147,40,13);" />
<polyline points="194 84,194 75, 202 82,202 84, 192 84"
style="fill:rgb(238,72,6);" />
<polyline points="174 84,174 53,175 55,175 84,174 84"
style="fill:rgb(216,52,4);" />
<polyline points="179 84,179 58,181 61,181 84,179 84"
style="fill:rgb(203,52,8);" />
```

```
<polyline points="81 84, 152 15, 206 84, 203 84, 156 32, 87 84"
style="fill:rgb(0,0,0);" />
</g>
<polyline points="0 0, 177 0,153 322,0 398, 0 0"
style="fill:rgb(198,33,0);" />
<polyline points="89 0, 136 0,150 240,0 231, 0 0, 89 0"
style="fill:rgb(255,168,0);" />
<polyline points="0 0, 133 24,150 240,0 231, 0 0"
style="fill:rgb(255,168,0);" />
<polyline points="0 0, 89 0,91 0,131 5,135 224,0 231, 0 0"
style="fill:rgb(255,112,23);" />
<polyline points="0 398, 143 410,125 671,0 671, 0 398"
style="fill:rgb(198,33,0);" />
<a xlink:href="CourseRegistration.html"><text x="10" y="40"
style="fill:white; font-size:9pt; letter-spacing:1;">Create Course</text></a>
<a xlink:href="..//template3/index.html"><text x="10" y="60"
style="fill:white; font-size:9pt; letter-spacing:1;">Student Site</text></a>
<a xlink:href="PrepareLesson.html"><text x="10" y="80"
style="fill:white; font-size:9pt; letter-spacing:1;">Create Lessons </text></a>
<a xlink:href="UploadTeacher.html"><text x="10" y="100"
style="fill:white; font-size:9pt; letter-spacing:1;">Upload Content</text></a>
<a xlink:href="TestTeacher.html"><text x="10" y="120"
style="fill:white; font-size:9pt; letter-spacing:1;">Create Test</text></a>
<a xlink:href="StudentRead.asp"><text x="10" y="140"
style="fill:white; font-size:9pt; letter-spacing:1;">Grade Work</text></a>
<a xlink:href="LogoutTeacher.html"><text x="10" y="160"
style="fill:white; font-size:9pt;
letter-spacing:1;">Logout</text></a>
<a xlink:href="HelpTeacher.html"><text x="10" y="180"
style="fill:white; font-size:9pt;
letter-spacing:1;">Help</text></a>
```

Next, you can try combining the XHTML tables and CSS to keep some structure and allow more control over placement, but there are browser issues again,
as shown in Figure 3-7.

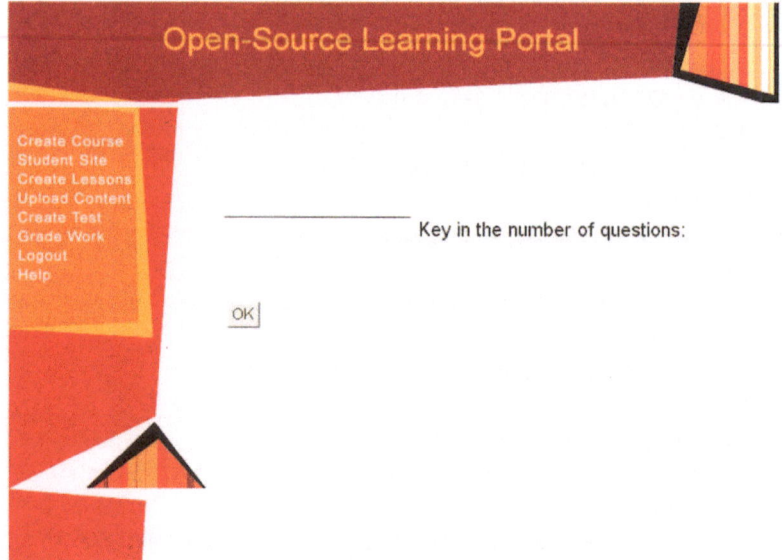

FIGURE 3-7 *Table/CSS browser implementation issues*

Listing 3-7 generates the Figure 3-7 graphic. The CSS remains the same as in Listing 3-4.

LISTING 3-7 *Combinging XHTML Tables and CSS*

```
<html>
<head>
<link rel="stylesheet" type="text/css" href="portal1.css">
</head>
<table border="0">
<tr>
<td class="rect"><object data="templateA.svg"
type="image/svg+xml" width="900" height="105">
<p>Sorry your browser does not support SVG</p>
</object></td>
</table>
<table>
<tr><td class="rect2"><object data="templateB1.svg"
type="image/svg+xml" width="225" height="700">
<p>Sorry, your browser does not support SVG</p>
</object></td>
```

```
<td><form action="createTest.asp" method="post">
<table border="0">
<tr>
<td class="text3">
<input type="text" name="countQ"> Key in the number of questions:</td>
</tr>
<tr>
<td> </td>
<td class="text6"><input type="submit" name="B1" value="OK"></td>
</tr></table></form>
<!--End-->
</td></tr></table></html>
```

Setting Interface Options

The second part of the interface, beyond the index page, is the registration page, as shown in Figure 3-8.

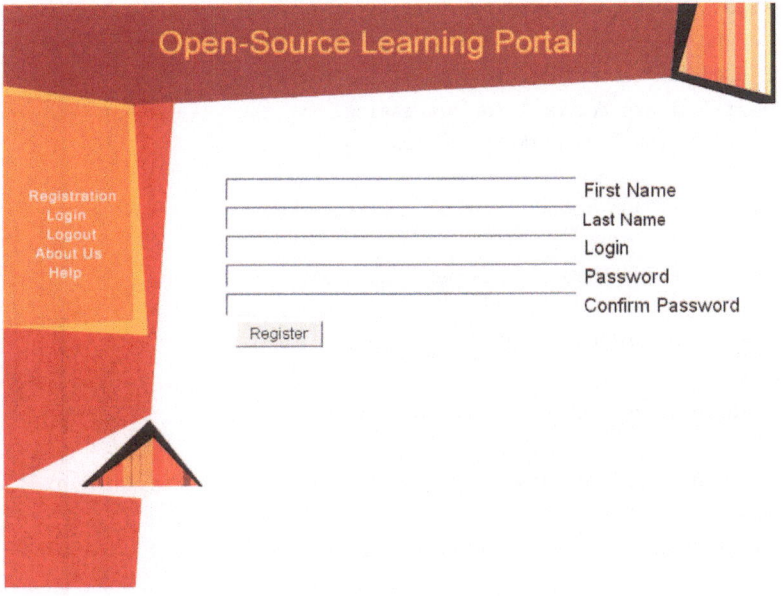

FIGURE 3-8 *The registration form*

Listing 3-8 generates the registration form using XHTML.

LISTING 3-8 *The Registration Form*

```
<?xml version="1.0" encoding="UTF-8"?>
<!DOCTYPE html
PUBLIC "-//W3C//DTD XHTML 1.0 Strict//EN"
"http://www.w3.org/TR/xhtml1/DTD/xhtml1-strict.dtd">
<html xmlns="http://www.w3.org/1999/xhtml" xml:lang="en" lang="en">
<head><title>Portal SVG</title>
<link rel="stylesheet" type="text/css"
href="portal1.css" />
</head>
<body>
<p class="svg1"><object data="templateA.svg"
type="image/svg+xml" width="900" height="105">
<p>Sorry, your browser does not support SVG</p>
</object></p>
<p class="svg2"><object data="templateB.svg"
type="image/svg+xml" width="225" height="700">
<p>Sorry, your browser does not support SVG</p>
</object></p>
<!--The form is used for teacher input. Data are
submitted to createTest.asp document for processing.-->
<form method="post" action="teacherRegistration.asp">
<p class="text1">
<input type="text" size="40" name="firstName"/>First Name</p>
<p class="text2">
<input type="text" size="40" name="lastName"/>Last Name</p>
<p class="text3">
<input type="text" size="40" name="ID" />Login</p>
<p class="text4">
<input type="password" size="40" name="password"/>Password</p>
<p class="text5">
<input type="password" size="40" name="confirmPassword"/>Confirm Password</p>
<p class="text6">
<input type="submit" name="B1" value="Register"/></p>
</form>
</body>
</html>
```

JavaScript creates the XML document in which data regarding registration resides. We elected to stay away from a database until such time that a student or teacher population makes it necessary. Listing 3-9 uses ASP and JavaScript for registration purposes. You can also use JSP or PHP.

LISTING 3-9 *Registration Logic*

```
<%@Language="JavaScript"%>
<%
teachXml=Server.CreateObject("Microsoft.XMLDOM")
/* Instantiates the Microsoft DOM object and assigns it reference teachXml.*/
teachXml.async=false
/* Loading is done synchronously.*/
teachXml.load(Server.MapPath("teacher.xml"))
/*Loading the XML document teacher.xml.*/
if (teachXml.parseError !=0)
{
Response.Write(teachXml.parseError.reason)
/*Messaging if there's an error in the XML document.*/
}
firstNameS=Request.Form("firstName")
lastNameS=Request.Form("lastName")
IDs=Request.Form("ID")
passwordS=new String(Request.Form("password"))
confirmPasswordS=new String(Request.Form("confirmPassword"))
/*If the password is correct, the XML document is updated
with the teacher's data using DOM -- new record added.*/
if(passwordS.toString()==confirmPasswordS.toString()){
root=teachXml.documentElement
/*Root element of the XML document.*/
var cTeacher=teachXml.createElement("teacher")
root.appendChild(cTeacher)
/*Adds this element to the XML document.*/
var cFirstName=teachXml.createElement("firstName")
/*Creates new element firstName.*/
var cLastName=teachXml.createElement("lastName")
/*Creates new element lastName.*/
var cTeacherId= teachXml.createElement("teacherId")
/*Creates new element teacherId.*/
var cPassword =teachXml.createElement("password")
/*Creates new element password.*/
var tFirstName=teachXml.createTextNode(firstNameS)
/*Creates text node firstNameS.*/
var tLastName=teachXml.createTextNode(lastNameS)
/*Creates text node lastNameS.*/
var tID=teachXml.createTextNode(IDs)
/*Creates text node IDs.*/
var tPassword=teachXml.createTextNode(passwordS)
/*Creates text node passwordS.*/
cTeacher.appendChild(cFirstName)
```

```
/*Appends element firstName to element teacher.*/
cFirstName.appendChild(tFirstName)
/*Appends text node firstNameS to element firstName.*/
cTeacher.appendChild(cLastName)
/*Appends element lastName to the element cTeacher.*/
cLastName.appendChild(tLastName)
/*Appends text node lastNameS to the element lastName.*/
cTeacher.appendChild(cTeacherId)
/*Appends element teacherId to the element teacher.*/
cTeacherId.appendChild(tID)
/*Appends text node tID to the element teacherId.*/
cTeacher.appendChild(cPassword)
/*Appends element password to the element teacher.*/
cPassword.appendChild(tPassword)
/*Appends text node password to the element password.*/
teachXml.save(Server.MapPath("teacher.xml"))
/*Saves updated document teacher.xml.*/
Response.Write("Your registration was successful
<a href='index1.html'>continue</a>")}
/*If password was not confirmed, the message 'Wrong data
and try again' displays.*/
else
Response.Write("Wrong Data<a href='RegTeacher.html'> and try again.</a>")
%>
```

The next component allows the user to generate tests, as shown in Figure 3-9.

Listing 3-10 generates the Create a Test form.

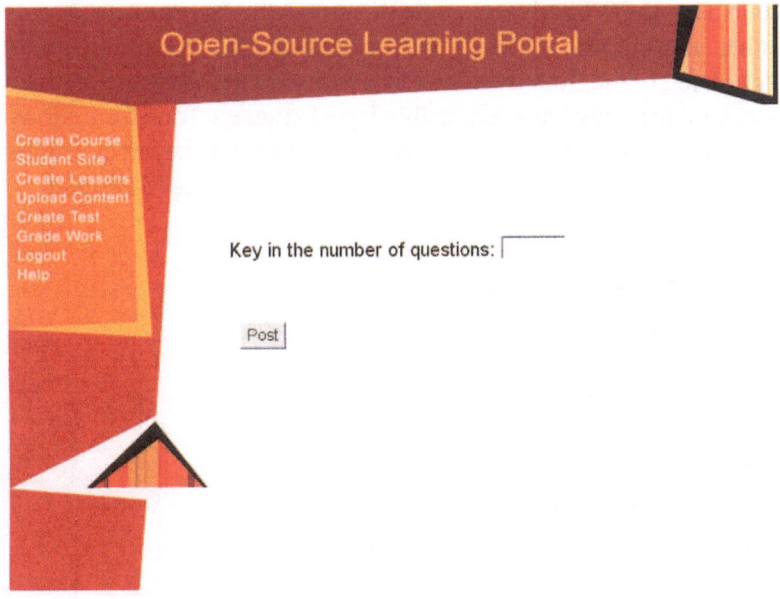

FIGURE 3-9 *A test entry*

LISTING 3-10 *The Form to Create Tests*

```
<?xml version="1.0" encoding="UTF-8"?>
<!DOCTYPE html
PUBLIC "-//W3C//DTD XHTML 1.0 Strict//EN"
"http://www.w3.org/TR/xhtml1/DTD/xhtml1-strict.dtd">
<html xmlns="http://www.w3.org/1999/xhtml" xml:lang="en" lang="en">
<head>
<title>Portal SVG</title>
<link rel="stylesheet" type="text/css" href="portal1.css"/>
</head>
<body>
<p class="svg1">
<object data="templateA.svg" type="image/svg+xml" width="900" height="105">
<p>Sorry your browser does not support SVG</p></object></p>
<p class="svg2">
<object data="templateB1.svg" type="image/svg+xml" width="225" height="700">
<p>Sorry your browser does not support SVG</p></object></p>
<form action="createTest.asp" method="post">
<p class="text3">Key in the number of questions:
<input type="text" size="3" name="countQ" /></p>
<p class="text6"><input type="submit" name="B1" value="Post" /></p>
</form>
</body>
</html>
```

The next code uses ASP/VBScript to create the test as the teacher keys in questions, possible answers, and marks the correct answer. The Document Object Model (DOM) is created in memory dynamically because of the varying possible number of questions a test may have. Extensible Style Language Transformations (XSLT) generates XHTML output to create a form where teachers key in questions and possible answers. At the same time, the form transfers the data to another ASP file where the data is stored, as shown in Listing 3-11.

LISTING 3-11 *Storing the Test Data Using VBScript*

```
<?xml version="1.0" encoding
<%@ Language=VBScript %>
<script language=VBscript RUNAT=Server>
create
Private Sub create()
countQ = Request.Form("countQ")+0
Set objDOM = Server.CreateObject("Microsoft.XMLDOM")
'Instantiates Microsoft DOM object and assigns it
'reference objDOM.
objDOM.async = False
'Loading is done synchronously.
Set objElementTest = objDOM.createElement("test")
'Creates element "test", root of the XML document.
 Set objAttr = objDOM.createAttribute("countQ")
'Creates new attribute "countQ".
  objElementTest.setAttribute "countQ", countQ
'Assigns value to "countQ".
objDOM.appendChild objElementTest
'Appends element "test" to the XML document.

For I = 0 To countQ-1
'Loop index goes over all questions.

Set objElementQuestion = objDOM.createElement("question")
'Creates element "question".
objElementTest.appendChild objElementQuestion
'Appends element "question" as a child of element "test" to the XML document.
'The element will contain question, possible answers, and correct answer.

Set objElementQ = objDOM.createElement("q")
'Creates element "q" that contains "question".
objElementQuestion.appendChild objElementQ
'Appends element "q" as a child of "question" to the XML document.
```

```
Set objElementA = objDOM.createElement("a")
'Creates element "a" to contain the first answer.
objElementQuestion.appendChild objElementA
'Appends element "a" as a child of "question" to the XML document.

Set objElementB = objDOM.createElement("b")
'Creates element "b" to contain the second answer.
objElementQuestion.appendChild objElementB*
'Appends element "b" as a child of "question" to the XML document.

Set objElementC = objDOM.createElement("c")
'Creates element "c" to contain the third answer.
objElementQuestion.appendChild objElementC
'Appends element "c" as a child of "question" to the XML document.

Set objElementD = objDOM.createElement("d")
'Creates element "d" to contain the fourth answer.
objElementQuestion.appendChild objElementD
'Appends element "d" as a child of "question" to the XML document.

Set objElementAnswer = objDOM.createElement("answer")
'Creates element "answer" to contain the label of
'correct answer (a or b or c or d).
objElementQuestion.appendChild objElementAnswer
'Appends element "answer" as a child of "question" to the XML document.
Next 'I

'Load XSL
set objXSL = Server.CreateObject("Microsoft.XMLDOM")
objXSL.async = false
objXSL.load(Server.MapPath("createTest.xsl"))

'Transform file
Response.Write(objDOM.transformNode(objXSL))
'Transforms the XML document using XSLT.

End Sub
</script>
```

Listing 3-12 demonstrates Listing 3-11, this time using ASP/JavaScript.

LISTING 3-12 *Scoring the Test Data Using JavaScript*

```
<%@ Language="JavaScript%>
<%
countQ = Request.Form("countQ")+0
objDOM = Server.CreateObject("Microsoft.XMLDOM")
objDOM.async = False

 objElementTest = objDOM.createElement("test")
 objAttr = objDOM.createAttribute("countQ")
  objElementTest.setAttribute "countQ", countQ

objDOM.appendChild(objElementTest)

for(i = 0;i<countQ;i++)
{
 objElementQuestion = objDOM.createElement("question")
objElementTest.appendChild(objElementQuestion)

objElementQ = objDOM.createElement("q")
objElementQuestion.appendChild(objElementQ)

objElementA = objDOM.createElement("a")
objElementQuestion.appendChild(objElementA)

objElementB = objDOM.createElement("b")
objElementQuestion.appendChild(objElementB)

objElementC = objDOM.createElement("c")
objElementQuestion.appendChild(objElementC)

objElementD = objDOM.createElement("d")
objElementQuestion.appendChild(objElementD)

objElementAnswer = objDOM.createElement("answer")
objElementQuestion.appendChild(objElementAnswer)
}
//Load XSL
objXSL = Server.CreateObject("Microsoft.XMLDOM")
objXSL.async = false
objXSL.load(Server.MapPath("createTest1List.xsl"))

//Transform file
Response.Write(objDOM.transformNode(objXSL))
%>
```

The user enters the text for each question and answer and selects a radio button for the correct answers, as shown in Figure 3-10. Students access the test from their portal entrance.

Listing 3-13 generates test question and answer input, as shown in Figure 3-10.

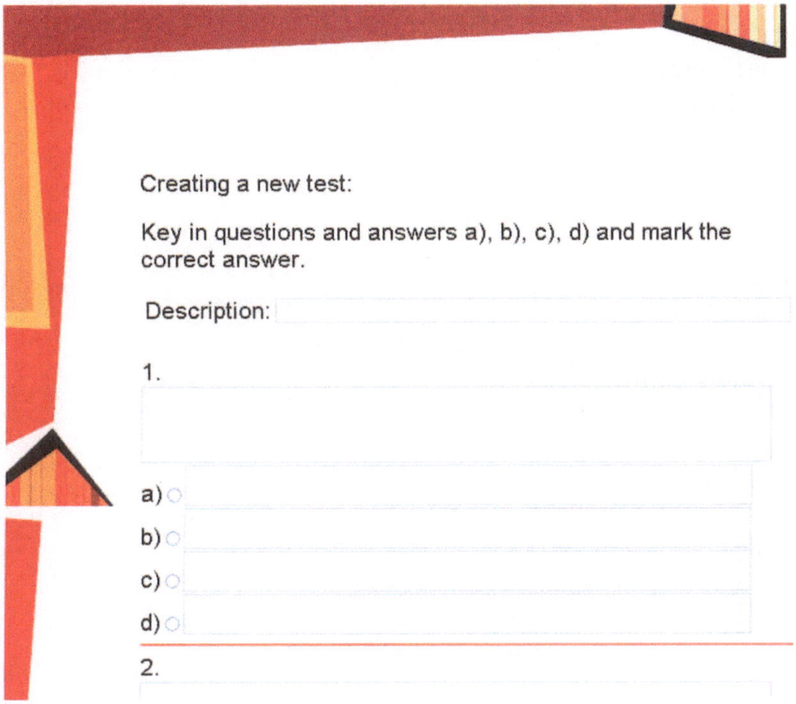

FIGURE 3-10 *The test form input*

LISTING 3-13 *Question and Answer Input*

```
<?xml version='1.0'?>
<xsl:stylesheet xmlns:xsl="http://www.w3.org/1999/XSL/Transform" version="1.0">
<xsl:template match="/">
<!-- The XSL document transforms the XML document to
HTML which displays the input form for keying in the
test's question, possible answers and correct answer.-->
<html>
<head>
<title>Open-Source Learning Portal</title>
<link rel="stylesheet" type="text/css"
href="portal1.css" />
</head>
<body>
<p class="svg1"><object data="templateA.svg"
type="image/svg+xml" width="900" height="105">
```

```
<p>Sorry, your browser does not support SVG</p>
</object></p>
<p class="svg2"><object data="templateB.svg"
type="image/svg+xml" width="225" height="700">
<p>Sorry, your browser does not support SVG</p>
</object></p>
<p class="text1">
<table width="500" border="0" cellspacing="0"
cellpadding="0" align="center">
<tr>
<td>
<p>
<br />
<p>Creating a new test:</p>
<xsl:for-each select="test">
<!--The form asks the user to key in all questions.-->
<xsl:variable name="countQ">
<xsl:value-of select ="@countQ" />
</xsl:variable>
<!--The form sends data document storeTest.asp for processing.-->
<form action="storeTest.asp" method="post">
<table border="0">
<tr>
<td>Description: </td>
<td><input type="text" size="70" name="desc" /></td>
</tr>
<tr>
<p>Key in questions and answers a), b), c), d) and mark the correct answer.</p>
</tr>
</table>
<br />
<xsl:for-each select="question">
<!--Definition of variables used for transfer of parameters.-->
<xsl:variable name="Radio">Radio<xsl:value-of select
="position()"/></xsl:variable>
<xsl:variable name="A">A<xsl:value-of select ="position()"/></xsl:variable>
<xsl:variable name="B">B<xsl:value-of select ="position()"/></xsl:variable>
<xsl:variable name="C">C<xsl:value-of select ="position()"/></xsl:variable>
<xsl:variable name="D">D<xsl:value-of select ="position()"/></xsl:variable>
<xsl:variable name="Q">Q<xsl:value-of select ="position()"/></xsl:variable>
```

```
<tr>
<!--Question input.-->
<td> <xsl:value-of select ="position()"/>.
<textarea name="{$Q}" rows="4" cols="67"></textarea>
</td>
</tr>

<tr>
<!--Input of the first possible answer label a, the correct
answer is checked in the radio box.-->
 <td>a)<input type="radio" name="{$Radio}" value="a" />
 <textarea name="{$A}" rows="2" cols="60"></textarea>
</td>
</tr>

<tr>
<!--Input of the second possible answer label b, the correct
answer is checked in the radio box.-->
<td>b)<input type="radio" name="{$Radio}" value="b" />
<textarea name="{$B}" rows="2" cols="60"></textarea>
</td>
</tr>

<tr>
<!--Input of the third possible answer label c, the correct
answer is checked in the radio box.-->
<td>c)<input type="radio" name="{$Radio}" value="c" />
<textarea name="{$C}" rows="2" cols="60"></textarea>
</td>
</tr>

<tr>
<!--Input of the fourth possible answer label d, the correct
answer is checked in the radio box.-->
<td>d)<input type="radio" name="{$Radio}" value="d" />
<textarea name="{$D}" rows="2" cols="60"></textarea>
</td>
</tr>

<tr>
<td><hr color='#ff3300' /></td>
</tr>
```

```
</xsl:for-each>
<tr>
<!--Hidden variable countQ equals the number of questions.-->
<td><input type="hidden" name="countQ"
value="{$countQ}" /></td>
</tr>
<tr>
<td><input type="submit" name="TestID2"
value="Create" /></td></tr></form>
</xsl:for-each>
</p></td></tr></table></p></body>
</html>
</xsl:template>
</xsl:stylesheet>
```

Students access a test from their side of the portal. You can get more portal code at http://www.praxis.ws.

Project 1 Axioms

Listening to clients and determining a set of representative words that translates into conceptual shapes and initial sketches can significantly shorten the design process and help ensure that a site reflects the client's intent. Browser issues can greatly influence design. However, initial sketches should be flexible enough so that you can develop a conceptual solution. Design elements such as line, type, shape, texture, space, size, and value—the details of a design—typically evolve as you start coding and adding content. And, yet, if you keep the concept, language, focal point, and design principles true, you can adjust the design elements without changing the interpretation of the site or product.

In the next chapter, you'll explore the design elements line, type, and shape and learn how to utilize code to keep as close as possible to the product's design concept. You'll also look at transitioning initial sketches to sketch prototypes.

Implementing Design Elements:

Line, Type, and Shape

We adore chaos because we love to produce order.

—M.C. Escher, artist (1898–1972)

Design elements visually communicate a design concept to the user. In Chapter 1, you focused on identifying language that best tells the client's story and enables a relationship between the client and the user. In Chapter 2, you focused on transitioning language to a design concept and incorporating the principles of balance, emphasis, rhythm, unity, and contrast. In Chapter 4, the design elements of line, type, shape, texture, space, size, and value represent the design concept and combine to become the layout in Chapter 5. Design elements in layout are an expression of the design concept, brought forward from the language of clients and users.

This process may seem unnecessarily complicated, but it's essential in creating a product that facilitates the user's understanding of the client. Therefore, it's important you don't attempt to separate or skip one of the phases of the process but rather see each phase as interconnected. In holding language, principles, and elements together, you create a layout and interface that transcends the momentary character of any single user event and create a reciprocal living text between the client and user.

Using Lines

Line is a constant companion in the visual world whether in the form of lines on the road, lines painted on store floors to draw in shoppers, or lines that represent direction, detail, and topography on maps. Lines in an interface, for example, separate columns and cells in a table or identify hyperlinks. Lines divide, organize, and connect; they enhance readability by giving users directional cues.

Lines are straight, curved, narrow, thick, pointed, rounded, short, long, dotted, dashed, and so on. Your decision regarding the choice and combination of lines should follow the design concept and its language. Think of the idea, concept, and language you want to convey. What type of line and in what position helps you to make the client's statement?

Off-balance lines convey language differently than thin horizontal lines. Simple x-axis lines, surrounded by space, convey comfort, calmness, and familiarity. Lines at angles convey action and uniqueness, and they tend to focus the user more intently. Curved lines convey a more natural, flowing, and softer space. Combinations of different types of lines, combined with a good use of whitespace, create interesting, contrasting shapes.

Thick lines separate and organize, and they create a strong focal point, as in Figure 4-1.

How do you interpret these lines?

a) A shape that conveys strength, direction, and organization and may evolve to a layout for a bandwidth company.

b) A shape that communicates sunshine, gardening, and outdoors and may evolve to a layout for a small neighborhood nursery.

c) A shape that communicates division, politics, action, and development and may evolve to a political association Web site.

FIGURE 4-1 *Thick lines and space*

A shape that conveys strength, direction, and organization and may evolve to a layout for a bandwidth company is the most likely response. The lines are solid, clean, technical, and bold. A shape that communicates sunshine, gardening, and a nursery would probably incorporate more natural lines with a lighter width. Finally, a political association Web site is a possibility. Conversations with members would help you to determine if this shape meshes with their interpretation of the association's cause. Listing 4-1 generates the Figure 4-1 shape.

LISTING 4-1 *Communicating with Lines*

```
<?xml version='1.0'?>
<svg width="400" height="400">
<rect x="50" y="50" width="300" height="300"
style="fill:none; stroke:black; stroke-width:2;" />
<defs>
<g id="thickLines">
<polyline points="13,56 145,300 178, 300 40,56"
style="fill:black; stroke:black;" />
<polyline points="11,139 250,53 256,73 10,162 10,139"
style="fill:black; stroke:black;" />
</g>
</defs>
<use xlink:href="#thickLines" x="50" y="50" />
</svg>
```

Varieties of lines also convey concepts such as density and weight. Figure 4-2 combines line varieties for text display purposes rather than for effective design development. Your design may use one or more line varieties depending on what language or metaphor you want to convey.

How do you interpret these lines?	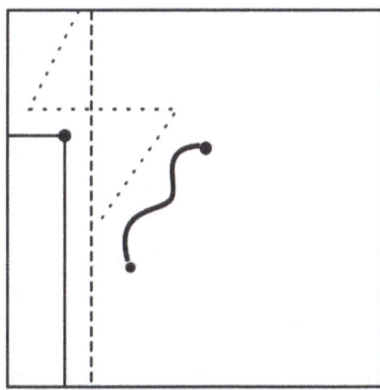
a) The variety reminds me of lines in a road. This is a potential layout for a road survey company.	
b) The variety of lines and their narrow width remind me of a movie theater. This is a potential layout for a cineplex.	
c) The variety and shape of the lines remind me of the quilts my aunt used to make. This is a potential layout for a quilting or needlework store.	

FIGURE 4-2 *Varied line styles and space*

The lines are a little light for a road survey company. Thicker lines, less variety, and bolder placement would be a closer match for that type of company. A cineplex is also off the mark. A quilting or needlework store is the closest because the lines are light, clear, and soft. Typically, you should keep line types to two per page to keep the intent of your design clear. Listing 4-2 generates the Figure 4-2 shape.

LISTING 4-2 *Communicating with Lines and Space*

```
<?xml version='1.0'?>
<svg width="400" height="400">
<rect x="50" y="50" width="300" height="300"
style="fill:none; stroke:black; stroke-width:2;" />
<defs>
<g id="lineVar">
<rect x="0" y="100" width="45" height="200"
style="fill:none; stroke:black; stroke-width:2;" />
<circle cx="45" cy="100" r="5" style="fill:black;" />
<circle cx="97" cy="205" r="4" style="fill:black;" />
<circle cx="157" cy="110" r="5" style="fill:black;" />
<line x1="66" y1="0" x2="66" y2="300" style="fill:none;
stroke:black; stroke-dasharray:8,4; stroke-width:2;" />
<polyline points="56,0 17,79 134,79 71,171" style="fill:none;
stroke:black; stroke-dasharray:3,8; stroke-width:2;" />
<path d="M95 200 C 82 153, 127 163,130 148 S 120 110, 152 108"
style="fill:none; stroke:black; stroke-width:4;" />
</g>
</defs>
<use xlink:href="#lineVar" x="50" y="50" />
</svg>
```

Line placement and design can convey a solid, immobile object or an object in motion, as in Figure 4-3.

How do you interpret these lines? ▶

a) The spiral of the line reminds me of a tornado. This is a potential layout for a weather association.

b) The spiral of the line cuts the box in half and reminds me of a drapery on the right and a window on the left. This is a potential layout for a drapery shop.

c) The spiral of the line reminds me of a telephone cord. This is a potential layout for a local phone/electronic store.

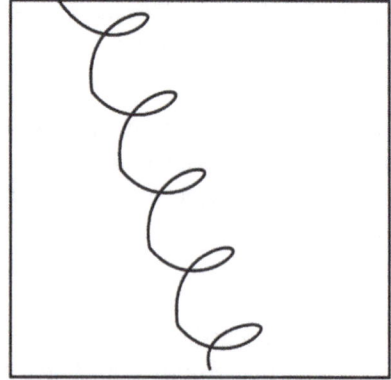

FIGURE 4-3 *Simple lines can convey movement.*

A weather association is a possibility. Different site pages could show subtle changes to the line. A drapery shop, a completely different kind of site, is also a possibility. In this case, the line separates color and texture to enhance product information. A phone/electronic store also works because the line could resemble a phone cord and "wind" through the site. In all three cases, varying the spring and density of the line connects the user to the design in a subtly different way. Listing 4-3 generates the Figure 4-3 shape.

LISTING 4-3 *Communicating Movement or Action*

```
<?xml version='1.0'?>
<svg width="400" height="400">
<rect x="10" y="45" width="300" height="300"
style="fill:none; stroke:black; stroke-width:2;" />
<g transform="rotate(70, 90,80)  scale(0.6)"
style="fill:none; stroke:#000000; stroke-width:4" >
<path d="M 70 180 c 150 160 150 100 135 80 s 100 160 200 180" />
<path d="M 200 180 c 60 -20 60 -80 45 -100 s -35 80 65 100" />
<path d="M 310 180 c 60 -20 60 -80 45 -100 s -35 80 65 100" />
<path d="M 420 180 c 60 -20 60 -80 45 -100 s -35 80 65 100" />
<path d="M 530 180 c 60 -20 60 -80 45 -100 s -35 80 25 80" />
</g>
</svg>
```

A minimalist approach to line, surrounded by whitespace, communicates lightness, as in Figure 4-4.

How do you interpret these lines? ▶

a) The simple lines, combined with whitespace, remind me of sound. The resulting light and space could be a layout for a classical music store.

b) The simple lines make me comfortable. With light colors and text, this is a potential layout for a crisis support organization.

c) The simple lines remind me of a quiet, natural place; this is a potential layout for a pizza/beer restaurant.

FIGURE 4-4 *Line shapes with space to convey lightness in weight*

Simple lines with an abundance of whitespace work for many different kinds of organizations and products. In the case of Figure 4-4, only the pizza/beer restaurant doesn't fit. New designers have a tendency to overdesign. If what you want to convey is open, free, light, and caring, a minimal amount of line surrounded by a significant amount of space works every time. Listing 4-4 generates the Figure 4-4 shape.

LISTING 4-4 *Communicating a Light or Heavy Design Concept*

```xml
<?xml version='1.0'?>
<svg width="300" height="300">
<rect x="50" y="50" width="200" height="200"
style="fill:none; stroke:black; stroke-width:2;" />
<polyline points="61 161, 100 157"
style="fill:none; stroke:black; stroke-width:2;" />
<polyline points="61 161, 100 157"
style="fill:none; stroke:black; stroke-width:2;" />
<polyline points="63 186, 96 183"
style="fill:none; stroke:black; stroke-width:2;" />
<polyline points="64 211, 107 207"
style="fill:none; stroke:black; stroke-width:2;" />
<path d="M59,101 A30,30  330 0, 0 91,63"
style="fill:none; stroke:black; stroke-width:2;" />
<path d="M63, 129 A40,40 330 0, 0 107,77"
style="fill:none; stroke:black; stroke-width:2;" />
</svg>
```

Sharp, angular lines organized in an orderly pattern communicate a technical, exacting product or company, as in Figure 4-5.

How do you interpret these lines? ▶

The angular line combinations communicate a sense of the sea and an island paradise. This is a potential layout for a holiday travel agency.

The angular line combinations communicate a technical product or organization. This is a potential layout for a telecommunications company.

The angular line combinations communicate a technical view of the earth and a mountain. This is a potential layout for an extreme sports organization.

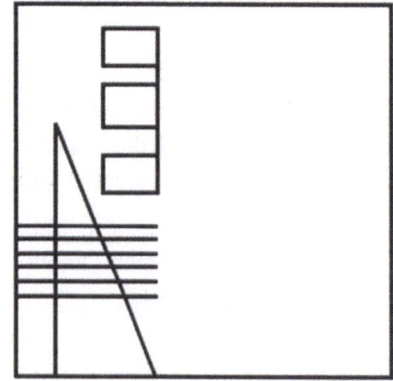

FIGURE 4-5 *Angular lines can communicate a harsher, technical, offbeat interface.*

If you're going to make boxes and lines orderly and exact, you may as well try to come up with a few interesting shapes. Some products and clients demand things perfectly spaced and compulsively ordered. If that's the case, try to make the negative space interesting and allow the line to tell your story. A telecommunications company is the best choice for Figure 4-5. Listing 4-5 generates the Figure 4-5 shape.

LISTING 4-5 *Communicating a Technical yet Interesting Concept*

```
<?xml version='1.0'?>
<svg width="300" height="300">
<rect x="50" y="50" width="200" height="200"
style="fill:none; stroke:black; stroke-width:2;" />
<rect x="96" y="63" width="29" height="20"
style="fill:none; stroke:black; stroke-width:2;" />
<rect x="96" y="93" width="29" height="23"
style="fill:none; stroke:black; stroke-width:2;" />
<rect x="96" y="131" width="29" height="20"
style="fill:none; stroke:black; stroke-width:2;" />
<line x1="125" y1="63" x2="125" y2="131"
style="fill:none; stroke:black; stroke-width:2;" />
<line x1="71" y1="250" x2="71" y2="114"
style="fill:none; stroke:black; stroke-width:2;" />
<line x1="124" y1="250" x2="71" y2="114"
style="fill:none; stroke:black; stroke-width:2;" />
<line x1="50" y1="169" x2="125" y2="169"
style="fill:none; stroke:black; stroke-width:2;" />
<line x1="50" y1="176" x2="125" y2="176"
style="fill:none; stroke:black; stroke-width:2;" />
<line x1="50" y1="184" x2="125" y2="184"
style="fill:none; stroke:black; stroke-width:2;" />
<line x1="50" y1="191" x2="125" y2="191"
style="fill:none; stroke:black; stroke-width:2;" />
<line x1="50" y1="199" x2="125" y2="199"
style="fill:none; stroke:black; stroke-width:2;" />
<line x1="50" y1="207" x2="125" y2="207"
style="fill:none; stroke:black; stroke-width:2;" />
</svg>
```

Angular lines with more whitespace soften the interpretation, as in Figure 4-6.

a) The lines remind me of mountains and ski lifts. This is a potential layout for a ski resort.

b) The lines remind me of mountains and wires. This is a potential layout for a radio tower and radio station.

c) The lines remind me of knives. This is a potential layout for a cooking store.

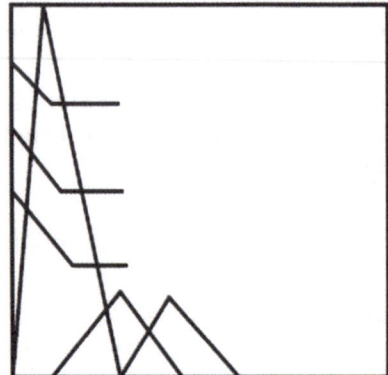

FIGURE 4-6 *Angular lines and space combine to create shape.*

Angular lines can open up a design for a landscaped, spatial perspective. This design can result in a layout for any of the three companies; however, a ski resort is the closest choice. Simple designs such as Figure 4-6 also allow room for interesting color and content possibilities. Listing 4-6 generates the Figure 4-6 shape.

LISTING 4-6 *Communicating Shapes with Lines and Space*

```
<?xml version='1.0'?>
<svg width="300" height="300">
<rect x="50" y="50" width="200" height="200"
style="fill:none; stroke:black; stroke-width:2;" />
<polyline points="50 250, 67 50, 107 250" style="fill:none;
stroke:black; stroke-width:2;" />
<polyline points="71 250, 107 204, 140 250, 170 250, 133 207,
107 250" style="fill:none; stroke:black; stroke-width:2;" />
<polyline points="50 81, 71 103, 107 103" style="fill:none;
stroke:black; stroke-width:2;" />
<polyline points="50 116, 76 150, 109 150" style="fill:none;
stroke:black; stroke-width:2;"/>
<polyline points="50 150, 82 190, 111 190" style="fill:none;
stroke:black; stroke-width:2;" />
</svg>
```

The differences between Figure 4-5 and 4-6 may appear nominal at first glance. However, they communicate a different story when shown again for comparison, as in Figure 4-7.

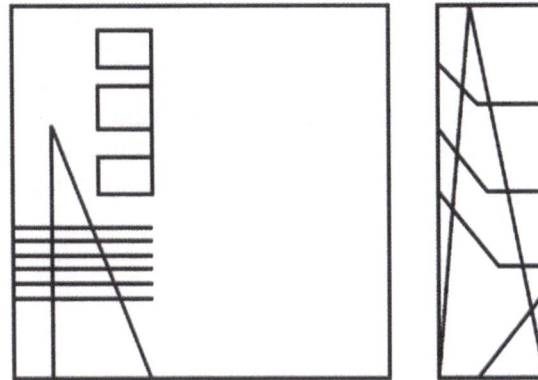 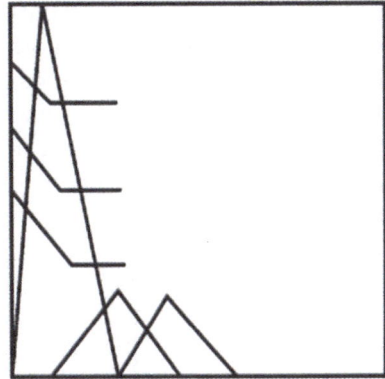

FIGURE 4-7 *Revisiting Figures 4-5 and 4-6 for contrast*

Slight differences in line width, space, shape combinations, and placement allow the same style to communicate a different product. Sketching five or six combinations for the same concept refines your idea and allows you to see one sketch in relation to others. This also helps you determine which is the strongest and leads to developing the best sketch for your concept. As a result, you'll feel more confident in the design as it progresses from shapes toward layout.

Using Line Combinations

Interesting combinations evolve as a result of combining smooth, natural lines with angular, technical lines. As before, remember that your goal is to translate the language and the design concept into an effective and suggestive layout by determining line shape and placement.

For example, if your language includes the words *clean, technical,* and *accurate* to describe a product and the words *supportive, friendly,* and *helpful* to describe a company, you need to somehow design for both sets of words. This is the kind of situation where combinations of lines can solve your problem and draw everything together.

A warm and fuzzy site doesn't emphasize the product's technical nature to the client's satisfaction. A crisp, high-tech site doesn't emphasize the company's sense of support and community to the client's satisfaction.

Consider what each line communicates. If you're having trouble, consider metaphors such as connections, bridges, or networks and try to convey these ideas with lines. Let your imagination flow. Don't revert to overused metaphors such as graphics of clasped hands or the everpresent globe. Instead, think of your own language, metaphors, and design concepts and let the lines fall where they best communicate your idea.

In Figure 4-8, angular lines support curved lines. The straight, horizontal portion of the curved lines conveys comfort; at a 90° angle to the left edge, the graphics speak differently. The curved ends are exaggerated in their curly shape and are supported by angular lines. Some whitespace shows through and adds texture and dimension to the shape made from the sum of the lines. Think of what your overall shape represents and how each line communicates the individual parts and the whole.

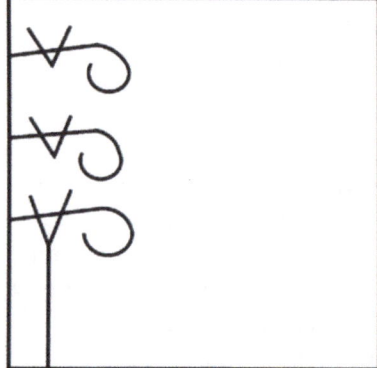

FIGURE 4-8 *Line combinations of angular and curved can create a sense of texture and space.*

Listing 4-7 generates the Figure 4-8 shape.

LISTING 4-7 *Communicating Texture and Space with Lines*

```
<?xml version='1.0'?>
<svg width="300" height="300">
<rect x="50" y="50" width="200" height="200"
style="fill:none; stroke:black; stroke-width:2;" />
<line x1="50" y1="82" x2="97" y2="76"
style="fill:none; stroke:black; stroke-width:2;" />
<line x1="50" y1="126" x2="97" y2="122"
style="fill:none; stroke:black; stroke-width:2;" />
<line x1="50" y1="170" x2="97" y2="164"
style="fill:none; stroke:black; stroke-width:2;" />
<line x1="71" y1="184" x2="71" y2="250"
style="fill:none; stroke:black; stroke-width:2;" />
<polyline points="60 67,73 87,83 66"
style="fill:none; stroke:black; stroke-width:2;" />
<polyline points="61 115,74 136,83 114"
style="fill:none; stroke:black; stroke-width:2;" />
```

```
<polyline points="61 157,71 184,83 154"
style="fill:none; stroke:black; stroke-width:2;" />
<path d="M97,76 A21,20 0 0, 1 113,86"
style="fill:none; stroke:black; stroke-width:2;" />
<path d="M94,86 A11,10 0 1, 0 113,86"
style="fill:none; stroke:black; stroke-width:2;" />
<path d="M97,122 A16,15 0 0, 1 109,134"
style="fill:none; stroke:black; stroke-width:2;" />
<path d="M89,134 A11,10 0 1, 0 109,134"
style="fill:none; stroke:black; stroke-width:2;" />
<path d="M97,164 A16,15 0 0, 1 116,177"
style="fill:none; stroke:black; stroke-width:2;" />
<path d="M90,177 A11,10 0 1, 0 116,177"
style="fill:none; stroke:black; stroke-width:2;" />
</svg>
```

Figure 4-9 incorporates angular and curved lines differently than the previous example. Here, the curved line is the focal point; it's stronger at its base and lighter in weight as it traverses upward. As mentioned in Chapter 2, vertical shapes convey upward movement. In this case, adding the line increases the upward movement. If the curve stood alone, it might look more like a swirl, precariously set to topple. The line holds it in place and conveys stability.

FIGURE 4-9 *Angular and curved used together can create a more natural shape when the curved shape overrides the angular.*

Listing 4-8 generates the Figure 4-9 shape.

LISTING 4-8 *Communicating a Peaceful Shape*

```xml
<?xml version='1.0'?>
<svg>
<?xml version='1.0'?>
<svg width="300" height="300">
<rect x="50" y="50" width="200" height="200"
style="fill:none; stroke:black; stroke-width:2;" />
<g transform="rotate(270,190,290) translate(210,195) scale(0.20) ">
<path d="M200,350 Q300,40 600,290"
style="fill:black; stroke:black; stroke-width:2" />
<path d="M200,400 Q320,90 590,290"
style="fill:white; stroke:black; stroke-width:2" />
<path d="M590,290 Q700,370 730,290"
style="fill:black; stroke:black; stroke-width:4" />
<path d="M600,290 Q700,350 720,290"
style="fill:white; stroke:black; stroke-width:4" />
<path d="M720,290 Q800,140 1000,290"
style="fill:black; stroke:black; stroke-width:2" />
<path d="M730,290 Q800,150 1000,290"
style="fill:white; stroke:black; stroke-width:2" />
<line x1="190" y1="290" x2="950" y2="290"
style="fill:none; stroke:black; stroke-width:8;" />
<rect x="200" y="340" width="50" height="60"
style="fill:white; stroke:white; stroke-width:5;" />
</g>
</svg>
```

Lines can physically support shapes. In this case, lines act to vertically and horizontally support and extend ellipses, as in Figure 4-10.

What layout may result from this simple combination? ▶

a) This is a potential layout for a cooking store; the ellipses remind me of chafing dishes, the covered serving platters used in restaurants.

b) This is a potential layout for a camping supply store; the ellipses remind me of tents in a forest.

c) This is a potential layout for a candy store; the lines and ellipses could represent licorice and gumdrops.

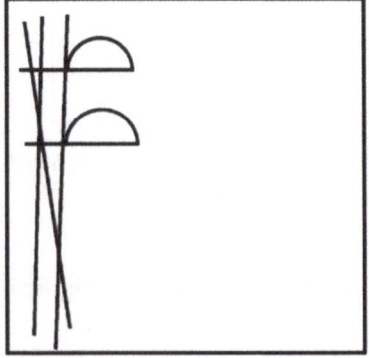

FIGURE 4-10 *These lines create physical vertical and horizontal support rather than the interpreted support shown in Figure 4-9.*

All three options can transition to a good layout when simple lines and shapes come together. The cooking store would look great with silver and black lines, some whitespace, and an elegant type. The camping supply store isn't as strong, but brown and green shapes with an outdoor-like font might work. The candy store works well with red, pink, orange, yellow, and other candy and gum-like colors. Listing 4-9 generates the Figure 4-10 shape.

LISTING 4-9 *Communicating Supported Shapes*

```
<?xml version='1.0'?>
<svg width="300" height="300">
<rect x="50" y="50" width="200" height="200"
style="fill:none; stroke:black; stroke-width:2;" />
<line x1="60" y1="63" x2="85" y2="236"
style="fill:none; stroke:black; stroke-width:2;" />
<line x1="70" y1="60" x2="65" y2="240"
style="fill:none; stroke:black; stroke-width:2;" />
<line x1="84" y1="59" x2="77" y2="248"
style="fill:none; stroke:black; stroke-width:2;" />
<line x1="57" y1="90" x2="121" y2="90"
style="fill:none; stroke:black; stroke-width:2;" />
<line x1="60" y1="132" x2="124" y2="132"
style="fill:none; stroke:black; stroke-width:2;" />
<path d="M84,90 A16,16  0 1, 1 120,90"
style="fill:none; stroke:black; stroke-width:2;" />
<path d="M83,133 A19,19  0 1, 1 123,132"
style="fill:none; stroke:black; stroke-width:2;" />
</svg>
```

Lines work well to communicate something simple without being entirely conservative. For instance, a slight offbeat placement of the line adds a bit of freedom or carefree nature to the resulting design. If you create a graphic with lines that match the language but the result is too static or dull, try moving one or two lines so they're not quite so geometric and even. The result adds a touch of creativity and fun to the overall design, as shown in Figure 4-11.

Listing 4-10 generates the Figure 4-11 shape.

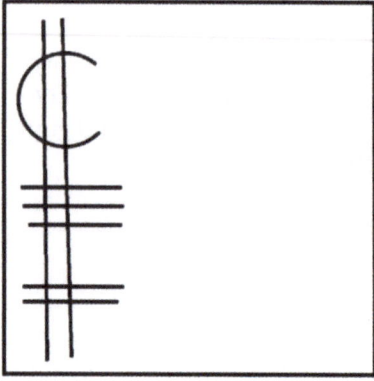

FIGURE 4-11 *Lines in combination, with slight variation in shape, convey an offbeat approach to simple design.*

LISTING 4-10 *Communicating Variation with a Combination of Lines*

```
<?xml version='1.0'?>
<svg width="300" height="300">
<rect x="50" y="50" width="200" height="200"
style="fill:none; stroke:black; stroke-width:2;" />
<line x1="71" y1="60" x2="73" y2="243"
style="fill:none; stroke:black; stroke-width:2;" />
<line x1="81" y1="59" x2="86" y2="241"
style="fill:none; stroke:black; stroke-width:2;" />
<line x1="60" y1="211" x2="111" y2="211"
style="fill:none; stroke:black; stroke-width:2;" />
<line x1="60" y1="203" x2="114" y2="203"
style="fill:none; stroke:black; stroke-width:2;" />
<line x1="63" y1="170" x2="113" y2="170"
style="fill:none; stroke:black; stroke-width:2;" />
<line x1="60" y1="160" x2="114" y2="160"
style="fill:none; stroke:black; stroke-width:2;" />
<line x1="59" y1="150" x2="113" y2="150"
style="fill:none; stroke:black; stroke-width:2;" />
<path d="M99,84 A25,25  45 1, 0 101,120"
style="fill:none; stroke:black; stroke-width:2;" />
</svg>
```

Using Type

Chapter 8 covers typography in greater depth. This short discussion describes type as a design element. Type, in design, communicates with both shape and meaning. Arranging type and determining its size, weight, and placement convey language and visual subtexts. Figure 4-12 displays the same word with the same meaning, but they're visually different. One interpretation is angular with a slightly offbeat, rounded shape, and the other is smooth, curved, and natural.

FIGURE 4-12 *Same word, different lines*

The same word, again, with repetition creates a rhythm. The bold signature on the left of Figure 4-13 portrays the word differently than the one on the right. These two words may visually attract a different audience even though the meaning is the same.

FIGURE 4-13 *Same word, different pattern and thickness*

As an exercise, from a visual perspective only, think about which of the previous presentations of the word *love* may attract the following audiences:

- 15–19 years old

- 20–30 years old

- 30–40 years old

Conveying Meaning with Type

Consider the meaning of a word as you work with the shape, size, spacing, and placement of its shape.

For example, Figure 4-14 could evolve into a layout where the left shapes resemble books on a shelf. The "books" can double as sections; clicking the words takes users to different areas of a bookshop. The familiar, horizontal lines in the top-right corner can become links to a search engine or an order status page. Subpages could use less space for navigation and could incorporate the book theme into their submenus.

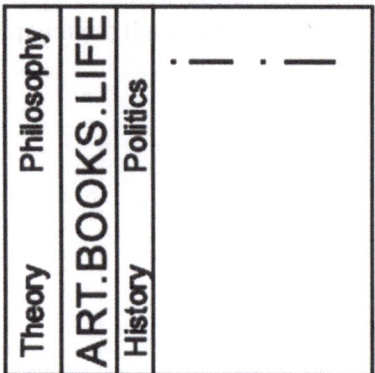

FIGURE 4-14 *Type organizes and doubles as graphical elements.*

Listing 4-11 generates the Figure 4-14 shape.

LISTING 4-11 *Communicating Products with Type and Lines*

```
<?xml version="1.0"?>
<svg>
<rect x="50" y="50" width="200" height="200"
style="fill:none; stroke:black; stroke-width:2;" />
<line x1="80" y1="50" x2="80" y2="250"
style="stroke:black; stroke-width:2;" />
```

```
<line x1="110" y1="250" x2="110" y2="50"
style="stroke:black; stroke-width:2;" />
<line x1="140" y1="80" x2="230" y2="80"
style="stroke:black; stroke-width:3;
stroke-dasharray:3,7,24,15,3,10,35" />
<line x1="130" y1="250" x2="130" y2="50"
style="stroke:black; stroke-width:2;" />
<text x="70" y="240" style="stroke:black;
font-size:16 pt;" transform="rotate(-90,70,240)">Theory</text>
<text x="70" y="140" style="stroke:black; font-size:16 pt;"
transform="rotate(-90,70,140)">Philosophy</text>
<text x="104" y="245" style="stroke:black; font-size:22
pt;letter-spacing:1;" transform="rotate(-90,104,245)">
ART.BOOKS.LIFE</text>
<text x="126" y="240" style="stroke:black; font-size:16 pt;"
transform="rotate(-90,126,240)">History</text>
<text x="126" y="140" style="stroke:black; font-size:16 pt;"
transform="rotate(-90,126,140)">Politics</text>
</svg>
```

Using Type As a Graphical Element

Angular, diagonal lines form the shape of Figure 4-15 as well as the shape of
the text. In this case, text happens to be a word, but it appears more a part of the
design than the site's content or navigation. Without the words, the triangle shape
communicates something different, but with the word, the strength of the
shape changes the meaning of the word to create something more powerful
than the word alone.

Always consider both the meaning and design of the type in your design and
how those elements change each other. The combination can lead to myriad
design options and solutions.

For instance, Figure 4-15 can evolve to a layout with content in the central
portion and a simple navigational menu on the right. The theme of triangles, diagonal lines, and lines as text can run throughout the site, changing as the meaning
of the content changes.

Listing 4-12 generates the Figure 4-15 shape.

FIGURE 4-15 *Type as a graphical element emphasizes language and lines.*

LISTING 4-12 *Communicating Shape with Type and Lines*

```xml
<?xml version="1.0"?>
<svg>
<rect x="50" y="50" width="200" height="200"
style="fill:none; stroke:black; stroke-width:2;" />
<line x1="56" y1="210" x2="64" y2="198"
style="stroke:black; stroke-width:2;" />
<line x1="78" y1="166" x2="82" y2="154"
style="stroke:black; stroke-width:2;" />
<line x1="50" y1="84" x2="110" y2="130"
style="stroke:black; stroke-width:2;" />
<line x1="128" y1="50" x2="120" y2="66"
style="stroke:black; stroke-width:2;" />
<path d="M90,50 A27,14 30 1,0 128,50"
style="fill:none; stroke:black; stroke-width:2;" />
<polyline points="50 250, 150 50,250 250"
style="fill:none; stroke:black; stroke-width:2;" />
<polyline points="66 222, 50 198,70 206"
style="fill:none; stroke:black; stroke-width:2;" />
<polyline points="74 202, 50 186,80 187,50 158, 86 176"
style="fill:none; stroke:black; stroke-width:2;" />
<polyline points="87 174, 50 138,94 158"
style="fill:none; stroke:black; stroke-width:2;" />
<polyline points="50 126, 58 110,98 152, 106 130"
style="fill:none; stroke:black; stroke-width:2;" />
<polyline points="113 123, 50 78,128 96, 50 50"
style="fill:none; stroke:black; stroke-width:2;" />
</svg>
```

Guiding User Attention with Type

In Figure 4-16, both the meaning of the text and its placement combine to communicate confusion, possibly to take the user by surprise. The goal is for the user to ask "Huh?" Organizing the words so that they all lead to the center brings the focal point around and into the center. This type concept can transition to a layout where a simple logo or graphic in the center acts as a link to subpages. You could also incorporate text and lines off-center throughout the site. Make sure you think through your concept well, though; this approach, if not carefully planned, can become annoying to the user.

FIGURE 4-16 *Type as shape and focal point, drawing the user to the center*

Listing 4-13 generates the Figure 4-16 shape.

LISTING 4-13 *Communicating Feeling with Type and Line*

```
<?xml version="1.0"?>
<svg>
<rect style="fill:none; stroke:black;
stroke-width:2;" x="50" y="50" width="200" height="200" />
<defs>
<path id="first" d="M60 100, L110 50"
style="stroke:white; fill:none;" />
<path id="second" d="M60 120, L130 50"
style="stroke:white; fill:none;" />
<path id="third" d="M180 60, L250 110"
style="stroke:white; fill:none;" />
<path id="fourth" d="M165 70, L250 130"
style="stroke:white; fill:none;" />
<path id="fifth" d="M240 180, L180 250"
style="stroke:white; fill:none;" />
<path id="sixth" d="M220 180, L160 250"
style="stroke:white; fill:none;" />
```

```
<path id="seventh" d="M120 240, L50 170"
style="stroke:white; fill:none;" />
<path id="eighth" d="M140 240, L50 148"
style="stroke:white; fill:none;" />
</defs>
<text style="font-size:10pt;">
<textPath xlink:href="#first">I find </textPath></text>
<text style="font-size:10pt;">
<textPath xlink:href="#second">myself going</textPath></text>
<text style="font-size:10pt;">
<textPath xlink:href="#third">in squares </textPath></text>
<text style="font-size:10pt;">
<textPath xlink:href="#fourth">at least there</textPath></text>
<text style="font-size:10pt;">
<textPath xlink:href="#fifth">are corners</textPath></text>
<text style="font-size:10pt;">
<textPath xlink:href="#sixth">and text</textPath></text>
<text style="font-size:10pt;">
<textPath xlink:href="#seventh">follows me</textPath></text>
<text style="font-size:10pt;">
<textPath xlink:href="#eighth">words language</textPath></text>
</svg>
```

Changing the shape of the lines and letters, their placement, and their density significantly changes the interpretation of a graphic. The design of Figure 4-17 suggests a shape with its use of softer, natural lines. The use of the dash mutes the effect of the line on the overall design. The words are disjointed and unbalanced. A small menu can work at the top of the site; its placement is important and may include two simple, light columns, just above the arches, rather than across the top of the site.

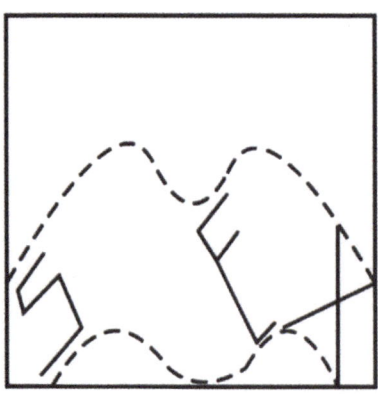

FIGURE 4-17 *Type with lines as language, graphic, and shape*

Listing 4-14 generates the Figure 4-17 shape.

LISTING 4-14 *Communicating Ideas with Lines As Type*

```
<?xml version="1.0"?>
<svg>
<rect x="50" y="50" width="200" height="200"
style="fill:none;
stroke:black; stroke-width:2;" />
<path d="M50 194 Q 110 90, 130 130 T 170 135"
style="stroke:black;fill:none;
stroke-width:2; stroke-dasharray: 9,5" />
<path d="M170 135 Q 190 90,  250 194"
style="stroke:black; fill:none;
stroke-width:2; stroke-dasharray: 9,5" />
<path d="M74 250 Q 105 195,  138 240"
style="stroke:black; fill:none;
stroke-width:2; stroke-dasharray: 9,5" />
<path d="M138 240 Q 155 255,  180 240"
style="stroke:black; fill:none;
stroke-width:2; stroke-dasharray: 9,5" />
<path d="M180 240 Q 205 195,  230 250"
style="stroke:black; fill:none;
stroke-width:2; stroke-dasharray: 9,5" />
<polyline points="70 178, 56 198,59 210,78 190, 90
218, 68 244" style="stroke:black;
fill:none; stroke-width:2;" />
<polyline points="170 146, 154 166, 164 182,
176 166, 164 182,186 226, 196 215"
style="stroke:black; fill:none;stroke-width:2;" />
<line x1="200" y1="218" x2="250" y2="194"
style="stroke:black; stroke-width:2;" />
<line x1="230" y1="250" x2="230" y2="163"
style="stroke:black; stroke-width:2;" />
</svg>
```

Supporting Backgrounds with Type

In Figure 4-18, lines create the background. A few colored icons as navigational links, placed at a diagonal, can draw users quickly toward their goal. In addition, icons would appear to sit on top of the lines and create depth. The text is actually vertical lines that don't comfort or totally disarm users. Their collected shape, as the word *NO*, can intrigue the user. If you use words in this manner, be sure to

select the critical keyword to your point. In this example, you see again the dual
concepts of type, meaning, and shape, which lend the design element such
power.

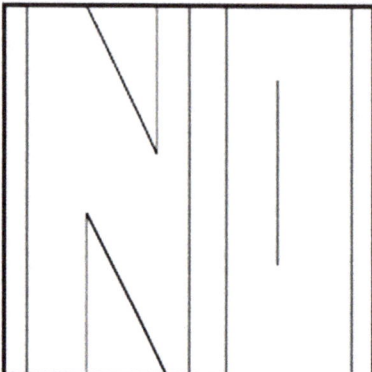

Type as a background that's angular and straight

Listing 4-15 generates the Figure 4-18 shape.

LISTING 4-15 *Communicating Metaphors with Lines As Type*

```xml
<?xml version="1.0"?>
<svg>
<rect x="50" y="50" width="200" height="200"
style="fill:none; stroke:black; stroke-width:2;" />
<line x1="62" y1="50" x2="62" y2="250"
style="stroke:black;stroke-width:1.2;" />
<line x1="198" y1="90" x2="198" y2="190"
style="stroke:black;stroke-width:1.2;" />
<line x1="150" y1="50" x2="150" y2="250"
style="stroke:black; stroke-width:1.2;" />
<line x1="170" y1="50" x2="170" y2="250"
style="stroke:black; stroke-width:1.2;" />
<line x1="238" y1="250" x2="238" y2="50"
style="stroke:black; stroke-width:1.2;" />
<polyline points="94 250,94 162, 138 250"
style="fill:none; stroke:black; stroke-width:1.2;" />
<polyline points="94 50,132 130, 132 50"
style="fill:none; stroke:black; stroke-width:1.2;" />
</svg>
```

Figure 4-19 uses words to create one simple statement: This is a poetry site. Buttons placed randomly suggest offbeat poetry. Buttons either placed in a linear order or placed as a group in the lower-right corner suggest different kinds of poetry.

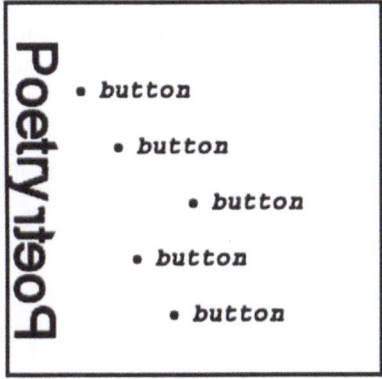

FIGURE 4-19 *Type as design*

Listing 4-16 generates the Figure 4-19 shape.

LISTING 4-16 *Communicating a Concept with Type*

```
<?xml version="1.0"?>
<svg>
<rect x="50" y="50" width="200" height="200"
style="fill:none; stroke:black; stroke-width:2;" />
<text x="56" y="70" style="stroke:black; font-size:30 pt;"
transform="rotate(90,56,70)">Poetry</text>
<defs>
<text id="a" x="-56" y="230" style="stroke:black;
font-size:30 pt;" transform="scale(-1,1)">Poetr</text>
</defs>
<g id="b">
<circle cx="90" cy="98" r="2" style="stroke:black; fill:black; " />
<text x="100" y="101" style="stroke:black; font-size:12;
font-family:courier; font-style:italic; letter-spacing:1;">button</text>
</g>
<use xlink:href="#b" transform="translate(20,30)" />
<use xlink:href="#b" transform="translate(60,60)" />
<use xlink:href="#b" transform="translate(30,90)" />
<use xlink:href="#b" transform="translate(50,120)" />
<use xlink:href="#a" transform="rotate(90,54,230)" />
</svg>
```

Setting Type in Motion

Fast, fun, low maintenance, plenty of room for content and color . . . site design doesn't always have to be a huge task. Clean style, simple navigation, and interesting content works. Placing the word *SKIING* at different angles in Figure 4-20 can convey different kinds of skiing. If the competition shows mountain photos, a different look can transition to a layout that grabs attention. Scenic photos can be included, but they don't need to dictate the layout.

FIGURE 4-20 *Type and motion or direction*

Listing 4-17 generates the Figure 4-20 shape.

LISTING 4-17 *Communication Action with Type*

```
<?xml version="1.0"?>
<svg>
<rect x="50" y="50" width="200" height="200"
style="fill:none; stroke:black; stroke-width:2;" />
<defs>
<path id="line" d="M 50 98 , L114 250"
style="stroke:white; fill:none;" />
</defs>
<text style="font-size:20pt; letter-spacing:9;">
<textPath xlink:href="#line">SKIING</textPath>
</text>
<g id="form">
<polyline points="70 62, 70 74,82 74"
style="fill:none; stroke:black; stroke-width:2;" />
```

```
<line x1="88" y1="74" x2="108" y2="74"
style="stroke:black; stroke-width:2;" />
</g>
<use xlink:href="#form" transform="translate(12,25)" />
<use xlink:href="#form" transform="translate(30,62)" />
<use xlink:href="#form" transform="translate(46,95)" />
</svg>
```

Using Shapes

Lines and blocks of text combine to become shapes, which is the next step in your design process. Shapes, lines, and text add an additional level of visual support to your original design concept. In other words, how you determine line form and placement conveys meaning at a micro level; how you place shapes created from line and text conveys meaning at a macro level.

In the design process, consider both the singular elements and the shapes they create. This approach to design, with its continued link back to language, plays a significant role in transitioning from concept to layout.

Shapes have height and weight. They may form a picture or simply suggest something familiar. As always, avoid clichés and let the shapes and their parts communicate your story naturally. Simple shapes often create good layouts that don't become stale within a few months.

The shapes in Figure 4-21, made from simple circle and line combinations, could transition to a layout for several sites.

How do you interpret these lines? ▶

a) Bubbles, candy, and toy store

b) A bulletin board with stick pins, added color in the pinheads

c) A martini olive collection

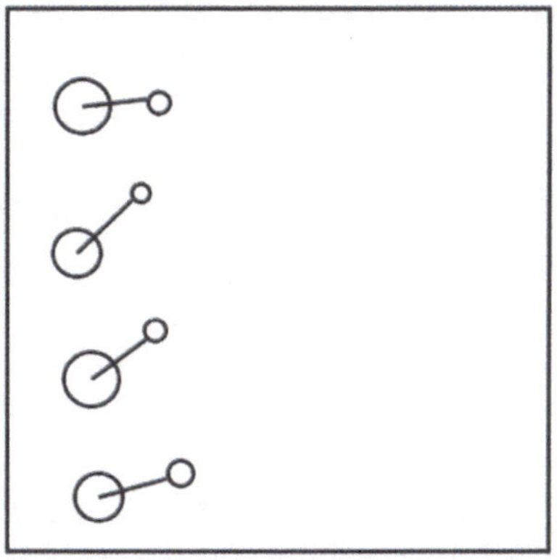

FIGURE 4-21 *Lines in combination with circles, slightly out of balance, portray whimsical shapes.*

Again, when answering questions like these and considering these issues, metaphors can be a powerful aid to the developer. For example, bubbles, candy, and a toy store could result in a design with light blue, orange, and white colors and an arrangement of the shapes to convey whimsical motion. A bulletin board could be realized with bright colored pins and square shapes resembling yellow small notes "posted" at slightly offset intervals on the page. The martini olive collection could work with olive green, orange, and a touch of pimento red combined with graphics, fun text, and a sophisticated use of space. Listing 4-18 generates the Figure 4-21 shape.

LISTING 4-18 *Communicating Whimsy with Line and Space*

```xml
<?xml version='1.0'?>
<svg width="400" height="400">
<rect x="50" y="50" width="300" height="300"
style="fill:none; stroke:black; stroke-width:2;" />
<defs>
<g id="circleLineCombo">
<circle cx="41" cy="54" r="15" style="fill:none;
stroke:black; stroke-width:2;" />
<circle cx="38" cy="135" r="13" style="fill:none;
stroke:black; stroke-width:2;" />
<circle cx="46" cy="205" r="15" style="fill:none;
stroke:black; stroke-width:2;" />
<circle cx="50" cy="270" r="13" style="fill:none;
stroke:black; stroke-width:2;" />
<circle cx="83" cy="52" r="6" style="fill:none;
stroke:black; stroke-width:2;" />
<circle cx="73" cy="102" r="5" style="fill:none;
stroke:black; stroke-width:2;" />
<circle cx="81" cy="178" r="6" style="fill:none;
stroke:black; stroke-width:2;" />
<circle cx="95" cy="257" r="7" style="fill:none;
stroke:black; stroke-width:2;" />
<line x1="41" y1="54" x2="76" y2="50" style="fill:none;
stroke:black; stroke-width:2;" />
<line x1="38" y1="135" x2="68" y2="106" style="fill:none;
stroke:black; stroke-width:2;" />
<line x1="46" y1="205" x2="76" y2="183" style="fill:none;
stroke:black; stroke-width:2;" />
<line x1="50" y1="270" x2="87" y2="260" style="fill:none;
stroke:black; stroke-width:2;" />
</g>
</defs>
<use xlink:href="#circleLineCombo" x="50" y="50" />
</svg>
```

Figure 4-22, made from simple circle and line combinations, could transition to a layout for several sites.

How do you interpret these lines? ▶

a) A cabinetmaker

b) A hardware store

c) A heavy-metal band

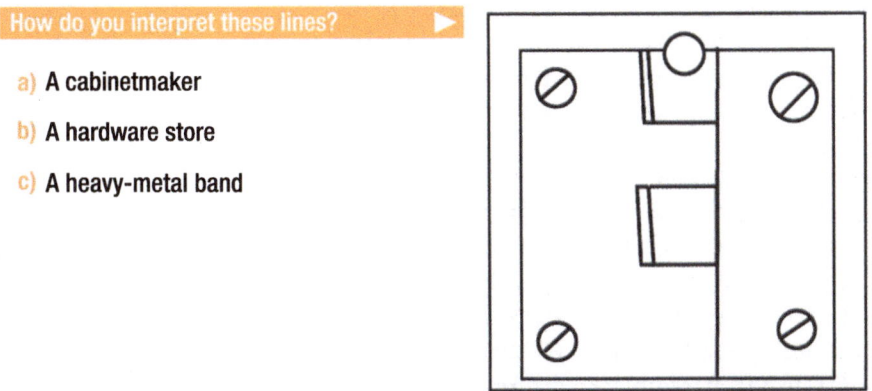

FIGURE 4-22 *Lines in combination become shapes that represent actual products.*

The shape of Figure 4-22 could be used as an accent on a simple site promoting a cabinetmaker and a hardware store. A selection of warm colors and detailed tools and gadgets made with line and space would convey a detailed, crafted approach to the user. A heavy-metal band could work as a spoof; however, a cabinetmaker and a hardware store are the obvious choices, and the heavy-metal band is a quirky attempt at humor. Remember not to overthink these things. With shapes, like code, simple is good. Listing 4-19 generates the Figure 4-22 shape.

LISTING 4-19 *Communicating a Client Product or Project with Lines and Shapes*

```
<?xml version='1.0'?>
<svg width="400" height="400">
<rect x="50" y="50" width="300" height="300"
style="fill:none; stroke:black; stroke-width:2;" />
<defs>
<g id="hinge">
<rect x="25" y="29" width="250" height="262"
style="fill:none; stroke:black; stroke-width:2;" />
<circle cx="53" cy="59" r="15"
style="fill:white; stroke:black; stroke-width:2;" />
<circle cx="53" cy="261" r="15"
style="fill:none; stroke:black; stroke-width:2;" />
<circle cx="243" cy="67" r="19"
style="fill:none; stroke:black; stroke-width:2;" />
```

```
<circle cx="245" cy="252" r="15"
style="fill:none; stroke:black; stroke-width:2;" />
<circle cx="155" cy="32" r="16"
style="fill:white; stroke:black; stroke-width:2;" />
<line x1="40" y1="69" x2="64" y2="47"
style="fill:none; stroke:black; stroke-width:2;" />
<line x1="43" y1="269" x2="64" y2="249"
style="fill:none;
stroke:black; stroke-width:2;" />
<line x1="231" y1="83" x2="259" y2="55"
style="fill:none; stroke:black; stroke-width:2;" />
<line x1="232" y1="259" x2="258" y2="242"
style="fill:none; stroke:black; stroke-width:2;" />
<line x1="182" y1="27" x2="181" y2="290"
style="fill:none; stroke:black; stroke-width:2;" />
<polyline points="126,28 130,87 181, 87"
style="fill:none; stroke:black; stroke-width:2;" />
<polyline points="120,28 123,87 130, 87"
style="fill:none; stroke:black; stroke-width:2;" />
<polyline points="126,138 130,200 181, 200 181,138 127,138"
style="fill:none; stroke:black; stroke-width:2;" />
<polyline points="126,138 117,138 120, 200 130,200"
style="fill:none; stroke:black; stroke-width:2;" />
</g>
</defs>
<use xlink:href="#hinge" x="50" y="50" />
</svg>
```

Shapes don't have to be an exact replication of something familiar; they can simply resemble an object and still have a powerful effect on a design. The shapes in Figure 4-23, made from simple curve and line combinations, can transition to a layout for a variety of clients.

How do you interpret these lines? ▶

a) A bird shop

b) A fencing company

c) A racetrack

d) A railroad company

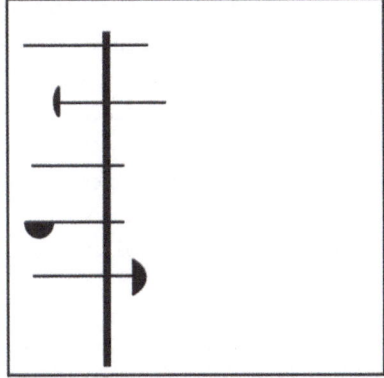

FIGURE 4-23 *Lines in combination become shapes that resemble, rather than represent, actual products and concepts.*

The main point with Figure 4-23 is that lines and space can create even a small amount of shape but still evoke a feeling of familiarity that works in an interesting fashion for several types of products and companies. It isn't necessary to have a top-flight illustrator to communicate to users. Listing 4-20 generates the Figure 4-23 shape.

LISTING 4-20 *Communicating Familiarity with Lines and Shapes*

```
<?xml version='1.0'?>
<svg width="400" height="400">
<rect x="50" y="50" width="300" height="300"
style="fill:none; stroke:black; stroke-width:2;" />
<defs>
<g id="pole">
<line x1="79" y1="26" x2="79" y2="293"
style="fill:none; stroke:black; stroke-width:6;" />
<line x1="13" y1="37" x2="112" y2="37"
style="fill:none; stroke:black; stroke-width:2;" />
<line x1="41" y1="83" x2="126" y2="83"
style="fill:none; stroke:black; stroke-width:2;" />
<line x1="19" y1="133" x2="93" y2="133"
style="fill:none; stroke:black; stroke-width:2;" />
<line x1="20" y1="221" x2="100" y2="221"
style="fill:none; stroke:black; stroke-width:2;" />
<line x1="41" y1="70" x2="41" y2="94"
style="fill:none; stroke:black; stroke-width:2;" />
```

```
<line x1="14" y1="178" x2="93" y2="178"
style="fill:none; stroke:black; stroke-width:2;" />
<path d="M14,178 A11,12 0 0,0 36,178"
style="fill:black; stroke:black; stroke-width:2;" />
<path d="M41,70 A17,19 0 0,0 41,94"
style="fill:black; stroke:black; stroke-width:2;" />
<path d="M99,208 A28,18 0 0,1 99,236"
style="fill:black; stroke:black; stroke-width:2;" />
</g>
</defs>
<use xlink:href="#pole" x="50" y="50" />
</svg>
```

Shapes can seem to take on a personality. In Figure 4-24, the circles appear to weigh down the curve because of the heaviness of the line. Upside down, this shape almost represents a happy face. As you see it here, the base holds up what may be a tree or a pole of some sort. The idea is that shapes can be simple and yet draw interest from the user. The combination of arcs, circles, a line, and a rectangle add more content and substance to the overall shape.

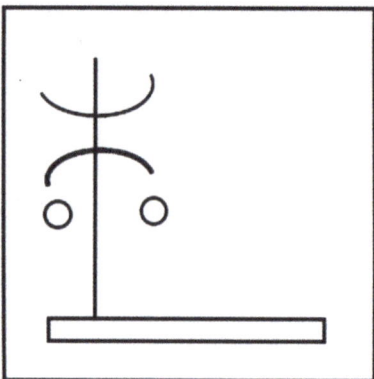

FIGURE 4-24 *Shapes can seem to have personality.*

Listing 4-21 generates the Figure 4-24 shape.

LISTING 4-21 *Communicating Personality with Lines and Shapes*

```
<?xml version='1.0'?>
<svg width="300" height="300">
<rect x="50" y="50" width="200" height="200"
style="fill:none; stroke:black; stroke-width:2;" />
<rect x="74" y="217"  width="149" height="12"
style="fill:none; stroke:black;stroke-width:2;" />
```

```
<line x1="99" y1="77" x2="99" y2="217"
style="fill:none; stroke:black;stroke-width:2;" />
<circle cx="79" cy="161" r="7"
style="fill:none; stroke:black;stroke-width:2;" />
<circle cx="131" cy="159" r="7"
style="fill:none; stroke:black;stroke-width:2;" />
<path d="M70, 96 A18,10 0 0, 0 129,86"
style="fill:none; stroke:black;stroke-width:2;" />
<path d="M74, 146 A18,10 0 1, 1 130,139"
style="fill:none; stroke:black;stroke-width:3;" />
</svg>
```

Conveying Abstract Concepts

The Figure 4-25 shape conveys an entirely different language than the representations in Figure 4-24. Bold, thick lines convey strength. When combined with angular placement and whitespace, the lines take on a geometric form. The base isn't as heavy as the top; the bottom lines are at a "springy" angle. If the bottom half of the shape mirrors the top half, the result is a solid, columnar object. When the bottom support is more springy than solid, the top appears to rest in equilibrium rather than being cemented in place.

FIGURE 4-25 *Shapes can portray strength.*

Listing 4-22 generates the Figure 4-25 shape.

LISTING 4-22 *Communicating Heavy or Solid with Lines and Shapes*

```
<?xml version='1.0'?>
<svg width="400" height="400">
<rect x="50" y="50" width="300" height="300"
style="fill:none; stroke:black; stroke-width:2;" />
```

```
<defs>
<g id="boldLines">
<line x1="34" y1="64" x2="34" y2="173"
style="fill:none; stroke:black; stroke-width:6;" />
<line x1="61" y1="63" x2="61" y2="173"
style="fill:none; stroke:black; stroke-width:6;" />
<line x1="89" y1="63" x2="89" y2="173"
style="fill:none; stroke:black; stroke-width:6;" />
<line x1="101" y1="35" x2="32" y2="65"
style="fill:none; stroke:black; stroke-width:6;" />
<line x1="144" y1="174" x2="168" y2="209"
style="fill:none; stroke:black; stroke-width:6;" />
<line x1="143" y1="175" x2="48" y2="237"
style="fill:none; stroke:black; stroke-width:6;" />
<line x1="133" y1="283" x2="90" y2="283"
style="fill:none; stroke:black; stroke-width:6;" />
<polyline points="12,17 129,16 101,35 12,35"
style="fill:black;" />
<polyline points="31,173 145,173 102,201 31,202"
style="fill:black;" />
<polyline points="10,279 15,295 132,295 100,280 10,279"
style="fill:black;" />
<polyline points="14,44 127,44 89,65"
style="fill:none; stroke:black; stroke-width:6;" />
<polyline points="101,35 130,33 61,65"
style="fill:none; stroke:black; stroke-width:6;" />
<polyline points="152,192 55,251 132,283"
style="fill:none; stroke:black; stroke-width:6;" />
<polyline points="164,207 60,269 107,283"
style="fill:none; stroke:black; stroke-width:6;" />
</g>
</defs>
<use xlink:href="#boldLines" x="50" y="50" />
</svg>
```

Conveying Emotion and Recollection

Figure 4-26 can transition to a layout with buttons in the angled rectangles and possibly other buttons in the circles. Mousing over the angles may allow the circles and their supporting lines to appear. The shape itself, reminiscent of a street lamp, offers the potential for simple navigation with a shape different from typical left menus. Color can thematically link the rectangles to the circles. Graphics can team with text in the rectangles to keep the background clean and simple. (You'll learn more about color in Chapter 9.)

FIGURE 4-26 *Shapes can be simple and imaginative.*

Listing 4-23 generates the Figure 4-26 shape.

LISTING 4-23 *Communicating Content with Simple Shapes As Buttons*

```
<?xml version='1.0'?>
<svg width="300" height="300">
<rect x="50" y="50" width="200" height="200"
style="fill:none; stroke:black; stroke-width:2;" />
<defs>
<g id="anglePole">
<line x1="61" y1="79" x2="61" y2="119"
style="fill:none; stroke:black;stroke-width:2;" />
<line x1="90" y1="70" x2="90" y2="104"
style="fill:none; stroke:black;stroke-width:2;" />
<line x1="61" y1="89" x2="90" y2="73"
style="fill:none; stroke:black;stroke-width:2;" />
<line x1="61" y1="107" x2="90" y2="90"
style="fill:none; stroke:black;stroke-width:2;" />
</g>
</defs>
<use xlink:href="#anglePole" x="0" y="57" />
<use xlink:href="#anglePole" x="0" y="0" />
<use xlink:href="#anglePole" x="0" y="112" />
<line x1="80" y1="61" x2="80" y2="79 "
style="fill:none; stroke:black; stroke-width:2;" />
```

```
<line x1="80" y1="97" x2="80" y2="137 "
style="fill:none; stroke:black; stroke-width:2;" />
<line x1="80" y1="154" x2="80" y2="191"
style="fill:none; stroke:black; stroke-width:2;" />
<line x1="80" y1="208" x2="80" y2="250"
style="fill:none; stroke:black; stroke-width:2;" />
<line x1="80" y1="110" x2="127" y2="110"
style="fill:none; stroke:black; stroke-width:2;" />
<circle cx="120" cy="100" r="7"
style="fill:none; stroke:black; stroke-width:2;" />
<circle cx="120" cy="120" r="7"
style="fill:none; stroke:black; stroke-width:2;" />
</svg>
```

Shapes that remind users of artwork, music, times, and sounds evoke memories and create a comfort level with their familiarity. Although the Figure 4-27 shape won't remind you of one specific picture, it's designed to be reflective of still-life artwork from the 1950s and 1960s and might transition to a nice layout for either.

How do you interpret these lines? ▶

a) An art supply store

b) A café

c) A retro site of collectibles

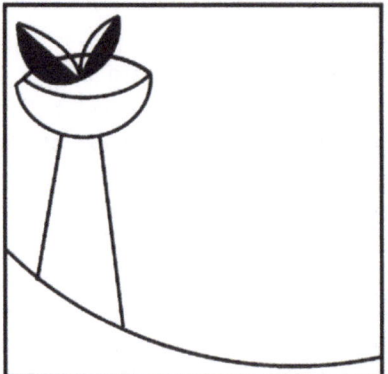

FIGURE 4-27 *Shapes remind users of other mediums of artwork.*

Listing 4-24 generates the Figure 4-27 shape.

LISTING 4-24 *Communicating Ideas or Shapes from a Previous Time or Style*

```
<?xml version='1.0'?>
<svg width="300" height="300">
<rect x="50" y="50" width="200" height="200"
style="fill:none; stroke:black; stroke-width:2;" />
<line x1="80" y1="120" x2="67" y2="198"
style="fill:none; stroke:black;stroke-width:2;" />
<line x1="100" y1="121" x2="112" y2="223"
style="fill:none; stroke:black;stroke-width:2;" />
<line x1="56" y1="93" x2="60" y2="90"
style="fill:none; stroke:black;stroke-width:2;" />
<path d="M50,181 A210,200 0 0, 0 250,239"
style="fill:none; stroke:black;stroke-width:2;" />
<path d="M56,93 A32,28 0 0, 0 127,87"
style="fill:none; stroke:black; stroke-width:2;" />
<path d="M60,90 A40,25 0 0, 0 127,87"
style="fill:none; stroke:black;stroke-width:2;" />
<path d="M60,90 A40,25 0 0, 1 127,87"
style="fill:none; stroke:black; stroke-width:2;" />
<path d="M60,90 A40,25 0 0, 1 127,87"
style="fill:none; stroke:black; stroke-width:2;" />
<path d="M57,60 A40,25 20 0, 1 90,90"
style="fill:none; stroke:black; stroke-width:2;" />
<path d="M57,60 A40,25 20 0, 0 90,90"
style="fill:none; stroke:black; stroke-width:2;" />
<path d="M90,90 A40,35 50 0, 1 110,56"
style="fill:none; stroke:black; stroke-width:2;" />
<path d="M90,90 A40,35 30 0, 0 110,56"
style="fill:black; stroke:black; stroke-width:2;" />
<path d="M90,90 A30,65 30 0, 1 110,56"
style="fill:black; stroke:black; stroke-width:2;" />
<path d="M57,60 A30,50 20 0, 0 90,90"
style="fill:black; stroke:black; stroke-width:2;" />
</svg>
```

NOTE Shapes that remind people too much of an object can result in a cliché—
the use of the sun, for example. Don't use an orange/yellow gradient. As in
Figure 4-28, keep the shape simple and experiment with color and type combinations for an overall aesthetic approach that happens to have a sun metaphor rather
than a depiction of the sun. Something unique in the final layout "warms" the user
without looking stale from the overused metaphor.

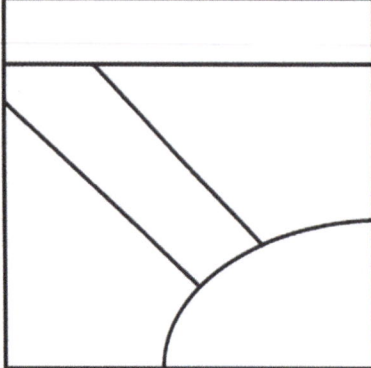

FIGURE 4-28 *Be careful with overused familiarity or clichés*

Listing 4-25 generates the Figure 4-28 shape.

LISTING 4-25 *Communicating Familiarity Without Sliding into Cliché*

```
<?xml version='1.0'?>
<svg width="300" height="300">
<rect style="fill:none;stroke:black; stroke-width:2;"
x="50" y="50" width="200" height="200" />
<line x1="50" y1="86" x2="250" y2="86"
style="stroke:black; stroke-width:2;" />
<line x1="50" y1="106" x2="155" y2="205"
style="stroke:black; stroke-width:2;" />
<line x1="98" y1="86" x2="190" y2="184"
style="stroke:black; stroke-width:2;" />
<path d="M 136,250 A 120,80 0 0,1 250,170"
style="fill:none; stroke:black; stroke-width:2;" />
</svg>
```

New designers tend to put a little of everything in, hoping to hit something. The simple shape of line and rectangle, combined with color and content, can result in a clean, readable site. Text placed at intermittent points in the rectangle can act as buttons. Simple shapes won't meet every client's needs. However, if your client's and users' language includes words such as *basic*, *simple*, and *easy*, a layout based on a minimalist concept might be a welcome relief from the client's design-challenged competition, as in Figure 4-29.

Listing 4-26 generates the Figure 4-29 shape.

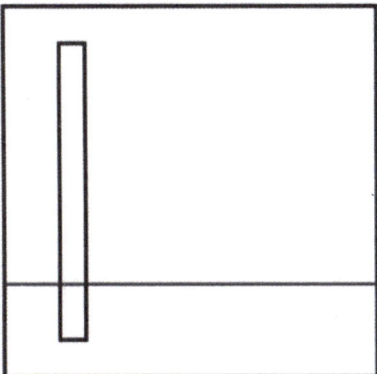

FIGURE 4-29 *Simple shapes can enhance content and result in great readability.*

LISTING 4-26 *Communicating Content with Minimalist Design*

```
<?xml version='1.0'?>
<svg>
<rect x="50" y="50" width="200" height="200"
style="fill:none; stroke:black; stroke-width:2;" />
<line x1="50" y1="200" x2="250" y2="200"
style="stroke:black; stroke-width:1.5;" />
<rect x="80" y="70" width="14" height="160"
style="fill:none; stroke:black; stroke-width:2;" />
</svg>
```

You can use rectangles, described in Chapter 2 as solid and comforting, to modernize the design by adjusting their placement and line density. This combination allows for both stability and a bit of uniqueness. Rectangles work well throughout this potential layout in slightly different combinations for buttons, navigation, and content. Rectangles can convey a fresh look for a traditional organization, as in Figure 4-30.

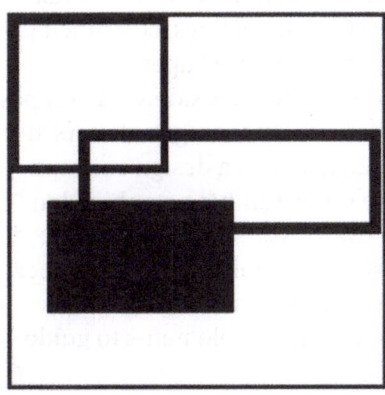

FIGURE 4-30 *Simple rectangles in an updated look*

Listing 4-27 generates the Figure 4-30 shape.

LISTING 4-27 *Communicating Familiarity with an Updated Approach*

```xml
<?xml version='1.0'?>
<svg>
<rect x="50" y="50" width="200" height="200"
style="fill:none; stroke:black; stroke-width:2;" />
<rect x="70" y="150" width="100" height="60"
style="fill:black;stroke-width:4;" />
<rect x="53" y="53" width="80" height="80"
style="fill:none; stroke:black; stroke-width:4;" />
<rect x="90" y="115" width="155" height="50"
style="fill:none; stroke:black; stroke-width:6;" />
</svg>
```

Design Element Axioms

In this chapter, you learned about lines, type, and shapes as design elements. Line facilitates user understanding of the design concept. Lines are straight, curved, narrow, thick, pointed, rounded, short, long, dotted, dashed, and so on. Your decision regarding the choice and combination of lines follows the design concept and the language from which it was derived. Think of the idea, concept, and language you want to convey. What type of line in what position helps you to tell the client's story? Do you want to hold, divide, organize, throw, connect, or lift them? Find the language, create the lines that symbolize your words, and bring them together to convey an idea.

Off-balance lines visually convey language differently than thin horizontal lines. Simple x-axis lines, surrounded by space, convey the language of the comfortable, calm, and familiar. Lines at angles convey action and uniqueness, and they tend to focus the user more intently. Curved lines convey a more natural, flowing, and softer space. Combinations of different types of lines, combined with a good use of whitespace, create interesting, contrasting shapes.

Type as a design element offers a design subtext when considered as shapes, angles, lines, ellipses, and space in addition to its literal meanings as letters and words. Type can add boldness, intimacy, and intelligence to a design concept. Language is the strongest tool humans have. The opportunity to combine language and the visual shape of words powerfully draws users to the world you create. Select the appropriate words, study the shape of their letters, and experiment with fonts, size, shape, and space to allow type to stimulate the users' imagination. Incorporate type into design and navigational elements to guide users through your client's story.

Shape groups of lines and blocks of text combine to become shapes. Plan and implement line and text use, as individual elements, to support the design concept. Ask yourself what language the individual elements create and what language their shapes communicate. Do you think serious, whimsical, bizarre, intent, interesting, hopeful, honest, comical, safe, or free? What shapes culturally remind users of the client's purpose? What combinations of line, space, and type make up the shape?

Shapes have height and weight. They may form a picture or simply suggest something familiar. Try to stay away from clichés and let the shapes and their parts communicate your story. Simple shapes often create good layouts that don't become stale within a few months. Try different combinations of shape and space. Try different kinds of line and type to create a shape.

The next chapter builds on this knowledge of line, type, and space by creating layout sketch prototypes.

Implementing Design Elements:
Texture, Space, Size, Value, and Layout

For the things we have to learn before we can do them, we learn by doing them.

—Aristotle, philosopher (384–322 B.C.)

As mentioned in Chapter 4, design elements visually communicate a design concept to the user. In this chapter, you'll learn about text, space, size, and value. In addition, you'll use these design elements and the ones from Chapter 4 (line, type, and shape) to create a layout. Design elements in layout are an expression of the design concept, brought forward from the language of clients and users.

Using Texture

Texture works with both focused, single elements and over the breadth of the design. Texture can add dimension and strength to a concept. Always begin any design critique by looking for weak elements in your design; then, work to eliminate them. In this section, look to the existing elements of line, shape, and type discussed in Chapter 4 and determine if you can enrich them with texture.

You can convey texture with slightly abstract rectangles placed at angles. In Figure 5-1, filled rectangles appear on the right side of the screen where content is often lost. The largest rectangle, the empty one on the left, can transition to the content portion of an eventual layout. Further, you could change the size of the filled rectangles depending upon the content needed for specific pages. Negative spaces, on the center-right side and lower-left corner of the design, enhance the depth already created by the weight of the filled shapes.

FIGURE 5-1 *Texture, depth, and weight*

Listing 5-1 generates the Figure 5-1 shape.

LISTING 5-1 *Communicating Texture with Space and Shape*

```
<?xml version='1.0'?>
<svg width="400" height="400">
<rect x="50" y="50" width="300" height="300"
style="fill:none; stroke:black; stroke-width:2;" />
<defs>
<g id="abstract">
<line x1="230" y1="90" x2="237" y2="180" style="fill:none;
stroke:black; stroke-width:2;" />
<line x1="0" y1="275" x2="81" y2="258" style="fill:none;
stroke:black; stroke-width:2;" />
<polyline points="170,0 155,90 300, 90 300,0"
style="fill:black; stroke:black;" />
<polyline points="72,213 91,300 300,300 300,164"
style="fill:black; stroke:black;" />
</g>
</defs>
<use xlink:href="#abstract" x="50" y="50" />
</svg>
```

Lines can convey texture without varying in weight. In Figure 5-2, lines resemble barbed wire. Barbed wire, although used daily in much of the world, also portrays a metaphor: the loss of freedom. This design conveys the idea that in its starkness, a user can almost feel the wire and its points. This design works well internationally—for the right project and the right client, of course. The content needs to be clean and consistent; placing attractive photos in any of the four sections would result in the design's loss of power.

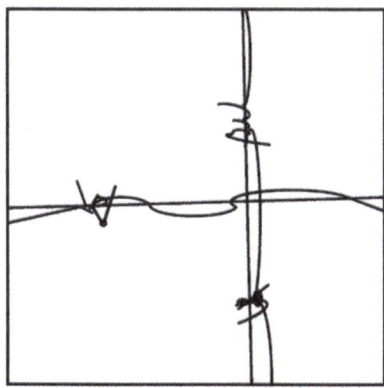

FIGURE 5-2   *Textured, hard, pointed objects*

Listing 5-2 generates the Figure 5-2 shape.

LISTING 5-2   *Communicating Texture and Meaning*

```
<?xml version='1.0'?>
<svg width="400" height="400">
<rect x="50" y="50" width="300" height="300"
style="fill:none; stroke:black; stroke-width:2;" />
<defs>
<g id="wire" style="fill:none; stroke:black;
stroke-width:2;">
<line x1="0" y1="159" x2="300" y2="150" />
<line x1="187" y1="0" x2="194" y2="300" />
<line x1="271" y1="150" x2="300" y2="161" />
<line x1="65" y1="160" x2="72" y2="148" />
<line x1="55" y1="137" x2="62" y2="157" />
<line x1="184" y1="237" x2="199" y2="233" />
<line x1="208" y1="220" x2="183" y2="240" />
<polyline points="86,141 76,172 67,157" />
<polyline points="86,141 76,172 67,157" />
<polyline points="0,171 58,158 68,163" />
<ellipse cx="199" cy="231" rx="3" ry="6"
style="fill:black; stroke:black;" />
<ellipse cx="187" cy="234" rx="4" ry="2"
style="fill:black; stroke:black;" />
<circle cx="76" cy="171" r="2"
style="fill:black; stroke:black;" />
<path d="M68,156 A23,8 0 0,1 113,157" />
<path d="M113,157 A35,9 0 0,0 182,158" />
<path d="M182,158 A45,9 0 0,1 271,150" />
<path d="M65,157 A3,1 0 0,0 71,150" />
```

```
<path d="M189,0 A5,38 0 0,1 187,76" />
<path d="M189,110 A6,57 0 0,1 198,224" />
<path d="M199,233 A12,63 0 0,1 210,300" />
<path d="M167,76 A8,3 10 0,1 187,88" />
<path d="M179,89 A8,3 10 0,1 190,95" />
<path d="M179,100 A6,3 10 0,1 193,100" />
<path d="M179,100 A20,2 10 0,0 209,108" />
<path d="M181,237 A15,4 340 0,1 183,251" />
</g>
</defs>
<use xlink:href="#wire" x="50" y="50" />
</svg>
```

Lines as shapes can convey direction or motion. The tracking at the top of Figure 5-3 can transition into a layout with color and graphics, or it can remain as is. The modified tracking on the left could house navigational links. The moderately off-center design is where the sense of direction or motion emanates. If the top and left tracks are flush with the edges and at right angles to each other, the design communicates something different. There's quite a bit of content space here, and there's room to move elements around.

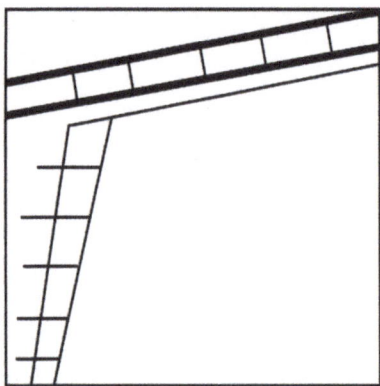

FIGURE 5-3 *Texture and direction/motion*

Listing 5-3 generates the Figure 5-3 shape.

LISTING 5-3 *Communicating Texture and Motion*

```
<?xml version='1.0'?>
<svg width="400" height="400">
<rect x="50" y="50" width="300" height="300"
style="fill:none; stroke:black; stroke-width:2;" />
<defs>
<g id="track" style="fill:none; stroke:black;
stroke-width:2;">
```

```
<line x1="0" y1="59" x2="279" y2="5"
style="fill:none; stroke:black; stroke-width:6;" />
<line x1="0" y1="85" x2="300" y2="30"
style="fill:none; stroke:black; stroke-width:6;" />
<line x1="53" y1="50" x2="57" y2="76" />
<line x1="97" y1="43" x2="101" y2="66" />
<line x1="204" y1="23" x2="208" y2="45" />
<line x1="155" y1="30" x2="159" y2="53" />
<line x1="8" y1="279" x2="43" y2="279" />
<line x1="257" y1="11" x2="261" y2="34" />
<line x1="9" y1="247" x2="50" y2="247" />
<line x1="14" y1="205" x2="57" y2="205" />
<line x1="12" y1="166" x2="67" y2="166" />
<line x1="25" y1="126" x2="76" y2="126" />
<line x1="38" y1="300" x2="84" y2="86" />
<polyline points="20,300 50,93 300,44" />
<polyline points="279,7 300,4 300,0 280,3 279,7"
fill="black" />
</g>
</defs>
<use xlink:href="#track" x="50" y="50" />
</svg>
```

Lines and space can also communicate direction and motion. In Figure 5-4, lines cross, parallel, divide, and combine across space. The direction is clearly vertical. The more the lines intersect, the more the motion slows. This design immediately draws a user's attention. This could result in a layout for a splash page with the simple addition of a line of text or a logo. Support pages for the site could incorporate the more focused use of lines.

FIGURE 5-4 *Texture and direction/motion, revisited*

Listing 5-4 generates the Figure 5-4 shape.

LISTING 5-4 *Communicating Motion with Texture and Line Variety*

```xml
<?xml version='1.0'?>
<svg>
<rect style="fill:none; stroke: black;
stroke-width:2;" x="50" y="50" width="200" height="200" />
<line x1="134" y1="50" x2="134" y2="250"
style="stroke:black; stroke-width:2;" />
<line x1="98" y1="250" x2="156" y2="50"
style="stroke:black; stroke-width:2;" />
<line x1="174" y1="250" x2="222" y2="50"
style="stroke:black; stroke-width:2;" />
<line x1="177" y1="250" x2="225" y2="50"
style="stroke:black; stroke-width:2;" />
<line x1="214" y1="250" x2="250" y2="130"
style="stroke:black; stroke-width:2;" />
<line x1="50" y1="170" x2="86" y2="90"
style="stroke:black; stroke-width:2;" />
<polyline points="50 150,50 130,94 50, 106
50,90 242,74 242,86 90, 94 74, 92 70, 50 150"
style="stroke:black; stroke-width:1;" />
<polyline points="179 242,190 247,250 114, 250 80,179 242"
style="stroke:black; stroke-width:1;" />
</svg>
```

Using Space

Space surrounds and fills design elements. Space is one of the most important elements of all design. Space enhances readability, leads to an understanding of scale, and creates a focal point as much as any shape. Open space provides a place for eyes to rest and allows users a pause to organize content visually.

Space isn't empty. It holds the same power as shape. You can often solve design problems by removing any noncritical elements and then creating a dynamic relationship between the remaining elements and the space. In many cultures, space communicates wealth. Open park space, space on airplanes, space in homes . . . most people treasure space and freedom. Don't fill your layout with cute or cool things it doesn't need. Your critical elements and your shapes, combined with a strong use of space, communicate a clear voice and richness in design.

The lines of Figure 5-5 can represent a simple logo, graphic, photo, or line of text. Sometimes a simple approach results in a layout that you code in a few minutes. The strength here is in the space and in how the objects communicate with each other and with the user. Take your time practicing with space and placement. In our society, we're bombarded with information, so space and readability often result in a site that's accessible and easy to view.

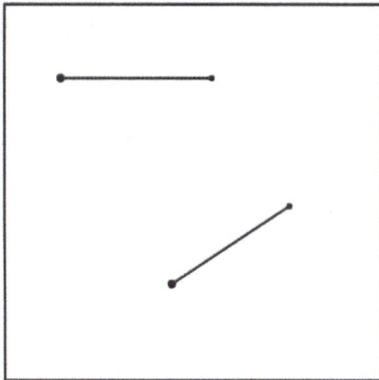

FIGURE 5-5 *Space and simple elements*

Listing 5-5 generates the Figure 5-5 shape.

LISTING 5-5 *Communicating Texture Using Minimal Design Elements*

```
<?xml version='1.0'?>
<svg width="400" height="400">
<rect x="50" y="50" width="300" height="300"
style="fill:none; stroke:black; stroke-width:2;" />
<defs>
<g id="line">
<line x1="45" y1="59" x2="165" y2="59"
style="fill:none; stroke:black; stroke-width:2;" />
<line x1="133" y1="223" x2="226" y2="161"
style="fill:none; stroke:black; stroke-width:2;" />
<circle cx="45" cy="59" r="3" style="fill:black;
stroke:black; stroke-width:1;" />
<circle cx="165" cy="59" r="2" style="fill:black;
stroke:black; stroke-width:1;" />
<circle cx="133" cy="223" r="3" style="fill:black;
stroke:black; stroke-width:1;" />
<circle cx="226" cy="161" r="2" style="fill:black;
stroke:black; stroke-width:1;" />
</g>
</defs>
<use xlink:href="#line" x="50" y="50" />
</svg>
```

In Figure 5-6, shape and space, made from a few lines, form dimension. Lines in perspective add the z-axis, resulting in a perception of depth. Combining color and simple navigation to this concept could transition into a layout suitable for either of the following:

- Products: The left and right shapes could be anything from software boxes to cans of food.

- Building maintenance or property management: The shapes also look like office buildings.

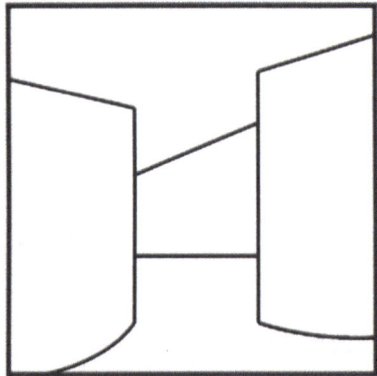

FIGURE 5-6 *Perspective and space convey dimension.*

Listing 5-6 generates the Figure 5-6 shape.

LISTING 5-6 *Communicating Dimension*

```
<?xml version='1.0'?>
<svg>
<rect x="50" y="50" width="200" height="200"
style="fill:none; stroke:black; stroke-width:3;" />
<line x1="50" y1="90" x2="118" y2="106" style="
stroke:black; stroke-width:2;" />
<line x1="118" y1="106" x2="118" y2="222"
style=" stroke:black; stroke-width:2;" />
<line x1="118" y1="142" x2="186" y2="114"
style="stroke:black; stroke-width:2;" />
<line x1="186" y1="86" x2="186" y2="222"
style="stroke:black; stroke-width:2;" />
<line x1="118" y1="186" x2="186" y2="186"
style="stroke:black; stroke-width:2;" />
<line x1="186" y1="86" x2="250" y2="66"
style="stroke:black; stroke-width:2;" />
```

```
<path d="M70, 250 A100,50 0 0,0 118,222"
style="fill:none; stroke:black; stroke-width:2;" />
<path d="M186, 222 A100,50 0 0,0 250,230"
style="fill:none; stroke:black; stroke-width:2;" />
</svg>
```

Organized space is important for some clients. Think of all of the information sites you see with columns of articles and advertisements. In Figure 5-7, lines build focal points for space. Negative space is less visible but offers room for secondary items.

 NOTE Positive space is the space occupied by your subject. Negative space is the space beyond the edges of the subject and within the borders or frame of the design. Both define the concept of your design.

For example, the *Wall Street Journal*'s front page pulls attention to article summaries through primary emphasis. Here, space and line guide the user to primary areas for your client.

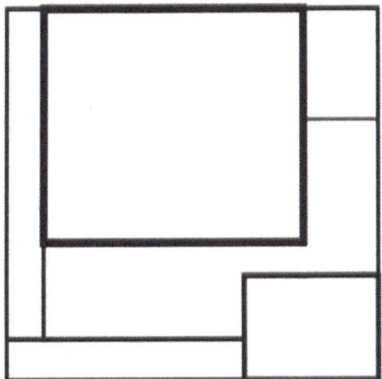

FIGURE 5-7 *Emphasized space*

Listing 5-7 generates the Figure 5-7 shape.

LISTING 5-7 *Communicating Space and Organization*

```
<?xml version='1.0'?>
<svg>
<rect x="50" y="50" width="200" height="200"
style="fill:none; stroke:black; stroke-width:2;" />
<rect x="70" y="50" width="140" height="126"
style="fill:none; stroke:black; stroke-width:4;" />
<rect x="178" y="194" width="72" height="56"
style="fill:none; stroke:black; stroke-width:3;" />
```

```
<path d="M 210 110, 250 110" style="fill:none;
stroke:black; stroke-width:1.5;" />
<path d="M 50 228,  178 228" style="fill:none;
stroke:black; stroke-width:2;" />
<path d="M 70 176,  70 228"  style="fill:none;
stroke:black; stroke-width:2;" />
</svg>
```

In Figure 5-8, space forms a "window" in the background. The foreground holds a vase and a shelf. This design might portray the inside of a house. Or, the "window" could be a photo, a graphic, or some content. Colors for the site could communicate a warm home or perhaps a funky apartment. The vase can be more geometric, balanced, or traditional to change the interpretation of the concept and reflect the personality of the client.

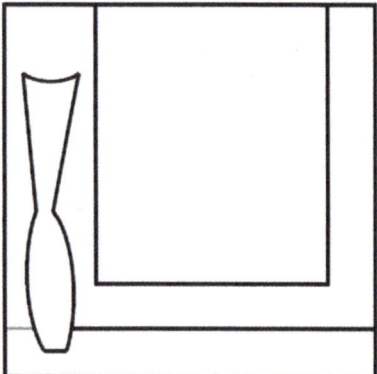

FIGURE 5-8 *Space in everyday life*

Listing 5-8 generates the Figure 5-8 shape.

LISTING 5-8 *Communicating Space and Familiarity*

```
<?xml version='1.0'?>
<svg width="300" height="300">
<rect x="50" y="50" width="200" height="200"
style="fill:none; stroke:black; stroke-width:2;" />
<rect x="99" y="50"  width="125" height="150"
style="fill:none; stroke:black; stroke-width:2;" />
<line x1="50" y1="224" x2="66" y2="224"
style="fill:none; stroke:black; stroke-width:2;" />
<line x1="85" y1="224" x2="250" y2="224"
style="fill:none; stroke:black; stroke-width:2;" />
<line x1="71" y1="236" x2="83" y2="236"
style="fill:none; stroke:black; stroke-width:2;" />
```

```
<line x1="60" y1="87" x2="67" y2="161"
style="fill:none; stroke:black; stroke-width:2;" />
<line x1="90" y1="87" x2="76" y2="161"
style="fill:none; stroke:black; stroke-width:2;"/>
<path d="M60,87 A18,10 0 0, 0 90,87"
style="fill:none; stroke:black; stroke-width:2;" />
<path d="M67,161 A50,20 90 0, 0 71,236"
style="fill:none; stroke:black; stroke-width:2;" />
<path d="M76,161 A50,20 90 0, 1 83,236"
style="fill:none; stroke:black; stroke-width:2;" />
</svg>
```

Setting Size

There are a few strange ideas about size and the Web. First, monitors are about 24 inches, or 60 centimeters, from the user. At that distance, people can read buttons, text, and links easily. Making these components large makes users want to "back away" from the monitor. Size is important in drawing users to objects you want them to see; however, size doesn't mean huge. Go to a bookstore and pick up a large-print book for readers with eyesight issues. These books are great for their intended audience. However, if you don't need the larger type, your eyes become overwhelmed after a few pages and the text becomes difficult to read.

Figure 5-9 shows a potential layout for an American flag. Here, lines are spaced in such a way that they visually double as stripes and as navigational areas. The size of the stars serves to divide the screen and draw attention to the flag metaphor. In this design, the size and the placement of the stars and stripes need to maintain a sense of relation—in other words, they need to maintain a familiarity to the proportions of an actual flag.

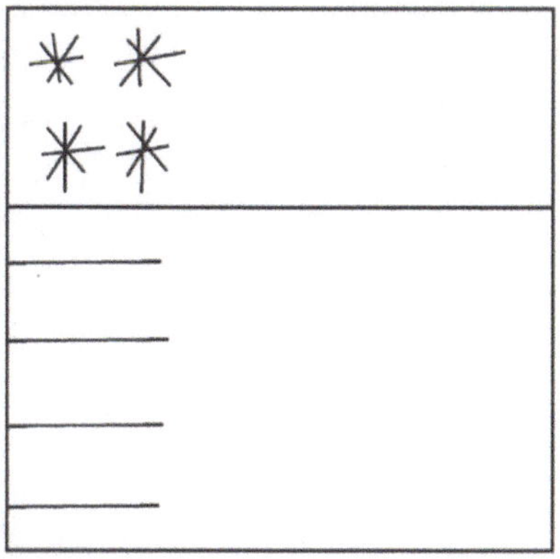

FIGURE 5-9 *Size and familiarity*

Listing 5-9 generates the Figure 5-9 shape.

LISTING 5-9 *Communicating Proportion and Familiarity*

```xml
<?xml version='1.0'?>
<svg width="400" height="400">
<rect x="50" y="50" width="300" height="300"
style="fill:none; stroke:black; stroke-width:2;" />
<defs>
<g id="flag">
<line x1="0" y1="110" x2="300" y2="110"
style="fill:none; stroke:black; stroke-width:2;" />
<line x1="0" y1="141" x2="85" y2="140"
style="fill:none; stroke:black; stroke-width:2;" />
<line x1="0" y1="184" x2="89" y2="183"
style="fill:none; stroke:black; stroke-width:2;" />
<line x1="0" y1="231" x2="86" y2="230"
style="fill:none; stroke:black; stroke-width:2;" />
<line x1="0" y1="276" x2="84" y2="275"
style="fill:none; stroke:black; stroke-width:2;" />
<line x1="22" y1="66" x2="43" y2="91"
style="fill:none; stroke:black; stroke-width:2;" />
<line x1="19" y1="81" x2="54" y2="77"
style="fill:none; stroke:black; stroke-width:2;" />
<line x1="22" y1="95" x2="41" y2="65"
style="fill:none; stroke:black; stroke-width:2;" />
<line x1="32" y1="63" x2="32" y2="102"
style="fill:none; stroke:black; stroke-width:2;" />
<line x1="60" y1="81" x2="89" y2="76"
style="fill:none; stroke:black; stroke-width:2;" />
<line x1="66" y1="93" x2="82" y2="66"
style="fill:none; stroke:black; stroke-width:2;" />
<line x1="66" y1="63" x2="88" y2="90"
style="fill:none; stroke:black; stroke-width:2;" />
<line x1="75" y1="62" x2="74" y2="102"
style="fill:none; stroke:black; stroke-width:2;" />
<line x1="18" y1="19" x2="36" y2="42"
style="fill:none; stroke:black; stroke-width:2;" />
<line x1="12" y1="31" x2="42" y2="27"
style="fill:none; stroke:black; stroke-width:2;" />
<line x1="22" y1="41" x2="39" y2="15"
style="fill:none; stroke:black; stroke-width:2;" />
<line x1="25" y1="14" x2="29" y2="41"
style="fill:none; stroke:black; stroke-width:2;" />
```

```
<line x1="66" y1="17" x2="90" y2="43"
style="fill:none; stroke:black; stroke-width:2;" />
<line x1="59" y1="31" x2="98" y2="24"
style="fill:none; stroke:black; stroke-width:2;" />
<line x1="62" y1="43" x2="84" y2="15"
style="fill:none; stroke:black; stroke-width:2;" />
<line x1="72" y1="11" x2="73" y2="43"
style="fill:none; stroke:black; stroke-width:2;" />
</g>
</defs>
<use xlink:href="#flag" x="50" y="50" />
</svg>
```

Figure 5-10 simply divides a screen and adds a circle. How you decide to size and place the division and the circle changes the concept from a bull's eye target for a shooting range to a moon viewed through a pane-glass window. Shapes can reflect objects or simply exist to draw interest. Although no color or line thickness has been added to Figure 5-10, there's a primary focal point (the crossed point of the lines) and a secondary focal point (the circle).

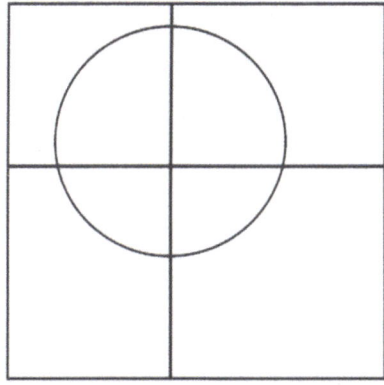

FIGURE 5-10 *Size and placement of design elements*

Listing 5-10 generates the Figure 5-10 shape.

LISTING 5-10 *Communicating a Focal Point Using Size and Placement*

```
<?xml version='1.0'?>
<svg width="400" height="400">
<rect x="50" y="50" width="300" height="300"
style="fill:none; stroke:black; stroke-width:2;" />
<defs>
<g id="target">
<circle cx="130" cy="110" r="92" style="fill:none;
stroke:black; stroke-width:2;" />
```

```
<line x1="131" y1="0" x2="131" y2="300"
style="fill:none; stroke:black; stroke-width:3;" />
<line x1="0" y1="130" x2="300" y2="130"
style="fill:none; stroke:black; stroke-width:3;" />
</g>
</defs>
<use xlink:href="#target" x="50" y="50" />
</svg>
```

The size of the Figure 5-11 clock face concept, in addition to the style of its "numbers," creates a sense of shape and time. Modern numerals, rather than these lines resembling Roman numerals, would change the user perception. In addition, the size of the graphics and the size of the intervening space tightens or loosens the clock face. The placement of the numerals—for example, their haphazard arrangement here vs. their perfect alignment—adds to the sense of these clocks.

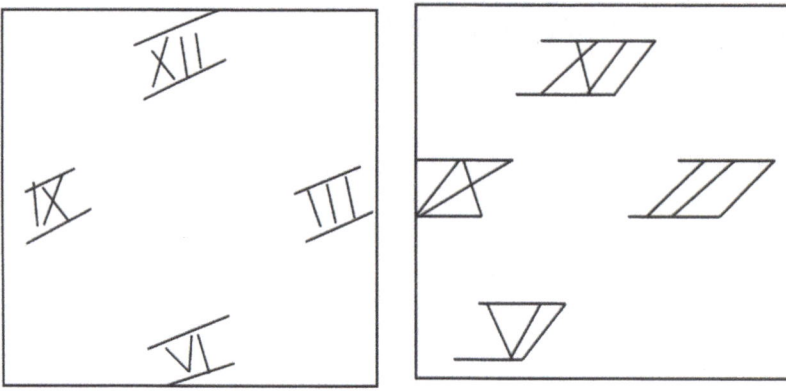

FIGURE 5-11 *Space, size, and placement*

Listing 5-11 generates the clock face on the left of Figure 5-11.

LISTING 5-11 *Communicating an Idea with Line and Space*

```
<?xml version='1.0'?>
<svg width="400" height="400">
<rect x="50" y="50" width="300" height="300"
style="fill:none; stroke:black; stroke-width:2;" />
<defs>
<g id="clock" style="fill:none; stroke:black;
stroke-width:2;">
<line x1="18" y1="146" x2="58" y2="127" />
<line x1="19" y1="187" x2="71" y2="159" />
```

```
<line x1="25" y1="138" x2="28" y2="173" />
<line x1="33" y1="172" x2="48" y2="132" />
<line x1="32" y1="142" x2="53" y2="169" />
<line x1="234" y1="147" x2="287" y2="125" />
<line x1="243" y1="185" x2="297" y2="161" />
<line x1="245" y1="144" x2="255" y2="173" />
<line x1="260" y1="139" x2="267" y2="170" />
<line x1="275" y1="133" x2="282" y2="166" />
<line x1="116" y1="271" x2="182" y2="244" />
<line x1="131" y1="300" x2="186" y2="282" />
<line x1="131" y1="270" x2="150" y2="289" />
<line x1="150" y1="289" x2="152" y2="260" />
<line x1="157" y1="259" x2="166" y2="290" />
<line x1="105" y1="29" x2="175" y2="0" />
<line x1="113" y1="72" x2="180" y2="40" />
<line x1="120" y1="33" x2="139" y2="56" />
<line x1="121" y1="62" x2="133" y2="22" />
<line x1="144" y1="22" x2="149" y2="54" />
<line x1="156" y1="19" x2="160" y2="47" />
</g>
</defs>
<use xlink:href="#clock" x="50" y="50" />
</svg>
```

Listing 5-12 generates the clock face on the right of Figure 5-11.

LISTING 5-12 *Communicating a Different Interpretation by Adjusting Line, Size, and Space*

```
<?xml version='1.0'?>
<svg width="400" height="400">
<rect x="50" y="50" width="300" height="300"
style="fill:none; stroke:black; stroke-width:2;" />
<defs>
<g id="clock" style="fill:none;
stroke:black; stroke-width:2;">
<line x1="0" y1="125" x2="78" y2="125" />
<line x1="3" y1="170" x2="77" y2="125" />
<line x1="53" y1="170" x2="38" y2="125" />
<line x1="0" y1="170" x2="35" y2="125" />
<line x1="0" y1="170" x2="53" y2="170" />
<line x1="210" y1="125" x2="287" y2="125" />
<line x1="243" y1="170" x2="286" y2="125" />
<line x1="205" y1="170" x2="255" y2="125" />
<line x1="170" y1="170" x2="243" y2="170" />
<line x1="185" y1="170" x2="231" y2="125" />
```

```
<line x1="50" y1="240" x2="120" y2="240" />
<line x1="30" y1="285" x2="85" y2="285" />
<line x1="120" y1="240" x2="85" y2="285" />
<line x1="100" y1="240" x2="75" y2="285" />
<line x1="57" y1="240" x2="77" y2="285" />
<line x1="100" y1="29" x2="193" y2="29" />
<line x1="159" y1="72" x2="192" y2="29" />
<line x1="80" y1="72" x2="160" y2="72" />
<line x1="140" y1="72" x2="129" y2="29" />
<line x1="100" y1="72" x2="146" y2="29" />
<line x1="137" y1="72" x2="169" y2="29" />
</g>
</defs>
<use xlink:href="#clock" x="50" y="50" />
</svg>
```

The Figure 5-12 shapes could change in size depending on their roles in a potential layout. They could be small and on the fringes of the site, taking on a thematic supporting role. On the other hand, they could be large, colorful, and significant, taking on the focal point of a splash page. They may appear alone or in various combinations as they interact with content. Their size and their placement significantly determine the level of whimsy the site projects.

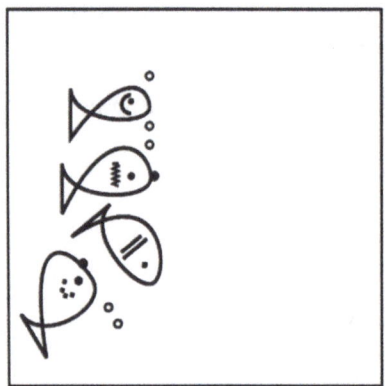

FIGURE 5-12 *Shape and size in relationship to character*

Listing 5-13 generates the Figure 5-12 shape.

LISTING 5-13 *Shape, Size, and Personality*

```
<?xml version='1.0'?>
<svg width="400" height="400">
<rect x="50" y="50" width="300" height="300"
style="fill:none; stroke:black; stroke-width:2;" />
```

```
<g transform="translate(-20,0)">
<g transform=" translate(0,-50) rotate(90, 120,163)
scale(1) " id="5" >
<path d="M140 115  A 4 4 3 0 1 125 115"
style="fill:none; stroke:black; stroke-width:3" />
<path style="fill:none; stroke:#000000; stroke-width:3"
d="M120 163 C 150 160 150 100 135 100  S 100 120 160 163 Z" />
<circle cx="130" cy="115" r="2" style="fill:black;
stroke:black; stroke-width:1;" />
<circle cx="110" cy="100" r="3" style="fill:none;
stroke:black; stroke-width:2;" />
<circle cx="150" cy="100" r="3" style="fill:none;
stroke:black; stroke-width:2;" />
<circle cx="165" cy="100" r="3" style="fill:none;
stroke:black; stroke-width:2;" />
<path style="fill:none; stroke:#000000; stroke-width:3"
d="M180 170 C 210 167 210 107 195 100  S 130 127 220 170 Z" />
<circle cx="190" cy="115" r="2" style="fill:black;
stroke:black; stroke-width:2;" />
<circle cx="190" cy="96" r="3" style="fill:black;
stroke:black; stroke-width:2;" />
<polyline points="180,125 180,130 182,125 184,130 186,125
188,130 190,125 192,130 194,125 196,130 198,125"
style="fill:none; stroke:black; stroke-width:2;" />
</g>
<g transform="translate(-40,130) rotate(60, 120,163)" id="5" >
<path style="fill:none; stroke:#000000; stroke-width:3"
d="M120 163 C 150 160 150 100 125 100  S 50 120 160 163 Z" />
<circle cx="120" cy="110" r="3" style="fill:black;
stroke:black; stroke-width:1;" />
<circle cx="120" cy="125" r="2" style="fill:black;
stroke:black; stroke-width:1;" />
<circle cx="125" cy="125" r="2" style="fill:black;
stroke:black; stroke-width:1;" />
<circle cx="127" cy="120" r="2" style="fill:black;
stroke:black; stroke-width:1;" />
<circle cx="115" cy="120" r="2" style="fill:black;
stroke:black; stroke-width:1;" />
<circle cx="110" cy="100" r="3" style="fill:black;
stroke:black; stroke-width:2;" />
<circle cx="150" cy="100" r="3" style="fill:none;
stroke:black; stroke-width:2;" />
<circle cx="165" cy="100" r="3" style="fill:none;
stroke:black; stroke-width:2;" />
```

```
</g>
<g transform="translate(0,115) rotate(140, 180,125) " id="5" >
<path style="fill:none; stroke:#000000; stroke-width:3"
d="M180 170 C 210 167 210 107 195 100  S 130 160 220 170 Z" />
<circle cx="190" cy="115" r="2" style="fill:black;
stroke:black; stroke-width:2;" />
<line x1="175" y1="130" x2="200" y2="130" style="fill:none;
stroke:black; stroke-width:3;" />
<line x1="177" y1="135" x2="198" y2="135" style="fill:none;
stroke:black; stroke-width:3;" />
</g>
</g>
</svg>
```

Understanding Value

Value expresses relationships between elements. Changes to texture, density, position, space, and other design elements alter a user's interpretation of a design. For example, a graphic of a chair shown in an empty tiny room with an undersized door communicates the familiar *Alice in Wonderland* metaphor. A graphic of a single chair on an expanse of beach or of a chair placed next to a casket covered with flowers convey different relationships. Graphically, elements that appear similar as an initial sketch can radically change the user's interpretation based on varying sizes, textures, positions, and other design elements you bring into the design. This chapter discusses the aspects of value not related to color. (Chapter 8 covers value expressed through color.) Specifically, value guides the eye to focal areas by combining black, white, and gray with the contrast of shapes, size, space, and placement. Value can convey a subtle feeling, a structured rhythm, a sense of drama, a perception of weight, or even emotion.

An important key to design is to develop a concept that works well in black and white and then to add color. Value allows you to strengthen your design idea to a point where your concept stands on its own. Adding color afterward completes and fine-tunes the design. For example, Figure 5-13 uses black, white, and two line widths to convey a sense of dimension. You can add focus by including gray areas. Changing the value of the lines subtly communicates layered shapes and results in depth or weight. Color, added later, should enhance the graphic rather than carry it.

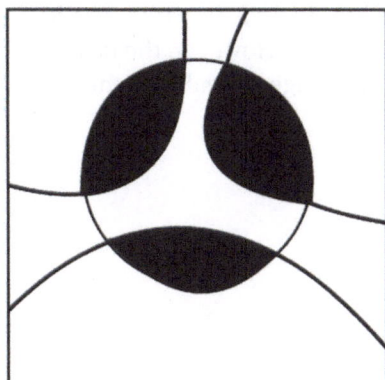

FIGURE 5-13 *Value and depth*

Listing 5-14 generates the Figure 5-13 shape.

LISTING 5-14 *Communicating Depth and Layers*

```
<?xml version='1.0'?>
<svg>
<rect x="50" y="50" width="300" height="300"
style="fill:none; stroke:black; stroke-width:2;" />
<circle cx="200" cy="180" r="90" style="fill:none;
stroke:black; stroke-width:2;" />
<path d="M50,190 Q200,230 190,50"
style="fill:none; stroke:black; stroke-width:3" />
<path d="M109,197 Q190,190 190,90"
style="fill:black; stroke:black; stroke-width:3" />
<path d="M109,197 Q110,100 190,90"
style="fill:black; stroke:black; stroke-width:3" />
<path d="M50,290 Q200,145 350,320"
style="fill:none; stroke:black; stroke-width:3" />
<path d="M130,235 Q200,210 260,247"
style="fill:black; stroke:black; stroke-width:3" />
<path d="M130,233 Q200,310 261,245"
style="fill:black; stroke:black; stroke-width:3" />
<path d="M240,50 Q170,190 350,220 "
style="fill:none; stroke:black; stroke-width:3" />
<path d="M223,93 Q170,190 290,204 "
style="fill:black; stroke:black; stroke-width:3" />
<path d="M223,93 Q300,119 290,204 "
style="fill:black; stroke:black; stroke-width:1" />
</svg>
```

Figure 5-14's concept is a minor modification of Figure 5-13 with one additional curved line and a slightly different line placement. However, the design
conveys an entirely different story. How could you change the value of this concept to reflect outer space or a kaleidoscope?

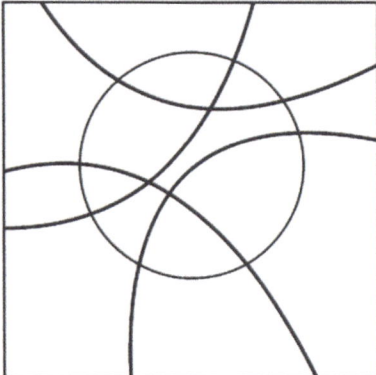

FIGURE 5-14 *Value and imagery*

Listing 5-15 generates the Figure 5-14 shape.

LISTING 5-15 *Communicating Modified Imagery*

```
<?xml version='1.0'?>
<svg>
<rect x="50" y="50" width="300" height="300"
style="fill:none; stroke:black; stroke-width:2;" />
<circle cx="200" cy="180" r="90" style="fill:none;
stroke:black; stroke-width:2;" />
<path d="M50,230 Q200,230 250,50"
style="fill:none; stroke:black; stroke-width:3" />
<path d="M150,350 Q140,120 350,160"
style="fill:none; stroke:black; stroke-width:3" />
<path d="M50,185 Q200,145 300,350"
style="fill:none; stroke:black; stroke-width:3" />
<path d="M80,50 Q170,190 350,100"
style="fill:none; stroke:black; stroke-width:3" />
</svg>
```

Value, in Figure 5-15, takes the form of shape, rather than color or shade. The
squiggling lines on the right appear light in weight. The curved shapes toward
the left appear textured and full. The negative space on the right appears interestingly flat in contrast to the shapes toward the left. The angular shape on the far left
and the negative space on the top left counter the heaviness of the curved spaces.

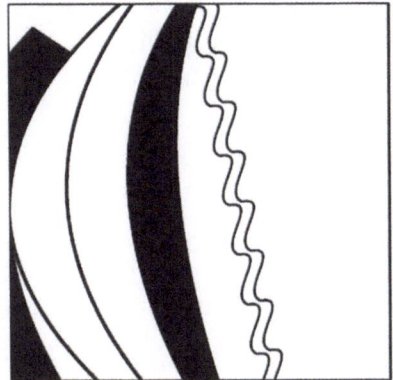

FIGURE 5-15 *Value and shape*

Listing 5-16 generates the Figure 5-15 shape.

LISTING 5-16 *Communicating a Symphony of Shape*

```
<?xml version='1.0'?>
<svg>
<rect x="50" y="50" width="300" height="300"
style="fill:none; stroke:black; stroke-width:2;" />
<path d="M70,70 Q -200,364 90,350 Q 5,200 100,90 Z"
style="fill:black; stroke:black; stroke-width:3" />
<path d="M140,50 Q -30,200 120,350 "
style="fill:none; stroke:black; stroke-width:3" />
<path d="M150,50 Q 40,200 155,350 "
style="fill:none; stroke:black; stroke-width:3" />
<path d="M200,30 Q 70,200 250,450 Q 150,200 200,50 Z"
style="fill:black; stroke:black; stroke-width:3" />
<g transform ="translate(-13,3) rotate(80,210,50)">
<path d="M 210,49 c0,-25 30,15 40 0 M 250,50 c0,-25 30,15 40 0
        M 290,50 c0,-25 30,15 40 0
        M 330,50 c0,-25 30,15 40 0
        M 370,50 c0,-25 30,15 40 0
        M 410,50 c0,-25 30,15 40 0
        M 450,50 c0,-25 30,15 40 0
        M 490,50 c0,-25 30,15 40 0"
style="fill:none; stroke:black; stroke-width:2;" />
</g>
<g transform =" translate(-3,0) rotate(80,210,50) ">
```

```
<path d="M 210,49 c0,-25 30,15 40 0 M 250,50 c0,-25 30,15 40 0
         M 290,50 c0,-25 30,15 40 0
         M 330,50 c0,-25 30,15 40 0
         M 370,50 c0,-25 30,15 40 0
         M 410,50 c0,-25 30,15 40 0
         M 450,50 c0,-25 30,15 40 0
         M 490,50 c0,-25 30,15 40 0"
style="fill:none; stroke:black; stroke-width:2;" />
</g>
<rect x="0" y="50" width="49" height="350"
style="fill:white; stroke:white; stroke-width:2;" />
<rect x="50" y="0" width="350" height="49"
style="fill:white; stroke:white; stroke-width:2;" />
<rect x="50" y="351" width="350" height="400"
style="fill:white; stroke:white; stroke-width:2;" />
</svg>
```

The layered shape of Figure 5-16 adds even more dimension with the addition of grays and textures. The diagonal placement of two rectangles and the diagonal supporting lines on the bottom left create a less structured environment. The solid, black rectangle in the background and the narrow black rectangle in the foreground hold the intermittent rectangles in place. The key to value is that the rectangles all reside on the same dimension, and only some appear to support the others.

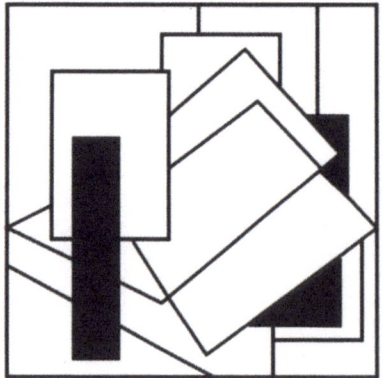

FIGURE 5-16 *Value and perception*

Listing 5-17 generates the Figure 5-16 shape.

LISTING 5-17   *Communicating Layers of Products, Projects, or Papers*

```
<?xml version='1.0'?>
<svg>
<rect style="fill:none; stroke:black; stroke-width:2;"
x="50" y="50" width="200" height="200" />
<rect style="fill:none; stroke:black; stroke-width:2;"
x="74" y="86" width="64" height="90" />
<rect style="fill:black; stroke:black; stroke-width:2;"
x="86" y="122" width="24" height="118" />
<line x1="50" y1="190" x2="162" y2="250"
style="stroke:black; stroke-width:2;" />
<line x1="154" y1="50" x2="154" y2="66"
style="stroke:black; stroke-width:2;" />
<line x1="218" y1="50" x2="218" y2="110"
style="stroke:black; stroke-width:2;" />
<line x1="194" y1="250" x2="194" y2="222"
style="stroke:black; stroke-width:2;" />
<polyline points="134 87,134 66, 198 66,198 94"
style="fill:none; stroke:black; stroke-width:2;" />
<polyline points="194 230,242 230, 242 175"
style="fill:none; stroke:black; stroke-width:2;" />
<polyline points="181 222,230 222, 230 186"
style="fill:black; stroke:black; stroke-width:2;" />
<polyline points="212 110 234 110, 234 153,220 140,232 130, 212 110"
style="fill:black; stroke:black; stroke-width:2;" />
<polyline points="118 177,158 238, 250 170,186 102,138 138"
style="fill:none; stroke:black; stroke-width:2;" />
<polyline points="74 158,50 170,134 210, 230 130,179 74,138
110" style="fill:none; stroke:black; stroke-width:2;" />
</svg>
```

Now that you have an idea of all the possibilities created and communicated with the design elements that you can incorporate into your design, it's time to start the layout of your site.

Designing the Layout

Layout, for Web development, is a little like watching the opening credits of a movie. Within a few seconds, you know if you're going to like it. You see type, space, and color; you hear sounds, music, or sometimes silence. Somehow, your eyes and mind grab the images, consider their significance, and determine in a moment how you interpret their meaning. Visual events—whether in a theater, a museum or gallery, a magazine, or on the Internet—attract, distract, or make no impact by the count of three.

Layout is what users see first when they encounter your design. Western eyes typically travel from left to right. However, focal points override tradition to guide the eye through design and content using design elements that are based on design concepts, which are in turn developed from the language determined by your client's and users' needs. The purpose of this section is to make the concept of layout seem so familiar that you don't panic and drop this design component altogether. Layout is where new designers typically fail. Often, they understand the client and user, they understand the concept, they understand the elements, but they somehow put it all together in a product that's flat-out ugly.

In fact, it's amazing to see layouts so filled with saturated, clashing colors they could almost be radioactive. It's bizarre to see characters or letters 1 inch, or 3 centimeters, high. It's ridiculous to see sites with misspelled words. In addition, there's no reason for anything to blink repeatedly. Good layout sets up the client's story for the user. In addition, good layout invites interaction and creates a comfortable, familiar space for finding products, accessing information, or having fun.

Begin designing your layout by verifying user priorities. What they want, in the order they want to access it, determines the foundation of your navigation. Consider also your client's needs. Do the client's expectations mesh or vary from a user's expectations? Typically, client and users have the same or similar priorities. You can address variations in submenus.

Everyone has an opinion about layout. Don't aim for comments such as "Oh, it's so cool" or "I like it!" Your task is to create a layout that clearly addresses client/user priorities and utilizes design principles and elements to communicate as directly as possible to the target audience. Remember the importance of purpose. For example, there are many portfolio sites on the Web where designers display work to attract future clients. How would you describe the purpose and audience of a portfolio site? You should say the purpose of a portfolio site is to communicate the range of the designer's work, to present examples from existing clients and products, and to serve as a marketing tool for future business.

However, if you explore Web design portfolios, you'll see something interesting. In a few cases, the current work of the designer is the focal point; in more cases, the designer has developed a bold, high-tech portfolio incorporating, graphics, animation, and sound. Your first thought is probably "Oh, it's so cool, I like it!" Your second thought is probably to go through the client/product examples that the portfolio highlights. After a few minutes, you realize the sounds of the site are a little irritating and the animation seems to go on for minutes. Furthermore, many showcase sites are often too small (some with windows that open to 3×3 inches, or 8×8 centimeters) to see any detail. After a few more clicks, you begin to think the work of the designer is somehow drowning in the portfolio shell. Finally, you leave without a real understanding of the designer's capability. Is this a problem? Absolutely—the purpose of the layout has failed.

Thus, start simply. Write down your purpose, your audience, and their priorities on a piece of paper. Keep it next to your computer. Look at it as you create. There's always someone on the team or possibly a stakeholder who wants to tell you what's right or wrong about your layout. If you stick with your purpose/audience/priority plan, you may need to make minor adjustments, but you won't be completely off target. As your layout evolves, you want your clients to say "That's what I wanted to say," and you want users to respond with "That's what I wanted to find."

Layout evolves. Take your time and have fun with it. Don't be intimidated by someone with three art degrees who has painted for 20 years, worked in graphic design for 30 years, and name-drops famous artists.

Sketching a Prototype

Starting with sketch prototypes allows you to try several different approaches in a small amount of time. Sketch prototypes are for your use; they don't need to be beautiful illustrations. Your focus is on the priorities and their arrangement.

For example, the Figure 5-17 sketch considers horizontal lines and rectangles as a possible layout. Here, graphics or content are in one main focal point and are supported by buttons underneath. A quick sketch with buttons on the top may follow. Your thought with this sketch is to determine how the shape, placement, rhythm, and space address the client/user priorities.

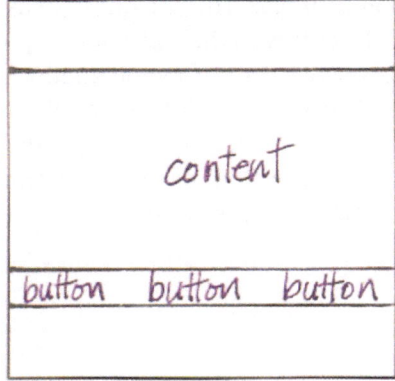

FIGURE 5-17 *Initial sketch layout, rectangles*

One consideration for Figure 5-17 is the number of buttons needed. This decision depends on the ways users want to access the site, not on how many buttons you think the design supports. Reference your notes on what users want to access and how. See if their needs fall into categories. If so, you may want three main buttons and can use other buttons on a linked page, or you may decide to incorporate a drop-down or rollover menu on the main page. If you need eight buttons, this layout may not work as shown. The large, bold graphic area, however, could support subnavigation. The questions to ask relate to design concepts and elements and to how the overall layout communicates your intent.

In Figure 5-18, you determine to break out of rectangle mode and yet need a lot of content area. The diagonal cutout and the diagonal line portray a different mood than a four-sided rectangle. You could build navigational elements in the space around and to the left of the diagonal line. On closer inspection, however, what happens with the left side of the content? Does each page somehow lean in on the left, and is that readable?

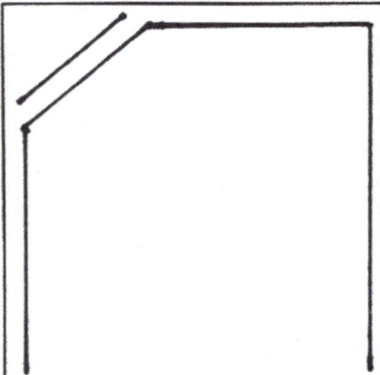

FIGURE 5-18 *Initial sketch layout, adding diagonals*

The large X in Figure 5-19 represents a logo or an image. This is a quasi-splash page. The lines represent the company's name. The dots with the small lines represent links to subpages. The trick to this layout is a great image or good quality logo and the time to fool around with spacing and positioning of the image, the text, and the links. The strength of this layout is the surrounding space; it quietly pulls the focus to the center and then right down to the links. Don't fill the background with tiled images or color. The background softly supports the image and text.

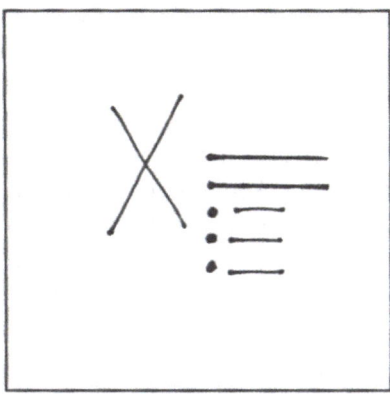

FIGURE 5-19 *Initial sketch layout, quasi-splash page*

Your first thought about the layouts in Figure 5-20 may be "Are you kidding?" Take a second look. Think images, color, positioning, and type. These elements relax the eye and yet don't put you to sleep. How could you evolve these simple presentations to a potential splash page? When does a client need a splash page vs. going directly to the text?

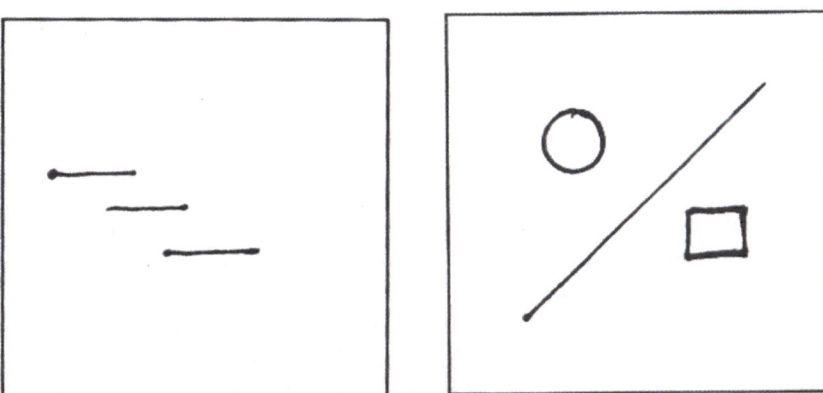

FIGURE 5-20 *Initial sketch layout (left) and splash page (right)*

Splash pages work when you want to make an initial impression on new customers and clients. Search engines pick up index pages. A few simple words, a good title, and appropriate meta-tags may help the client achieve a goal. On the other hand, splash pages are redundant and tedious for repeat customers who want to get to business. The decision, once again, goes back to the purpose and audience of the site.

The Figure 5-21 sketches reflect subtle variations of the rectangle theme. Here, you're working to avoid creeping back to the top and left bar layout and navigation. You can complete several variations of these sketches quickly to help you visualize content, layout, and how you want the site to "work." Sketches can be simple and rushed, such as Figure 5-21, and still focus your vision of how lay-out and content will work together. The functionality of the navigation should make accessing and retrieving priority information easy.

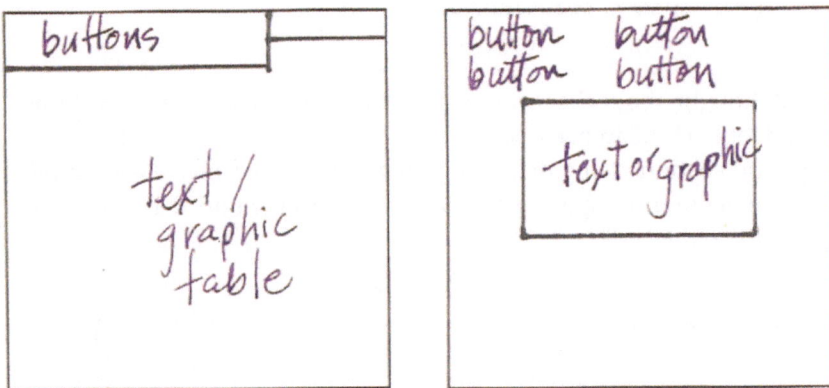

FIGURE 5-21 *Initial sketch layout, no splash page*

Most sites have only a few styles of pages. Typically, they include a possible splash page, a subpage for major content, and subpages for specific actions such as purchasing, forums, forms, and search retrieval. Subpages thematically follow the entry point of the site, whether that's a splash page or a content page. As you sketch entry-point pages, make sure to play around with potential subpages.

Figure 5-22 offers a small amount of navigation and significant space for an image or artwork on the left. On the right, Figure 5-22 offers significant space for content. The left sketch can also double as one-column content, with the addition of a table. The right sketch can act as the entry point and as subpages for an information site.

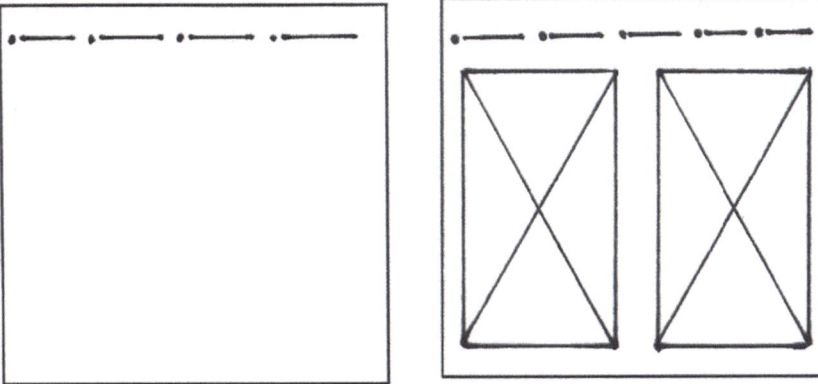

FIGURE 5-22 *Initial sketch layout (left) and content (right)*

Once a sketch layout seems that it'll fit a client's needs, you can quickly draw up and code additional subpages when needed. The sketch on the left of Figure 5-23 shows a potential data page, and the sketch on the right shows a potential search return or forum layout.

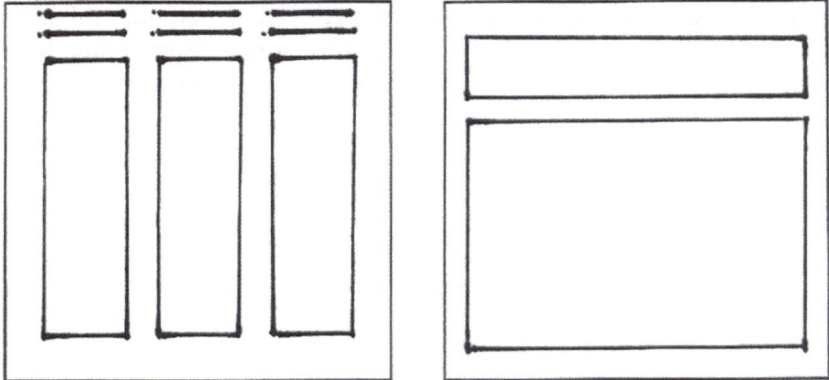

FIGURE 5-23 *Initial sketch layout (left) and additional content (right)*

Concepts for layouts that address the language of clients and users are simple to create. Figure 5-24 can begin to take shape as a layout with the inclusion of buttons and may result in an interesting approach to communicating with users.

Don't look to the Web for your layout ideas. Look to the language, ideas, and purpose you understand and then play with concepts and elements that interest clients and users into interacting with the site.

FIGURE 5-24 *Initial sketch layout (left) and unusual layout shapes (right)*

Sometimes initial sketches can resemble something you think the site could metaphorically portray, as in Figure 5-25 where a television metaphor might parody the media, Hollywood, or people who sit for hours in front of their television sets.

FIGURE 5-25 *Initial sketch layout for portraying a television metaphor*

Finally, sketch prototypes are also a good idea because of the following reasons:

No limitations: You avoid subconsciously designing to the level of your coding abilities, rather than for the user's expectations. For example, you want to position images and text at different locations. This is easy to sketch, but it's not so easy to code with Cascading Style Sheet (CSS) space and positioning properties in combination with previous platform and browser issues. A sketch prototype is a statement of the design concept requiring that you find the necessary coding solutions; in other words, it prevents the layout from being "dumbed down" to existing coding skills.

Flexibility: On a group project, other members are comfortable drawing on your sketch or suggesting variations on a separate piece of paper. Sometimes when you're already at the digital prototype stage and your layout is off a bit, team members don't speak out about moving items slightly because of the time involved. On the reverse, team members may think their idea is better and once drawn on paper, this turns out not to be the case.

Immediacy: There's often one person affiliated with a project who loves to talk, professes to know all, and deluges the designer and other project members with ideas. Give them a pen, ruler, and paper. Maybe they can deliver, maybe not.

Time: Significant changes at the sketch prototype stage take only a few minutes. This is better than coding a page to find out that you have an old logo, that your contact person didn't understand the target audience, or that you need to satisfy two marketing stakeholders you didn't expect to be a part of the approval process.

Brainstorming: Even if no one ever sees your sketch prototype, your understanding of the client and level of intimacy with the project's content improves during this thinking, playing, planning, and creating process.

Creating the Navigation

Designing and adjusting navigation takes place at several points in the design process. As you talk initially with clients and users, look for keywords and patterns that help determine buttons and categories of buttons. As an example, on an art site, users may want to access products by the artist, product type (painting, sculpture, and photography), price, or size. Have clients and users discuss what they would like to find, how they think about accessing information, and the prioritized order of their searches.

Your focus should be designing accessibility to what users want in a way that's clean and simple. Poorly designed buttons are irritating. If you click an

Artist button and then need to hold down the mouse and move to an artist by name and the menu is jumpy, it's easy to miss the correct entry. Sometimes the menu pops in and out if you move one pixel too far to the right or left. The user shouldn't have to stop, focus, and point precisely to access information. Make sure to test your button access with a couple of people new to the Web. They should be able to select an item while talking to you at the same time.

The order of navigational elements directly links to the purpose of the site. For example, there's a site for finding telephone numbers of people who live overseas. Users who access this site want to do one thing: find a number that goes with a name. Instead, users must wade through a couple of levels of information about the Telekom to find the phone directory and through another level or two to the information. The Telekom probably thinks this forces users to read their history. Untrue—the way to encourage users to read the company history is to make the site so usable that users become regulars, get curious, and decide to learn more about who created a great site and service.

Don't expect someone to tell you how many buttons to use or how to set up sublinks. You want to be in a position to make these decisions based on your understanding of the design problem. Clients and users want to access information. Your job is to design the navigation that makes that access easier. (Chapter 7 covers how to fine-tune navigation and content.)

Creating a Digital Prototype

Designers typically create digital prototypes in Adobe Photoshop or a similar application. On projects involving detailed, complex graphics with an abundance of curved lines or subtle shifts in color, Adobe Illustrator or Macromedia Fireworks communicate better. Also, Extensible HTML (XHTML), Extensible Markup Language (XML), Scalable Vector Graphics (SVG), and CSS work well for this purpose.

Digital prototypes don't actually "work." You may activate one or two links to demonstrate what a subpage looks like, but the purpose of a digital prototype is to realize the sketch prototype and to allow an agreement to be reached on layout, including fine-tuning the design elements. Working from a sketch allows you to work in more of a functional mode than in a "code it, move it, code it, delete it" mode. Although design is primary, browser and platform issues should be in the back of your mind as you create your digital prototype.

Clients often expect several choices for a digital prototype. These choices typically represent minor variations of a central concept. In some cases, color or font may be the only differences. In other cases, one prototype may be a little more conservative than another. Your focus is to give a complete idea of how the layout appears and to work with the stakeholders to make as many adjustments as possible before the build begins.

Prototype approval is key to the process. Any stakeholders missing in the prototype approval process can later stop and redirect the process. Post the prototypes on the Internet. Make sure all stakeholders have the Uniform Resource Locator (URL). This way, they can see your presentation and have the opportunity to look at each option once or twice on a monitor. After prototype approval, changes become time consuming, frustrating, and expensive.

Figure 5-26 shows digital prototypes of three splash pages and their accompanying subpages. Chapter 11 defines and explores the client for these examples; the purpose here is to demonstrate a digital prototype example.

A_simp_splash1.jpg   B_simp_splash2.jpg   C_simp_splash3.jpg

D_simp_layout1.jpg   E_simp_layout2.jpg   F_simp_layout3.jpg

FIGURE 5-26 *Digital prototype examples*

Color, typography, and content are also important aspects of layout. Initial sketch prototypes are often in black and white with swatches of possible color combinations penciled into the prototype. You adjust the color and type as a final layout evolves. A modern, minimalist layout calls for a different type and color combination than does a whimsical, avant-garde, or conservative layout. Each aspect of the layout expects consideration; your thought process should move from one possibility to another and back again, rather than through a linear approach to design. Keeping language and client/user expectations at the forefront results in a thematically cohesive site design that maintains its design integrity as it evolves to a final product.

Design Element Axioms

In this chapter, you learned about design elements. Specifically, texture adds the sense of touch to a design. Shapes can convey thickness and weight, smoothness or roughness, and depth, among other things. You may hear designers talking about a work looking "flat." Carelessly placed elements in a layout create a one-dimensional look that has no depth. The thoughtfully planned use of texture and space can transform a flat layout into one with a much higher level of interactivity and interest.

Space is critical to the design process. If your design isn't working, select all nonessential items and begin, one by one, to delete them. When you have the minimum amount of design elements that you need to communicate the client's story, try moving elements around to enhance the use of space. More space opens the design to more interesting possibilities. In other words, space isn't a negative element; your layout has shapes and space, each carrying important weight and playing equal roles in the design process.

Users understand items in relationship to the size of other items. A word of warning: Too big is too much. Remember, the user isn't much farther from a screen than from a book. Use size to emphasize, not to communicate.

Value guides the eye to focal areas of interest by combining black, white, and shades of gray with shape, size, space, and placement. If your design seems almost perfect, but not quite there, think of value and experiment with subtly different contrasts in line, color, and density.

Layout is key to good user interest. Don't look to the Web for layout. Listen to the client and user. Think about the product. Users expect the same service from a site that they do from a physical location. Have you set up products and information so they're easy to find? Does the overall design of the site communicate the intent of the client? Does it invite the user to come in and look around? Start simple; some layouts are incredible, most aren't. Place items carefully, avoid clichés, and remember that layout evolves. A few months after the site is finished, revisit the layout. A little bit of time away allows you to continue to ask if the layout supports the relationship, the story, and the language of the site. Regarding navigation, keep it simple. Keep it clean. Prioritize navigational elements in the order that the user wants to access the information.

Chapter 6 incorporates design elements and layout principles into a commercial project.

Project 2:
Building an Online Resource Center

Science does not know its debt to imagination.
—Ralph Waldo Emerson, writer (1803–1882)

The Converging Technologies Center is an online resource project designed for educators, students, and community members interested in learning about the next wave of technology (nanotechnology, biotechnology, bioinformatics, and micromachining) and gaining a deeper relationship with Information Technology (IT) networks. Once again, familiarize yourself with the project using this chapter's mini-requirements document, which is based on the Volere Requirements Specification Template.

Creating a Mini-Requirements Specification for the Online Resource Center

The following sections define the requirements specification for the online resource center.

The Purpose of the Product

The purpose of the product is as follows:

The user problem or background to the project effort: The technologies involved in the next wave of innovation are significantly more complex than those involved in the first wave of the Internet. Staffing this workforce will pose significant problems. American colleges and universities will be over-crowded from "Tidal Wave 3," the high number of college entrants expected in the next decade because of the age bracket population swell. The purpose of the product is to offer ideas, information, and resources to educators, students, and organizations related to the transdisciplinary topics connected to nanotechnology, biotechnology, bioinformatics, micromachining, and complex IT networks.

The goal of the project: The goal of the product is to present materials from educators, industries, and associations regarding the technologies and products of the next wave of innovation. The product also provides a forum for the discussion of related ideas. Another goal is to encourage the exchange of ideas and resources between individuals and organizations interested in participating in the planning and growth of converging technologies.

Clients, Customers, and Other Stakeholders

The clients, customers, and other stakeholders are as follows:

The client (the people paying for the development and the owners of the delivered system): The client is West Valley College, a community college in California. West Valley College is located in Silicon Valley and educates students for workforce development and for transferring to universities in the United States and abroad.

The customer (the people who will buy the product from the client): The potential customer base comprises secondary and/or post-secondary educators, students, and nonprofit organizations interested in learning about the next wave of ideas and their potential curriculum.

Other stakeholders: Additional schools, colleges, universities, organizations, and companies are encouraged to participate. West Valley College will begin the project but it most likely will be a long-term joint effort. These other stakeholders' ideas will be added to the project over time but don't need to be considered in the original design process.

Users of the Product

The following sections detail the users of the product.

The Users of the Product

Potential users of the product are secondary and post-secondary faculty and students, nonprofit organizations, and for-profit companies, not defined by any specific demographics. The product must conform to the Federal Regulations Section 508 of the Rehabilitation Act of 1973 (accessibility), and the minimum technological experience of the user is "novice." The product will be customizable to allow for a range of users.

All users are assumed to have basic computer skills including the ability to point and select items in a graphical user interface. Users are expected to be able to use standard Internet browsers. The second version of the product will incorporate voice and Braille-based technologies.

The Priorities Assigned to Users

The key users are as follows:

- Teachers
- Other individuals including those affiliated with nonprofit organizations and companies
- Students

User Participation

Feedback from primary users (see the previous section) is necessary in assessing the viability of the product interface.

Mandated Constraints

The following sections describe the mandated constraints of the product.

Solution Constraints

The solution constraints are as follows:

- The product must be accessible via a 56kbps modem, a 15-inch monitor, Internet Explorer 5+/Netscape 4.76+ or Opera 5+/America Online 7+, and Windows 9.*x*, Windows NT, Windows 2000+, Windows ME, Windows XP, or Mac OS 8+.

- The final product must be available for free.

- Faculty and students must use the same conceptual interface.

- The underlying code will be Extensible Markup Language (XML) based or XML compatible.

Implementation Environment of the Current System

The product will be "upload ready" to a server running an Apache or Windows 2000+ server.

Partner Applications

The partner applications are a Scalable Vector Graphics (SVG) viewer and Adobe Acrobat Reader 4+ if any materials are uploaded as Portable Document Format (PDF) file links.

Commercial Off-the-Shelf Packages

The online resource center must support the browser software as described in the "Solution Constraints" section. Users will also need access to the Internet.

Anticipated Workplace Environment

A typical workplace will be in a home, educational institution, or job environment; this includes any suitable indoor environment for a personal computer (including such requirements as adequate power supply, telephone or other Internet access line, raised work surface, and seating). Content will be delivered from the Internet, from a hard drive, or from a disk/CD-ROM/DVD.

Development Period

The beta is due in July 2003. Version 1 is due in January 2004. Version 2 is due in July 2004.

Naming Conventions and Definitions

The product will use the following naming conventions and definitions:

- **Designer**: This person constructs the product interface.

- **Developer**: This person generates the source code to implement the product.

- **Technical writer**: This person generates the original copy for the documentation and technical support.

- **Interface**: This is the product/user online interface.

- **Prerelease product**: This is any form of the product that hasn't been beta tested.

- **Product**: This is the complete, user-ready, beta-tested product.

Relevant Facts and Assumptions

The process includes the facts and assumptions in the following sections.

External Factors

If the product grows, additional forum/discussion threads will need to be added. Possible copyright issues need to be considered when linking to resource materials. Gaining author permissions may be time consuming. Categories of the resource center's content may overlap, and there may need to be a clear definition of what keywords are available in the search engine. Students and some educators may not understand or be frustrated by downloading the SVG viewer.

Assumptions

The team is making the following assumptions:

- Time will be available to meet production deadlines and maintain the site.

- Time will be available for locating and assessing resource materials.

- Maintaining current content will be critical to user interest levels of the project.

- Participating teachers, educational institutions, and nonprofit organizations will participate on a long-term basis.

- The skill levels of users will vary widely.

Considering Design Elements

In conversations with the site's clients and with users, the following ideas arose:

- The site design shouldn't focus on one aspect of converging technologies and should be open to ideas from the arts as well as from the sciences and mathematics.

- The site should support ideas from individuals of different nations, and, as such, the design shouldn't be too "American."

- The strength of the site is in the content material. The interface should be simple and support the content.

Language used to describe the site included a few obvious and a few subtle keywords:

- Technical (but approachable)

- Engaging

- Interdisciplinary

- Arts and sciences

- Intriguing

- Evolving

Language used to describe what users are interested in learning and experiencing include the following:

- Innovation

- Creativity

- Future

- Ideas

- Patents

- Products

- Cooperation

- Research

In addition, the client wanted the design to portray education as a partner with industry in the next wave of innovation. As such, the product shouldn't resemble a typical college Web site.

Sketching Prototypes

This site could easily fall into being a cliché. To avoid this, it was determined early that no typical symbols associated with physics, mathematics, information technology, chemistry, biology, art, philosophy, or anthropology would be used.

Stepping away from clip art and avoiding designs with ones and zeros representing bytes led the designers back to simple line and space. We decided to conceptualize the site in black and white and then explore color after settling on the design. The design concept was to incorporate lines in one thickness and in various lengths to resemble converging or unique shapes, as shown in Figure 6-1.

FIGURE 6-1 *Line concept*

From these sketches, it became immediately clear that the design demanded a thicker line and that an infinite number of combinations of lines and space would be possible. To speed up the process, we used a ruler and matte knife to cut white squares from printer paper that were 5×5 inches (18×18 centimeters) and to cut black strips from construction paper that were .5 inches (1.2 centimeters) wide and the length of the construction paper, in this case, 11.5 inches. Using the paper squares and strips and a glue stick with removable adhesive, we created a much faster representation of the sketches in Figure 6-1. Typically, hand-drawn sketches are easier than working with cut paper. In this case, however, we found ourselves trying to make the squares square and clean with a black felt pen and only creating a smeared, inky mess.

In the end, we created the concepts shown in Figure 6-2 for the splash page (the buttons and splash text were keyed, printed, cut, and glued down after moving them around a few times).

The idea is to use both lines and space. The top-right quarter of the design shows dense lines. The top-left quarter uses approximately half the number of lines as the quarter to its right. The bottom-left quarter uses approximately half the number of lines as the top left, and space becomes the predominant element. The bottom-right quarter uses still more space and even fewer lines.

Converging
Technologies Center

FIGURE 6-2 *Line concept splash page*

The rhythm of line and space adds the element of motion. When the splash page opens, the title appears. Eyes typically go to the text, then up and around to return to the text. The concept implies change and evokes interest. We decided to go with a splash page because of the number of newbies the client wants to draw in and to identify the site as a "center" rather than an educational institution.

We made support pages with different designs (again with the black-and-white paper) to incorporate the words *interdisciplinary* and *technical*. The support shapes are designed to be created in SVG. They can reside on the left side of the page and curve as a group to support content. Figure 6-3 shows the concept support page.

FIGURE 6-3 *Line concept for a support page*

Unfortunately, SVG creates some problems when introducing content. SVG text isn't as easy to read as is Extensible HTML (XHTML), and it isn't easy for client users to maintain and update unless they know how to code SVG. Eventually, you can use Cascading Style Sheets (CSS) or Extensible Stylesheet Language: Formatting Objects (XSL-FO) properties to set up the correct space and positioning. This client, however, expects some educators to use fifth-generation browsers, and, as such, the SVG needs to be designed as a graphic brought into XHTML tables.

A couple of content page options can enhance the communication of change and convergence; Figure 6-4 utilizes a metaphor for intelligence. The buttons, simple and easily accessed, can vary from page to page, driven by the numbers and categories of research. This concept works well for navigating resources in art, science, or mathematics. In art, the squares resemble the familiarity of tiles or of modern art. In math and science, they resemble the building blocks of logic or a chessboard. To you, they may not represent either of these examples. They're a reminder of building and changing, and they're easy to read and use.

FIGURE 6-4 *Line concept for a content page*

Figure 6-5 is consistent with the site's need for simple, unobtrusive navigation on the pages with higher levels of content. The site can retain its simplicity by utilizing the Figure 6-4 and 6-5 concepts.

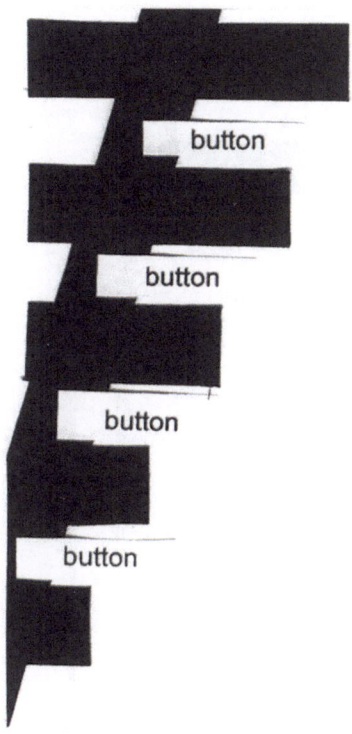

FIGURE 6-5 *Line concept for pages with high content*

Transitioning from Concept to Layout

With the concept approved, the layout comes next. Sketches are typically created for a layout, once again allowing creativity rather than coding skill to determine design. In this case, we continued to play with the construction paper. Additionally, we asked Steve Contreras (the Web mechanic from Chapter 1) to come up with a few layout ideas based on the site concepts.

Steve came up with the following four digital prototypes (Figures 6-6 through 6-9) as prototypes for a splash page that can be simplified for thematically similar content pages. Remember, this first phase isn't the final Web screen. Your purpose is to transition from concept to layout. It's important to take your time to move shapes around and consider different combinations. Creating several prototype examples will place you in a better position to choose what works and what doesn't. Which of the following layouts meets your understanding of the client and user needs and expectations?

FIGURE 6-6 *Digital concept shapes*

FIGURE 6-7 *Digital concept shapes with a different balance*

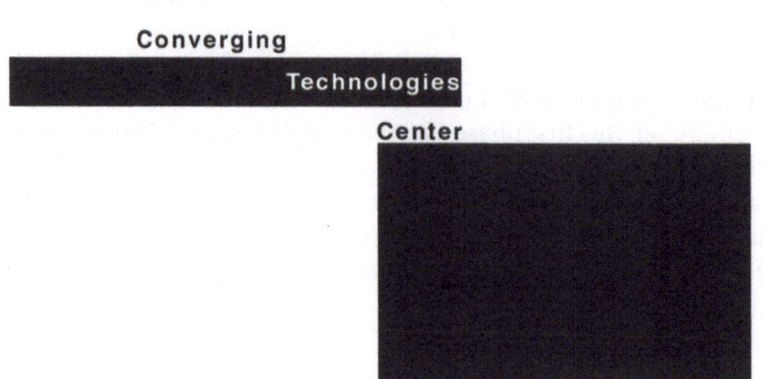

FIGURE 6-8 *Digital concept with fewer shapes, type, and space as elements*

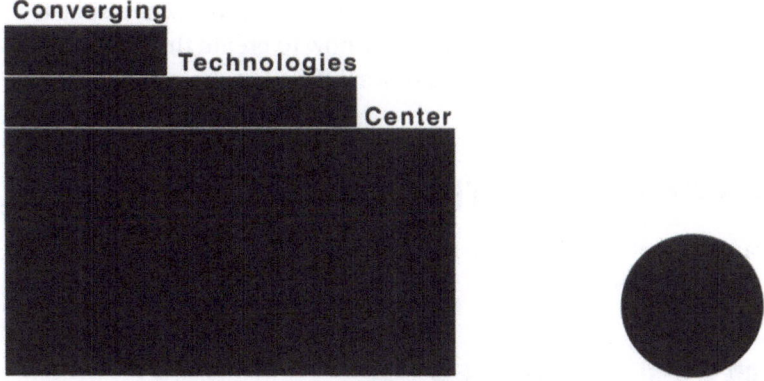

FIGURE 6-9 *Digital concept with simple shapes and space*

Determining which layout meets the needs of the user is key. We liked the design of Figure 6-10 and yet weren't ready to let go of the original paper concept shown in Figure 6-2.

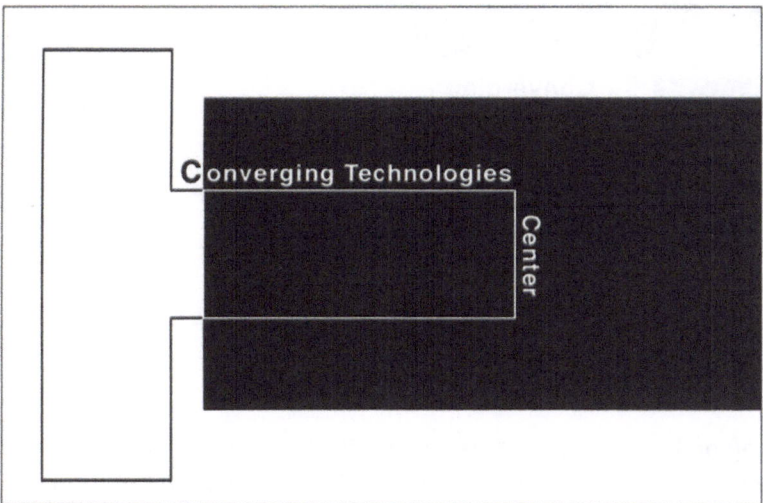

FIGURE 6-10 *Digital concept with lines, shapes, type, and space*

For this chapter, we created phases of the original concept of line and motion. The final Web layout may vary between the two or combine aspects of each.

The important aspect of the digital prototype is to narrow down the designs to one or two to take to the next level. If one design is clearly the winner, you can begin to include content and functionality. If two designs may merge to become the final layout, you need to make a mock-up of both and plan to create three or four pages with a minimal amount of content.

The first step, in the case of this Web site, is to see if SVG works as a splash page graphic. The following section demonstrates how to create the lined concept drawing (the left one in Figure 6-1), the more difficult of the two to create.

Creating a Working Prototype

The first SVG graphic, shown in Figure 6-11, is based on the initial concept made from the black strips of paper.

Converging
Technologies Center

FIGURE 6-11 *First splash SVG page*

The first draft of the graphic needs more density. Figure 6-12 shows how a quick sketch communicates changes to the SVG. It's important to fine-tune all graphics, use pencils and pens, scan drawings, and photocopy examples; in other words, there's no best practice for editing shapes. Use whatever tools seem appropriate for the type of design you want to create. This is an in-house document, so communicate your intent; don't worry about making it beautiful.

FIGURE 6-12 *Edited SVG, on paper*

The graphic is crowded at the top and closer to the left than the right. This approach enhances the feel of density at the top of the graphic. Positioning the graphic in the center makes it look as though it's just floating. More space on the bottom right and below the graphic supports the rhythm of dense elements on the top and the space on the bottom. The graphic is closer to the left than the right side of the screen because it opens to text on the right and allows the eyes to easily travel in the lower-right quadrant, as shown in the layout positioning of Figure 6-13.

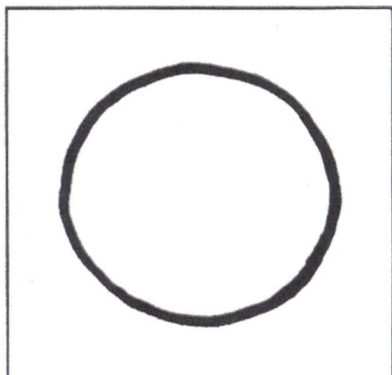 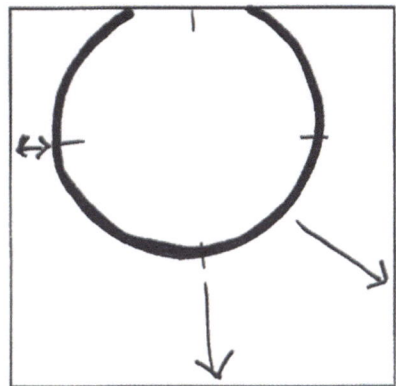

FIGURE 6-13 *Open placement (left) and a center placement that seems open but pulls focus inward (right)*

As a result, the placement of Figure 6-13 evolves to Figure 6-14.

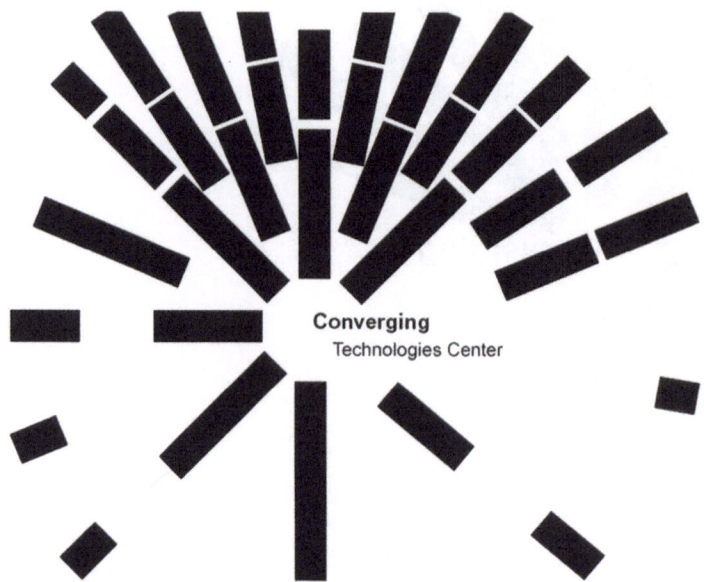

Converging
Technologies Center

FIGURE 6-14 *Finding balance*

The top-right quarter, however, isn't as dense as the sketch conveyed. At this point, it's easy to say "good enough." With design, as with code, the last 2 percent matters. Try to take a design as far as you can, considering time and technology issues. The next pass, Figure 6-15, is close but needs one more line section on the right. In addition, the right edge of the graphic is a little out of shape; instead, the lines should follow an invisible, straight, vertical line.

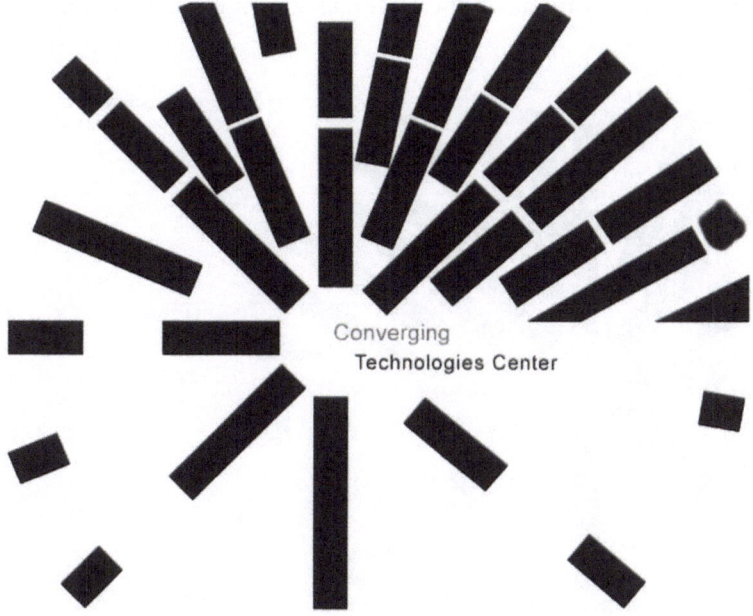

FIGURE 6-15 *Almost . . .*

Finally, Figure 6-16 works for the final prototype and the initial build.

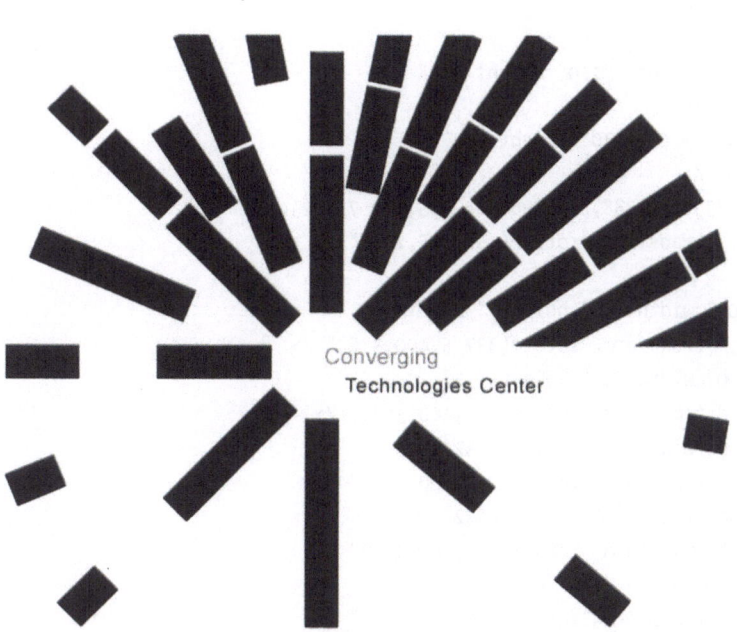

FIGURE 6-16 *Selected graphic for the final prototype*

The prototype graphic positions on the screen as shown in Figure 6-17.

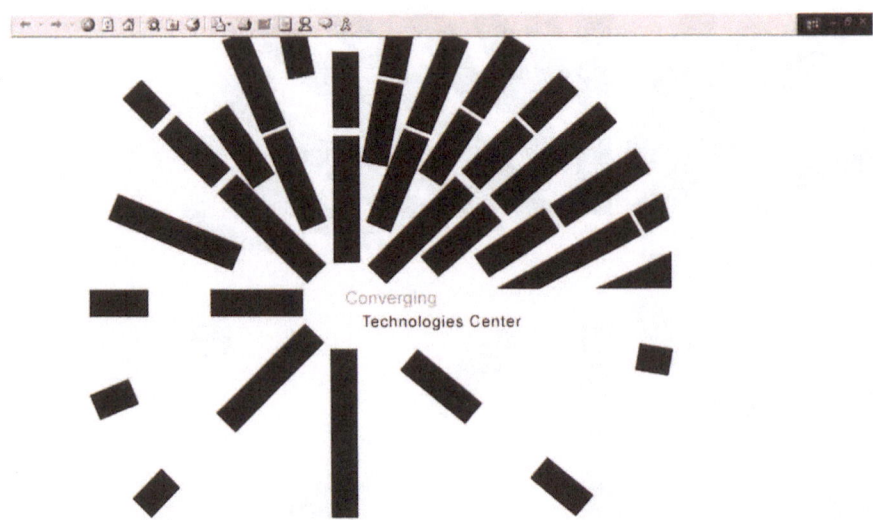

FIGURE 6-17 *Final prototype splash window*

Listing 6-1 generates the Figure 6-17 shape.

LISTING 6-1 *Prototype Splash Graphic*

```
<svg>
<rect x="240" y="300" width="110" height="32"
style="fill:black;" />
<rect x="95" y="300" width="70" height="32"
style="fill:black;" />
<polyline points="755,234 788,234 796,204 755,204 755,234"
style="fill:black;" transform="rotate(-30,755,235)" />

<rect x="77" y="300" width="50" height="32"
style="fill:black;" transform="rotate(337.5,400,318)" />
<rect x="57" y="300" width="50" height="32"
style="fill:black;" transform="rotate(315,400,318)" />
<rect x="30" y="300" width="70" height="32"
style="fill:black;" transform="rotate(220,400,318)" />
<rect x="10" y="300" width="40" height="32"
style="fill:black;" transform="rotate(190,400,318)" />
<rect x="200" y="300" width="148" height="32"
style="fill:black;" transform="rotate(135,400,318)" />
<rect x="147" y="300" width="200" height="32"
style="fill:black;" transform="rotate(270,400,318)" />
```

```
<rect x="200" y="300" width="150" height="32"
style="fill:black;" transform="rotate(90,400,318)" />
<rect x="200" y="300" width="150" height="32"
style="fill:black;" transform="rotate(45,400,318)" />
<rect x="200" y="300" width="100" height="32"
style="fill:black;" transform="rotate(220,400,318)" />
<rect x="200" y="300" width="150" height="32"
style="fill:black;" transform="rotate(315,400,318)" />
<rect x="180" y="300" width="120" height="32"
style="fill:black;" transform="rotate(112.5,400,318)" />

<rect x="180" y="300" width="120" height="32"
style="fill:black;" transform="rotate(67.5,400,318)" />
<rect x="140" y="250" width="100" height="32"
style="fill:black;" transform="rotate(146.5,400,318)" />
<rect x="55" y="300" width="120" height="32"
style="fill:black;" transform="rotate(112.5,400,318)" />
<rect x="100" y="300" width="160" height="32"
style="fill:black;" transform="rotate(22.5,400,318)" />
<rect x="55" y="300" width="120" height="32"
style="fill:black;" transform="rotate(67.5,400,318)" />
<rect x="12" y="250" width="120" height="32"
style="fill:black;" transform="rotate(146.5,400,318)" />
<rect x="130" y="300" width="100" height="32"
style="fill:black;" transform="rotate(101.5,400,318)" />
<rect x="130" y="298" width="90" height="32"
style="fill:black;" transform="rotate(123,400,318)" />
<rect x="195" y="270" width="100" height="32"
style="fill:black;" transform="rotate(139,400,318)" />
<rect x="125" y="300" width="100" height="32"
style="fill:black;" transform="rotate(56,400,318)" />
<rect x="25" y="300" width="100" height="32"
style="fill:black;" transform="rotate(79,400,318)" />
<rect x="25" y="300" width="100" height="32"
style="fill:black;" transform="rotate(101.5,400,318)" />
<rect x="25" y="298" width="100" height="32"
style="fill:black;" transform="rotate(123,400,318)" />
<rect x="15" y="270" width="170" height="32"
style="fill:black;" transform="rotate(139,400,318)" />
<rect x="100" y="300" width="90" height="32"
style="fill:black;" transform="rotate(90,400,318)" />
<rect x="100" y="300" width="90" height="32"
style="fill:black;" transform="rotate(45,400,318)" />
```

```
<rect x="40" y="300" width="50" height="32"
style="fill:black;" transform="rotate(45,400,318)" />
<rect x="100" y="300" width="90" height="32"
style="fill:black;" transform="rotate(135,400,318)" />
<rect x="25" y="300" width="70" height="32"
style="fill:black;" transform="rotate(135,400,318)" />
<polyline points="580,300 630,300 750,236 735, 210 580,300"
style="fill:black;" />
<polyline points="580,300 630,300 750,236 735, 210 580,300"
style="fill:black;" />
<polyline points="695,300 785,300 785,256  695,300"
style="fill:black;" />
<text x="400" y="318" font-size="16pt" font-weight="normal"
style="fill:#669999;">
<animate id="c" attributeName="font-size" begin="0s;4s"
dur="2s" from="16pt" to ="20pt" />
<animate  attributeName="font-size" begin="c.end" dur="2s"
from="20pt" to ="16pt" /> Converging</text>
<a xlink:href="ct2a.html"><text x="420" y="345"
style="font-size:14pt; fill:black;letter-spacing:1">
<animateColor begin="mouseover" dur="0.1s"
attributeName="fill" from="black" to="orange" fill="freeze" />
<animateColor begin="mouseout" dur="0.1s"
attributeName="fill" from="orange" to="black" fill="freeze" />
Technologies Center</text></a>
</svg>
```

The splash page is entirely SVG. The linked page uses XHTML tables, and the graphic is an SVG image within one table cell. The code uses tables for ease of maintenance. Eventually, CSS or XSL:fo positioning properties can replace the tables. The World Wide Web Consortium (W3C) doesn't recommend tables for positioning; this is no problem when positioning properties are strongly supported. However, this client needs backward compatibility to fifth-generation browsers, so positioning is unreliable at best.

Figure 6-18 shows the next page of the site. The lines form a ladder; they interconnect with categories of content and allow room for introductory content.

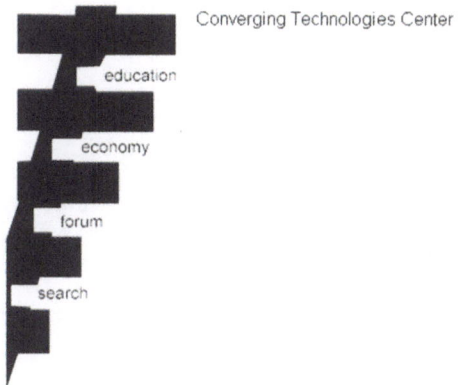

Converging Technologies Center

education

economy

forum

search

FIGURE 6-18 *The second page of the final prototype*

The XHTML includes three columns. The leftmost columns holds the SVG, the small, narrow column spaces the graphic from the content table, and the rightmost column holds the text *Converging Technologies Center* and can nest additional content tables.

Listing 6-2 generates the Figure 6-18 XHTML.

LISTING 6-2 *First Navigation XHTML*

```
<html>
<table border="0" style="font-family:arial, helvetica, sans-serif;">
<tr><td><embed src="ctc2.svg" width="150" height="512"
type="image/svg+xml" />
<td width="10" />
<td width="600"><p style="position: absolute;
top:20px;">Converging Technologies Center</p></td>
</tr>
</table>
</html>
```

We didn't use a Document Type Definition (DTD) here because of updates; the code meets the well-formed and validation standards. You'll need to add a DTD if you want to validate this document. We try to set all code up using a strict DTD. In some cases, backward compatibility forces us to go to a transitional DTD. Generally, we start with strict, do as much as we can, and go to transitional for a few deprecated tags. The stricter your code is, the more recoding you avoid and the fewer browser issues you produce. Validation seems to change regularly, so try to keep your code as clean and simple as possible.

Listing 6-3 generates the SVG for Figure 6-18.

LISTING 6-3 *First Navigation Graphic*

```xml
<?xml version='1.0'?>
<svg width="150" height="512">
<g transform="scale(0.5)">
<g id="tx" style="fill:black; font-size:30;">
<a xlink:href="education.html"><text x="173" y="133">
<animateColor begin="mouseover" dur="0.1s"
attributeName="fill" from="black" to="orange" fill="freeze" />
<animateColor begin="mouseout" dur="0.1s"
attributeName="fill" from="orange" to="black" fill="freeze" />
education</text></a>
<a xlink:href="economy.html"><text x="132" y="261">
<animateColor begin="mouseover" dur="0.1s"
attributeName="fill" from="black" to="orange" fill="freeze" />
<animateColor begin="mouseout" dur="0.1s"
attributeName="fill" from="orange" to="black" fill="freeze" />
economy</text></a>
<a xlink:href="forumD.asp"><text x="95" y="395">
<animateColor begin="mouseover" dur="0.1s"
attributeName="fill" from="black" to="orange" fill="freeze" />
<animateColor begin="mouseout" dur="0.1s"
attributeName="fill" from="orange" to="black" fill="freeze" />
forum</text></a>
<a xlink:href="searchDB.html"><text x="55" y="523">
<animateColor begin="mouseover" dur="0.1s"
attributeName="fill" from="black" to="orange" fill="freeze" />
<animateColor begin="mouseout" dur="0.1s"
attributeName="fill" from="orange" to="black" fill="freeze" />
search</text></a>
</g>
<polyline points="123,0 121,17 19,15 19,85 99,85 81,149 19,149
19,223 59,223 43,277 19,279 19,349 23,349 0,419 0,687 21,621
77,621 77,543 43,543 43,539 9,537 9,499 55,499 59,485 133,485
133,413 81,413 81,405 49,405 49,361 97,361 97,353 199,353
199,279 119,279 119,276 81,276 81,237 133,237 135,225 261,225
261,153 159,153 155,143 125,143 125,109 165,107 175,87 319,87
319,15 193,15 195,0 123,0" style="fill:black;" />
</g>
</svg>
```

The second page links to multiple content pages within a category. Figure 6-19 shows the word button for each icon; the idea is to offer a template so that buttons can be organized differently within the different technology categories. It's important to keep the buttons simple and consistent; they don't change order from page to page, but they can change from category to category. Typically, buttons are made as images and changes involve deleting the GIF or JPG file, reworking the graphic in Adobe Photoshop as an original PSD file, and saving it again as a GIF or JPG. Problems can arise if you can't find the original graphic file. SVG allows you to change button text as simply as changing any text.

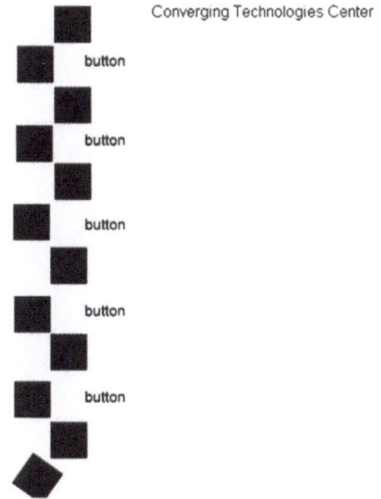

FIGURE 6-19 *Content page, final prototype*

Again, you can add content to the rightmost tables, including additional nested tables. Listing 6-4 generates the XHTML for Figure 6-19.

LISTING 6-4 *Second Navigation XHTML*

```
<html>
<table border="0" style="font-family:arial, helvetica, sans-serif;">
<tr><td><embed src="button.svg" width="130" height="512"
type="image/svg+xml" />
<td width="10" />
<td width="600"><p style="position: absolute;
top:20px;">Converging Technologies Center</p></td>
</tr>
</table>
</html>
```

Listing 6-5 generates the SVG for Figure 6-19.

LISTING 6-5 *Second Navigation Graphic*

```
<?xml version='1.0'?>
<svg width="260" height="512">
<g transform="scale(0.5)">
<defs>
<g id="sq">
<rect x="0" y="0" width="74" height="74"
style="fill:black; stroke:black; stroke-width:1;" />
</g>
</defs>
<defs>
<g id="tx">
<text x="0" y="0" style="fill:black; stroke:black;
font-size:30; stroke-width:1;">button</text>
</g>
</defs>
<use xlink:href="#sq" x="99" y="12" />
<use xlink:href="#sq" x="23" y="94" />
<use xlink:href="#sq" x="99" y="178" />
<use xlink:href="#sq" x="21" y="258" />
<use xlink:href="#sq" x="99" y="336" />
<use xlink:href="#sq" x="15" y="420" />
<use xlink:href="#sq" x="91" y="510" />
<use xlink:href="#sq" x="17" y="610" />
<use xlink:href="#sq" x="91" y="688" />
<use xlink:href="#sq" x="17" y="786" />
<use xlink:href="#sq" x="91" y="870" />
<use xlink:href="#tx" x="160" y="134" />
<use xlink:href="#tx" x="160" y="298" />
<use xlink:href="#tx" x="160" y="472" />
<use xlink:href="#tx" x="160" y="650" />
<use xlink:href="#tx" x="160" y="828" />
<rect x="55" y="934" width="74" height="74"
style="fill:black; stroke:black; stroke-width:1;"
transform ="rotate(35,55,934)" />
</g>
</svg>
```

A forum on the site acts as a simple conversation area. At some point, you can replace the forum with a multithreaded discussion board if participation warrants it. The forum consists of the page to post a topic and a returned page to display previous topics. This forum prototype uses Active Server Pages (ASP). You can adjust the server-side code for non-Windows servers with either JavaServer

Pages (JSP) or PHP. Server-side code typically depends on the client's server possibilities. Figure 6-20 shows the forum and how to post a topic.

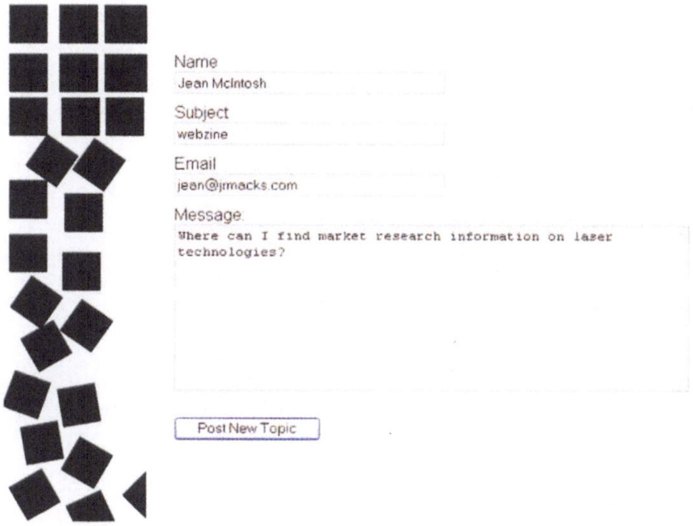

Name
Jean McIntosh

Subject
webzine

Email
jean@jrmacks.com

Message:
Where can I find market research information on laser technologies?

Post New Topic

FIGURE 6-20 *Forum page, final prototype*

The forum uses ASP, XML, and XSLT. The data are saved in the XML file and display using XSLT. ASP processes the data.

The starting page is generated by the ASP document, as shown in Listing 6-6.

LISTING 6-6 *Forum Input Using ASP*

```
<%@Language="JavaScript"%>
<?xml version="1.0" encoding="UTF-8"?>
<!DOCTYPE html
PUBLIC "-//W3C//DTD XHTML 1.0 Strict//EN"
"http://www.w3.org/TR/xhtml1/DTD/xhtml1-strict.dtd">
<html xmlns="http://www.w3.org/1999/xhtml" xml:lang="en"
lang="en">
<head>
<title>Converging Technologies Center Forum Display</title>
<link rel="stylesheet" type="text/css" href="ctc.css" />
</head>
<body>
<table border="0">
<tr>
<td><p class="svg1"><object  data="ctForum1.svg"
type="image/svg+xml" width="140" height="612">
```

```
<p>Sorry, your browser does not support SVG</p>
</object></p></td>
<td width="10" />
</td>
<%
var xmlDoc= Server.CreateObject("Microsoft.XMLDOM")
xmlDoc.async=false
xmlDoc.load(Server.MapPath("ctc.xml"))
var xslDoc=Server.CreateObject("Microsoft.XMLDOM")
xslDoc.async=false
xslDoc.load(Server.MapPath("ctc.xsl"))
Response.Write(xmlDoc.transformNode(xslDoc))
%>
</tr>
</table>
</body>
</html>
```

The data are saved in the XML document, as shown in Listing 6-7.

LISTING 6-7 *Forum Output*

```
<?xml version="1.0"?>
<messages>
<message>
<title>Laser Technology</title>
<email>werner@laserwave.com</email>
<date>date</date>
<author>Werner</author>
<text>I would like to connect a white paper
on our latest laser test results.</text>
</message>
<message><title>webzine</title>
<email>jean@jrmacks.com</email>
<date>Mon Jan 6 18:36:51 PST (date example)</date>
<author>Jean</author>
<text>I am writing a feature on marketing converging
technologies. Can you connect me to potential
interviews?</text>
</message>
</messages>
```

Listing 6-8 shows the XSLT document that generates HTML output.

LISTING 6-8 *Forum Transformation Using XSLT*

```
<?xml version="1.0"?>
<xsl:stylesheet
xmlns:xsl="http://www.w3.org/1999/XSL/Transform"
version="1.0">
<xsl:template match="/">
<html>
<head>
<title>Convergence Technlogies Community</title>
<link rel="stylesheet" type="text/css" href="ctc.css" />
</head>
<body>
<table class="text1" border="0" width="600">
<tr><td><p style="font-weight:bold;">Converging Technologies
Center</p><br />
<p><a href="forum.html">Add a Post</a></p></td></tr>
<xsl:for-each select="messages/message">
 <tr>
  <td><br /><br />
    <p>
   Title:<xsl:value-of select="title"/></p>
    <p>
   Date:<xsl:value-of select="date"/></p>
    <p>
   Email:<xsl:value-of select="email"/></p>
    <p>
   Author:<xsl:value-of select="author"/></p>
    <p>
    Message:<xsl:value-of select="text"/></p>
  <br />
    <p>_____</p>
  </td>
 </tr>

</xsl:for-each>
</table>
</body>
</html>
</xsl:template>
</xsl:stylesheet>
```

Listing 6-9 generates the SVG for Figure 6-20.

LISTING 6-9 *SVG Forum Input*

```
<?xml version='1.0'?>
<svg width="260" height="512">
<g transform="scale(0.5)" style="fill:black;
stroke:black; stroke-width:1;">
<defs>
<g id="sq">
<rect x="12" y="10" width="74" height="74" />
</g>
</defs>
<use xlink:href="#sq" x="0" y="0" />
<use xlink:href="#sq" x="98" y="0" />
<use xlink:href="#sq" x="0" y="96" />
<use xlink:href="#sq" x="98" y="96" />
<use xlink:href="#sq" x="186" y="96" />
<use xlink:href="#sq" x="260" y="96" />
<use xlink:href="#sq" x="186" y="0" />
<use xlink:href="#sq" x="260" y="0" />
<use xlink:href="#sq" x="334" y="0" />
<use xlink:href="#sq" x="408" y="0" />
<use xlink:href="#sq" x="0" y="182" />
<use xlink:href="#sq" x="102" y="182" />
<use xlink:href="#sq" x="188" y="182" />
<use xlink:href="#sq" x="0" y="344" />
<use xlink:href="#sq" x="108" y="370" />
<use xlink:href="#sq" x="0" y="450" />
<use xlink:href="#sq" x="104" y="486" />
<use xlink:href="#sq" x="98" y="0" />
<use xlink:href="#sq" x="0" y="96" />
<use xlink:href="#sq" x="98" y="96" />
<rect x="86" y="264" width="74" height="74"
transform ="rotate(35,86,264)"  />
<rect x="178" y="272" width="74" height="74"
transform ="rotate(35,178,272)" />
<rect x="56" y="542" width="74" height="74"
transform ="rotate(35,56,542)" />
<rect x="154" y="588" width="74" height="74"
transform ="rotate(35,154,588)" />
<rect x="34" y="666" width="74" height="74"
transform ="rotate(-30,34,666)" />
```

```
<rect x="24" y="728" width="74" height="74"
transform ="rotate(20,24,728)" />
<rect x="106" y="766" width="74" height="74"
transform ="rotate(-10,106,766)" />
<rect x="34" y="840" width="74" height="74"
transform ="rotate(-10,34,840)" />
<rect x="12" y="958" width="74" height="74"
transform ="rotate(-30,12,958)" />
<rect x="114" y="922" width="74" height="74"
transform ="rotate(-60,114,922)" />
<rect x="124" y="994" width="74" height="74"
transform ="rotate(-25,124,994)" />
<rect x="234" y="972" width="74" height="74"
transform ="rotate(-45,234,972)" />
<rect x="362" y="1024" width="74" height="74"
transform ="rotate(-45,362,1024)" />
</g>
</svg>
```

Slightly different code displays the forum content. The screen appears as in Figure 6-21.

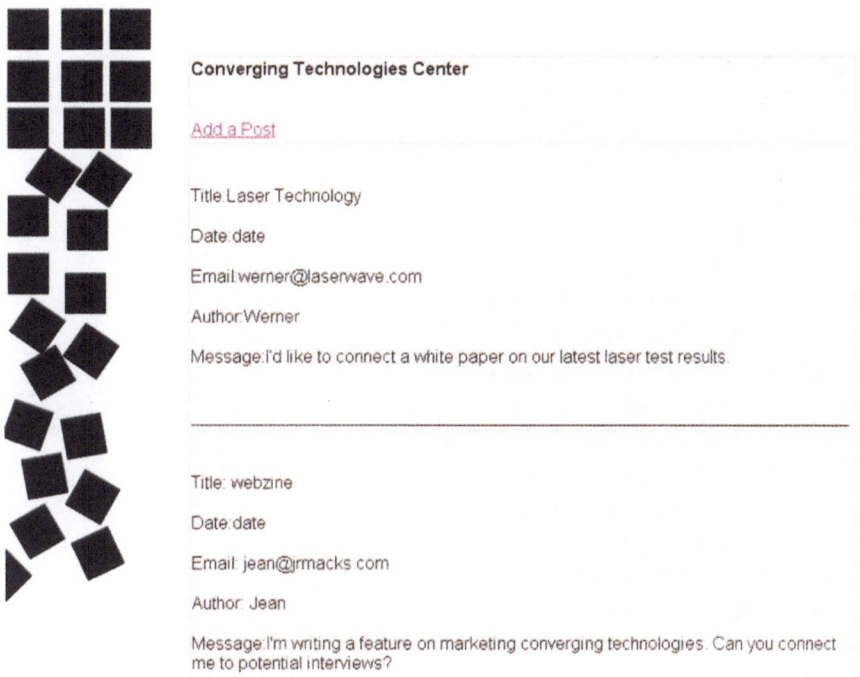

FIGURE 6-21 *Returned forum page, final prototype*

Listing 6-10 generates the SVG for Figure 6-21.

LISTING 6-10 *SVG Forum Output*

```xml
<?xml version='1.0'?>
<svg width="140" height="612">
<g transform="scale(0.5)" style="fill:black;
stroke:black; stroke-width:1;">
<defs>
<g id="sq">
<rect x="12" y="10" width="74" height="74" />
</g>
</defs>
<use xlink:href="#sq" x="0" y="0" />
<use xlink:href="#sq" x="98" y="0" />
<use xlink:href="#sq" x="0" y="96" />
<use xlink:href="#sq" x="98" y="96" />
<use xlink:href="#sq" x="186" y="96" />
<use xlink:href="#sq" x="186" y="0" />
<use xlink:href="#sq" x="0" y="344" />
<use xlink:href="#sq" x="0" y="450" />
<use xlink:href="#sq" x="0" y="182" />
<use xlink:href="#sq" x="102" y="182" />
<use xlink:href="#sq" x="188" y="182" />
<use xlink:href="#sq" x="108" y="370" />
<use xlink:href="#sq" x="104" y="486" />
<use xlink:href="#sq" x="98" y="0" />
<use xlink:href="#sq" x="0" y="96" />
<use xlink:href="#sq" x="98" y="96" />
<rect x="86" y="264" width="74" height="74"
transform ="rotate(35,86,264)"  />
<rect x="178" y="272" width="74" height="74"
transform ="rotate(35,178,272)" />
<rect x="56" y="542" width="74" height="74"
transform ="rotate(35,56,542)" />
<rect x="154" y="588" width="74" height="74"
transform ="rotate(35,154,588)" />
<rect x="34" y="666" width="74" height="74"
transform ="rotate(-30,34,666)" />
<rect x="24" y="728" width="74" height="74"
transform ="rotate(20,24,728)" />
<rect x="106" y="766" width="74" height="74"
transform ="rotate(-10,106,766)" />
```

```
<rect x="34" y="840" width="74" height="74"
transform ="rotate(-10,34,840)" />
<rect x="12" y="958" width="74" height="74"
transform ="rotate(-30,12,958)" />
<rect x="114" y="922" width="74" height="74"
transform ="rotate(-60,114,922)" />
<rect x="124" y="994" width="74" height="74"
transform ="rotate(-25,124,994)" />
<rect x="0" y="1000" width="74" height="74"
transform ="rotate(45,0,1000)" />
</g>
</svg>
```

Two additional documents display the forum. Listing 6-11 shows the XHTML for the forum form.

LISTING 6-11 *Forum Output XHTML*

```
<?xml version="1.0" encoding="UTF-8"?>
<!DOCTYPE html
PUBLIC "-//W3C//DTD XHTML 1.0 Strict//EN"
"http://www.w3.org/TR/xhtml1/DTD/xhtml1-strict.dtd">
<html xmlns="http://www.w3.org/1999/xhtml" xml:lang="en"
lang="en">
<head>
<title>Converging Technologies Center Forum Form</title>
<link rel="stylesheet" type="text/css" href="ctc.css" />
</head>
<body>
<p class="svg1"><object  data="ctForum.svg"
type="image/svg+xml" width="140" height="512">
<p>Sorry, your browser does not support SVG</p>
</object></p>
</object></p>
<form action="forum.asp"  method="post" id="form1"
name="form1">
<p class="text1">Name<br /><input type="text" name="author"
size="40"/></p>
<p class="text2">Subject<br /><input type="text" name="title"
size="40"/></p>
<p class="text5">Email<br /><input type="text" name="email"
size="40"/></p>
<p class="text3">Message:<br /><textarea rows="10" name="text"
cols="60"></textarea><br /></p>
```

```
<p class="text4"><br><input type="submit" value="Post Your
Message" name="gb_submit"/></p>
</form>
</body>
</html>
```

Listing 6-12 shows the ASP document for processing and saving input data using the Document Object Model (DOM).

LISTING 6-12 *Data Using the DOM and JavaScript*

```
<%@Language="JavaScript"%>
<?xml version="1.0" encoding="UTF-8"?>
<!DOCTYPE html
PUBLIC "-//W3C//DTD XHTML 1.0 Strict//EN"
"http://www.w3.org/TR/xhtml1/DTD/xhtml1-strict.dtd">
<html xmlns="http://www.w3.org/1999/xhtml" xml:lang="en"
lang="en">
<head>
<title>Converging Technologies Center Forum Processing</title>
<link rel="stylesheet" type="text/css" href="ctc.css" />
</head>
<body>
<table border="0">
<tr>
<td><p class="svg1"><object  data="ctForum1.svg"
type="image/svg+xml" width="140" height="612">
<p>Sorry, your browser does not support SVG</p>
</object></p></td>
<td width="10" />
</td>
<%
var xmlDoc= Server.CreateObject("Microsoft.XMLDOM")
xmlDoc.async=false
xmlDoc.load(Server.MapPath("ctc.xml"))
var xslDoc=Server.CreateObject("Microsoft.XMLDOM")
xslDoc.async=false
xslDoc.load(Server.MapPath("ctc.xsl"))
title=Request.Form("title")
date1=new Date()
email=Request.Form("email")
author=Request.Form("author")
textA=Request.Form("text")
root=xmlDoc.documentElement
```

```
messageE=xmlDoc.createElement("message")
titleE=xmlDoc.createElement("title")
emailE=xmlDoc.createElement("email")
dateE=xmlDoc.createElement("date")
authorE=xmlDoc.createElement("author")
textE=xmlDoc.createElement("text")
titleT=xmlDoc.createTextNode(title)
emailT=xmlDoc.createTextNode(email)
dateT=xmlDoc.createTextNode(date1)
authorT=xmlDoc.createTextNode(author)
textT=xmlDoc.createTextNode(textA)
titleE.appendChild(titleT)
emailE.appendChild(emailT)
dateE.appendChild(dateT)
authorE.appendChild(authorT)
textE.appendChild(textT)
messageE.appendChild(titleE)
messageE.appendChild(emailE)
messageE.appendChild(dateE)
messageE.appendChild(authorE)
messageE.appendChild(textE)
a=root.firstChild
root.insertBefore(messageE,a)
xmlDoc.save(Server.MapPath("ctc.xml"))
Response.Write(xmlDoc.transformNode(xslDoc))
%>
</td>
</tr>
</table>
</html>
```

The site CSS document, shown in Listing 6-13, includes rules for simple text properties. You must test the positioning.

LISTING 6-13 *Web Site CSS*

```
.svg1 {position: absolute; top: 0 px; left:0;}
.text1 {position:absolute; left:170px; right:100px;
top:50px; font-family: arial, helvetica, sans-serif; font-size:12pt;}
.svg2 {position: absolute; top:80px; left:170;}
.text2 {position:absolute; left:170px; top:100px;
font-family: arial, helvetica, sans-serif;
font-size: 12pt;}
```

```
.text3 {position:absolute; left:170px; top:200px;
font-family: arial, helvetica, sans-serif;
font-size: 12pt;}
.text4 {position:absolute; left:170px; top:390px;
font-family: arial, helvetica, sans-serif;
font-size: 12pt;}
.text5 {position:absolute; left:170px; top:150px;
font-family: arial, helvetica, sans-serif; font-size:12pt;}
.text6 {position:absolute; left:170px; top:330px;
font-family: arial, helvetica, sans-serif; font-size: 12pt;}
.text1a {position:absolute; left:30px; right:100px; top: 50px;
font-family: arial, helvetica, sans-serif; font-size:12pt;}
```

The site includes a simple search engine to find links to documents described by keywords. XML saves documents, and the DOM searches documents. Figure 6-22 shows the search engine entry form.

FIGURE 6-22 *Search entry form*

Listing 6-14 shows the search entry form.

LISTING 6-14 *Search Entry XHTML*

```
<?xml version="1.0" encoding="UTF-8"?>
<!DOCTYPE html
PUBLIC "-//W3C//DTD XHTML 1.0 Strict//EN"
"http://www.w3.org/TR/xhtml1/DTD/xhtml1-strict.dtd">
<html xmlns="http://www.w3.org/1999/xhtml" xml:lang="en"
lang="en">
<link rel="stylesheet" type="text/css" href="ctc.css"/>
<head>
<title>Converging Technologies Center Search Form</title>
</head>
```

```
<body>
<table border="0" style="font-family:arial, helvetica, sans-serif;">
<tr>
<td><p class="svg1"><object  data="ctSearch.svg"
type="image/svg+xml" width="98" height="98">
<p>Sorry, your browser does not support SVG</p>
</object></p></td>
<td width="10" />
</td>
<td><p>Converging Technologies Center</p></td></tr>
<tr>
<td width="98"></td>
<td width="10" />
<td width="600"><form action="searchDB.asp"  method="post"
id="form1" name="form1">
<p class="text1">Enter your keyword<br /><input type="text"
name="searchWord" size="40"/></p>
<p class="text4"><br /><input type="submit" value="Search"
name="gb_submit"/></p>
</form>
</td>
</tr>
</table>
</html>
```

Listing 6-15 shows the data stored in the XML document.

LISTING 6-15 *Search Entry Data XML*

```
<?xml version="1.0"?>
<documents>
<source>
<address>www.yahoo.com</address>
<keyword>biodiversity</keyword>
<keyword>nanotechnology</keyword>
<keyword>bioinformatics</keyword>
<keyword>biotechnology</keyword>
</source>
<source>
<address>www.cnn.com</address>
<keyword>convergence</keyword>
<keyword>micromachine</keyword>
<keyword>biotechnology</keyword>
<keyword>nanotechnology</keyword>
</source>
```

```
<source>
<address>www.ibm.com</address>
<keyword>genetics</keyword>
<keyword>biotechnology</keyword>
<keyword>nano</keyword>
<keyword>nanotechnology</keyword>
</source>
<source>
<address>www.eon.si.com</address>
<keyword>bioenergy</keyword>
<keyword>biotechnology</keyword>
<keyword>mind</keyword>
<keyword>nanomachine</keyword>
</source>
</documents>
```

Data is processed using the DOM in the ASP document, as shown in Listing 6-16.

LISTING 6-16 *Data Using DOM and JavaScript*

```
<%@Language ="JavaScript"%>
<?xml version="1.0" encoding="UTF-8"?>
<!DOCTYPE html
PUBLIC "-//W3C//DTD XHTML 1.0 Strict//EN"
"http://www.w3.org/TR/xhtml1/DTD/xhtml1-strict.dtd">
<html xmlns="http://www.w3.org/1999/xhtml" xml:lang="en"
lang="en">
<link rel="stylesheet" type="text/css" href="ctc.css" />
<head>
<title>Converging Technologies Center Search
Processing</title>
</head>
<body>
<table border="0" style="font-family:arial, helvetica,
sans-serif;">
<tr>
<td><p class="svg1"><object  data="ctSearch.svg"
type="image/svg+xml" width="98" height="98">
<p>Sorry, your browser does not support SVG</p>
</object></p></td>
<td width="10" />
</td>
<td><p>Converging Technologies Center</p></td></tr>
```

```
<tr>
<td width="98" />
<td width="10" />
<td width="600">
<%
var xmlDoc=Server.CreateObject("Microsoft.XMLDOM")
xmlDoc.async=false
xmlDoc.load(Server.MapPath("keybase.xml"))
root=xmlDoc.documentElement
searchWord=Request.Form("searchWord")
keywordsList=root.getElementsByTagName("keyword")
lenList=keywordsList.length
for(i=0;i<lenList;i++)
{
keyword=keywordsList.item(i).firstChild.nodeValue
if(keyword==searchWord)
{
 source=keywordsList.item(i).parentNode
 address=source.firstChild.firstChild.nodeValue
 Response.Write("<br> Address of source<a href='"+address+"'>  "+address+"</a>")
}
}
%>
</td>
</tr>
<tr height="50"><td width="98" /><td width="10" /><td>
<a href="searchDB.html">New Search</a></p></td></tr>
</table>
</html>
```

The returned search appears as shown in Figure 6-23.

Converging Technologies Center

Address of source www.yahoo.com
Address of source www.cnn.com
Address of source www.ibm.com
Address of source www.eon.si.com

New Search

FIGURE 6-23   *Search entry data results*

Listing 6-17 shows the SVG for the returned search.

LISTING 6-17 *Returned Search Graphic*

```
<?xml version='1.0'?>
<svg width="98" height="98">
<g transform="scale(0.5)">
<defs>
<g id="sq">
<rect x="12" y="10" width="74" height="74"
style="fill:black; stroke:black; stroke-width:1;" />
</g>
</defs>
<use xlink:href="#sq" x="0" y="0" />
<use xlink:href="#sq" x="98" y="0" />
<use xlink:href="#sq" x="0" y="96" />
<use xlink:href="#sq" x="98" y="96" />
</g>
</svg>
```

The purpose of this simple SVG is to remind users which site they're viewing. Simple cues such as these lines keep the theme of the site consistent.

Working forums or search engines aren't typically included in a final prototype. A working prototype does include links, or a sampling of links, so that users can interact with the site. You can include a main feature of the site in a final prototype depending on the client and your payment arrangements.

Project 2 Axioms

Requirements specifications help you understand clients who work in a niche market. For the Converging Technologies Center, a thorough understanding of biotechnology or nanotechnology isn't required. However, an understanding of how the client wants to communicate biotechnology or nanotechnology is nearly as important as the actual content selection. In this case, the design elements need to communicate the words *technical*, *new*, and *edgy*, and at the same time emanate the words *comfortable*, *informative*, and *supportive*. The only way to mesh these two sets of disparate words is with the right combination of design elements. Assumptions about scientists and mathematicians don't help. Clip art with science and mathematic products and symbols doesn't help. The right design elements, including an effective use of space and visual presentation of typographic elements, succeed in conveying the uniqueness that this niche product offers.

The next chapter explores how content supports design and interests users.

Working with Content and Typography

The text is the very place where the author appears.

—Paul Ricoeur, French philosopher (1913–)

Reading is the act that brings the Internet to the world of discourse. Text begins the conversation of clients and users. Quality content brings users back to a site. Text, supported by design, forms the core of the relationship between clients and users.

Site design offers, embraces, holds, and encourages users to enter the world of the client. Content reaches out, in partnership with design, to invite conversation, interpretation, and appropriation. Users always enter discourse with prejudgments based on their history, traditions, and experiences. Design and content interacting with user needs and expectations play a significant role in how users grow or terminate the relationship and shared world that discourse creates.

When designing an online project, your general content and typography considerations are as follows:

- **Content design**: What content (Web copy and graphics) looks like

- **Content meaning**: How content is interpreted

- **Content management**: How content is collected, written, edited, and organized

- **Typography selection**: What typeface to use and where to use it

All four considerations are key because without good content, there's no reason for users to return.

Understanding Content Design

Blocks of content form shapes of their own; it's important to represent these content shapes in your layout sketch to see if the result communicates the design's intent. Getting to a layout that satisfies the client is important, but the design job isn't complete without the content. In some cases, unexpected problems arise:

Incomplete content: At the beginning of the job, the client has great ideas for articles, resources, press releases, product specifications, and editorials. You base your content design on these ideas. Halfway through the project, the client prepares one editorial, gives you notes on Post-its, and sends you old brochures. The client announces there's no time to prepare more content.

Significant content changes: At the beginning of the job, the client approves your layout and sends in content, so you begin the build. You then get a phone call that the client needs a banner on the top and three ads on the right side of the screen. This completely changes what fits in the approved layout.

Poorly executed content: The client sends the content you need, and all is well. You begin transferring the content to the Web and realize the grammar is bad, the articles aren't well written, and the photos look greenish. You determine that the content problems are the client's and continue to build the site. However, the content looks so bad that the design can't support it, and the overall results appear thrown together. The site doesn't communicate the expertise the client wants to convey.

All of these examples change the way the content looks as it interacts with the layout. In other words, be aware of content issues. Begin thinking about content the minute you start working on a project. Consider how organized or unorganized the client seems to be. You may decide to create sketches of your layout with a few content possibilities, perhaps one with the expected content and one with half the content the client plans on developing. Unfortunately, it seems no one has time for content. Many specialists working with the Internet are interested in design or code, not in writing page after page about what clients offer. Marketing departments can help in some cases; in other cases, you may be handed documentation, brochures, and corporate paperwork that you need to rewrite for readability and sustainability on the Web.

Presenting Content in Layout Sketches

It's important to consider how content looks in a layout. You can quickly and easily redraw concept sketches with content. This approach allows you to immediately visualize potential layout with content problems. The Figure 7-1 layout appeared in Chapter 5 and potentially incurs display problems because of the left angle in the content box. The amount of text and the number, size, and position of graphics you plan to introduce plays a significant role in determining content placement. Taking a layout and adding a few buttons and then entering text and highlighting a few words in bold doesn't adequately address the design perspective of content. How can added content allow users to view the client as open and innovative? Figure 7-2 shows one possibility.

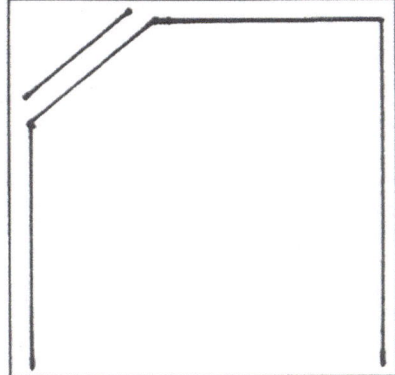

FIGURE 7-1 *An initial sketch layout*

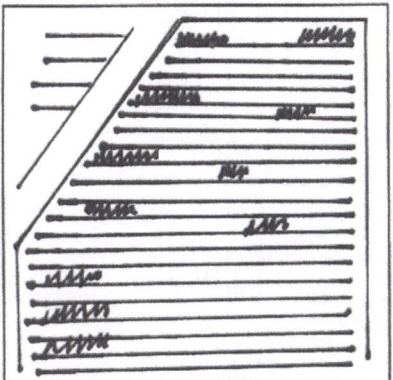

FIGURE 7-2 *Possible content addition to Figure 7-1*

As you finalize potential layouts and consider their navigation, it's important to visualize content. Sketches allow you to think about how to position and space assets that clients expect to see on their site. In some cases, editing text into chunks and manipulating images allows you to fit the story into the design. In some cases, you may need to throw out a layout for something simpler if the content doesn't work well with the design. If you can't seem to find a balance between concept and content, simplify the content and the design. Editing some content and allowing space to work with the text opens up the design and allows users to see text and graphics as partners in the layout, as shown in Figure 7-3.

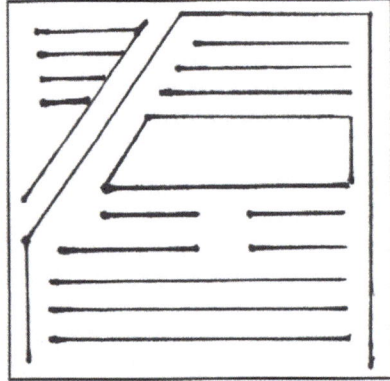

FIGURE 7-3 *A content alternative*

Open space supports a strong focal point, as shown in Figure 7-4 (also first presented in Chapter 5). In Figure 7-5, content has "room to breathe" with space on the top and bottom and a graphic or photo. As users navigate through sub-pages, the photo may change or more content could take its place.

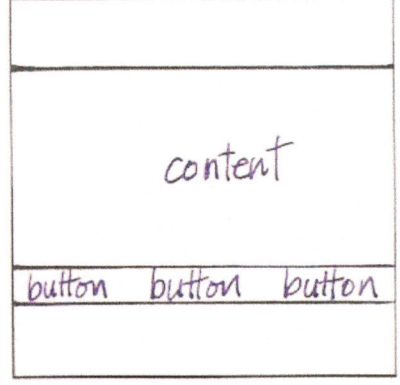

FIGURE 7-4 *Simple approach*

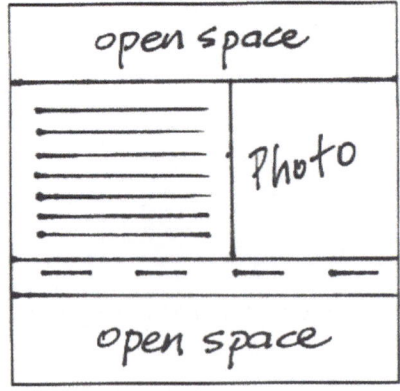

FIGURE 7-5 *Simple content*

Some designers recommend cutting Web copy into paragraphs of 10 to 25 lines in length. Text that's 25 lines long can overload a user and need to include considerations such as space between characters and space between lines as resting points. Good use of space and chunked information makes screen text less tiring on the eyes and conveys a relaxed openness to users.

Figure 7-6 shows navigation at the top and links to resources at the bottom for a content-heavy site. You should select one or the other. Don't move links from the bottom to the top within one site. Users like to see variation in the content area but not in the navigation. Keep navigation consistent, keep space for weary eyes, and focus on content presentation.

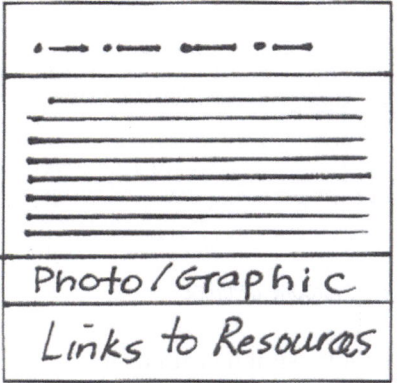

FIGURE 7-6 *Heavier content, same concept*

Content-heavy sites tend to become overwhelmed with links, bullets, text, and advertisements. Columns are often created and regularly overdone. Light-colored lines are supposed to separate ideas in tables; this may work for newspapers, but it doesn't work for the Web. Even sites with substantial information need to be delivered in such a way that users read and think, not just skim content and read only one or two lines.

Printed newspapers and advertising materials often present content with small, crowded characters. This content approach is because of printing costs, not because of preferred readability. Centuries of requests for smaller texts such as handheld books and newspapers (rather than the first texts, which were large manuscripts read from a lectern) have resulted in a cultural expectation of small, crowded words and graphics. The Web isn't constricted by paper formats or printing costs. Therefore, don't copy and paste from existing print materials. Think of the user, think Web copy, and determine how to best offer content to users so that they read it, appreciate it, and stay for longer periods.

Figure 7-7 presents links on the left, ads on the right, and three columns of text. Tabs on the top of the content suffice for navigation. The company logo displays on the top left, next to a banner. Clients with heavy content may press for everything to be available from one page. However, overwhelming, crowded content doesn't work any better than going into a store and not being able to navigate the aisles because of crowded conditions. Where's the focal point of this page? Users eyes will look and then gloss over dense content. Some users will try to read each line, but most will find one or two points of interest and then leave.

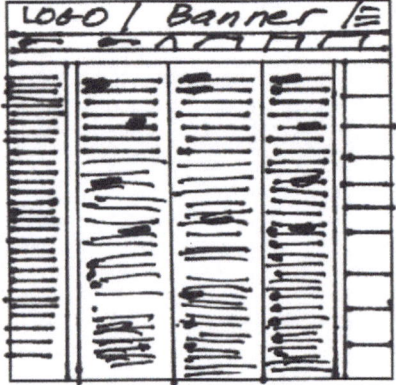

FIGURE 7-7 *Overdone columns*

Categorize and prioritize content based on conversations with users. Determine how users want to move through the site. Notice when the words users describe imply geographic ideas such as aisles, departments, and areas and then set up navigation accordingly. Keep content simple, and keep space a priority over some content items. Offer archived materials for older content. Your goal is to keep them coming, not to drown them with information.

The sketches in Figure 7-8 offer ideas for substantial content with whitespace for readability.

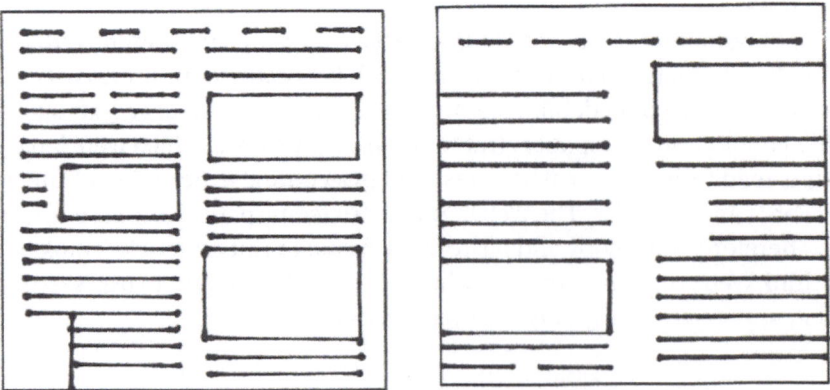

FIGURE 7-8 *Two columns, more space, and still a lot of information*

Consider how the layout works with the statements you want read. You may have a great relationship with a client who enthusiastically supports your design but who bores users with the company's history, mission statement, employment opportunities, and marketing strategy. How often when you go to a site to buy, to be entertained, or to learn do you want to stop and spend 15 minutes reading about the company's background? For example, you go to your favorite auction site to bid on a newly released game system. How important is it to you to read the chief executive officer's presentation from the last shareholder meeting or a press release on the company's plans for warehouse expansion? In the case of bidding on a game system, company background is probably of little interest to you. Price, shipping costs, and delivery dates are your priorities.

If, however, you want to apply for a job with the auction company, you would have cause to delve into the corporate background and the company's future plans. Users who go to a site to find data about a company don't mind digging into second or third levels of information on a site. One small About Us button, quietly positioned somewhere on the first page, can link to a site-within-the-site where a plethora of corporate information, current and archived, is available. The question for you to ask, as the designer or developer, is for every 1,000 users, how many want to buy and how many want corporate history? The answer to this and similar questions leads you toward obvious navigation categories. User priorities trump client priorities. Find quiet ways such as submenus and secondary links to support client content in which most users aren't interested.

Be careful to leave enough time in your schedule for client content issues. Always start gathering content *immediately* upon signing the contract. Waiting for client content, nagging for client content, and begging for client content always results in incorporating client content without having enough time to set it up as it should be.

Multiple column sites such as the Figure 7-9 layout are possible. Content works well in a three-column layout, as shown in Figure 7-10. Find out ahead of time if the client intends to place ads or banners on the site. Empty space should remain empty. Clients may decide empty space is a great spot for an ad after the prototypes are approved and you're in the build phase. Convincing clients of the need for space is one of the most difficult aspects of design.

Both sketches in Figure 7-11 contain a lot of content. You don't need to go to the extremes from dense content to minimalist design. The left sketch is too heavy with content. The right sketch uses space and yet continues to hold a lot of information on many topics.

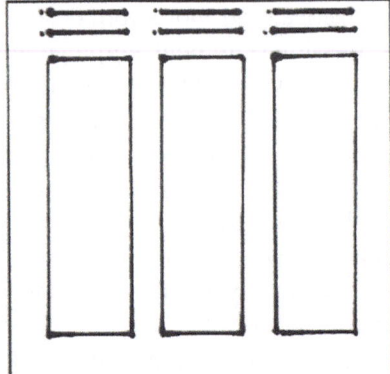

FIGURE 7-9   *Three columns and space*

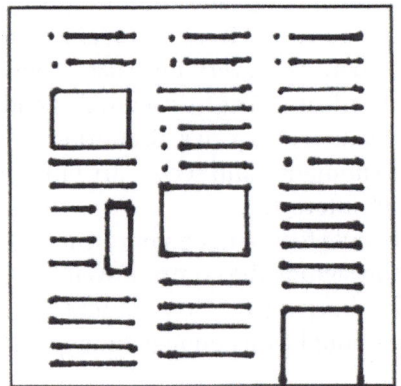

FIGURE 7-10   *Three columns with content*

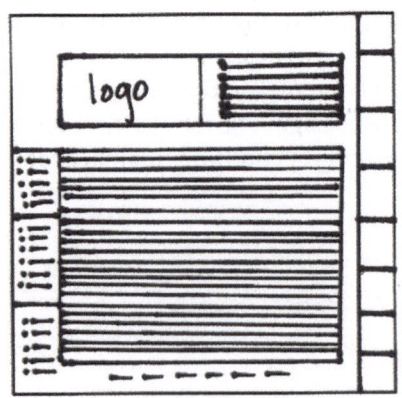

FIGURE 7-11   *Too dense (left) and heavy content with room to breathe (right)*

Unusually shaped layouts may dictate that content be set up in only one way or it may allow for several possibilities. Make sure, when sketching initial layouts out of the norm, that you consider content possibilities. Figure 7-12 shows a concept layout (a sketch originally shown in Chapter 5), and Figures 7-13, 7-14, and 7-15 show three potential content layouts.

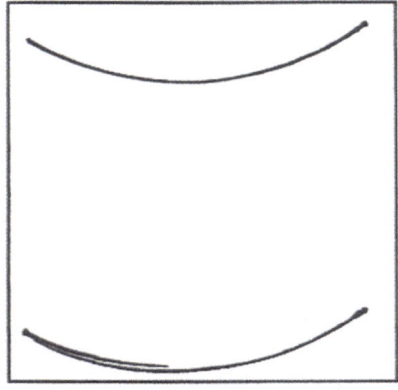

FIGURE 7-12 *Concept layout*

FIGURE 7-13 *Content layout with simple text and graphics*

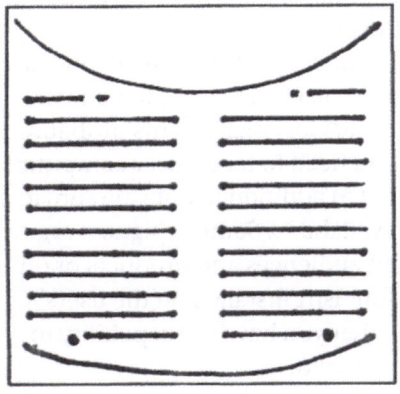

FIGURE 7-14 *Content layout with heavy text*

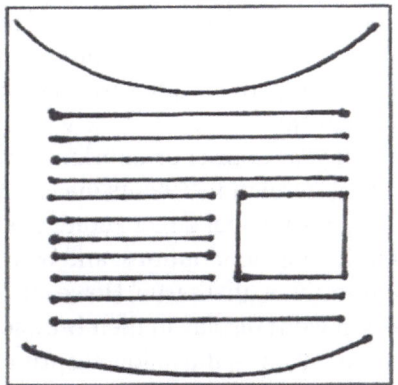

FIGURE 7-15 *Content layout with moderate text and graphic*

Unusual shapes can be interesting if their content remains usable and readable. The Figure 7-16 concept can contain a unique approach to content.

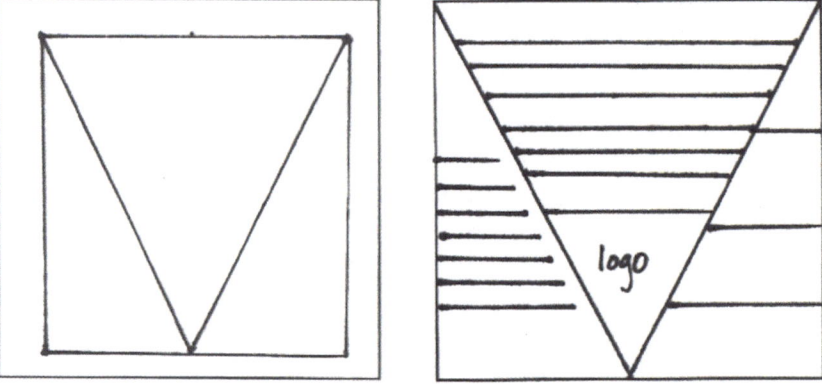

FIGURE 7-16 *An unusual shape (left) and an unusual shape with unique content (right)*

Using Typography

Many books cover type as a design element. Great fonts, available from many sources, make for great design. With code (as opposed to graphics), font choice is limited to the available browser fonts on the user's computer. Even so, type as a design element remains a key element in your overall design approach.

You don't need access to 150 fonts to create a good layout. Most everyone has access to two basic fonts, Times New Roman and Arial. On a Mac, Times substitutes for Times New Roman and Helvetica substitutes for Arial. Clients probably have fonts such as Courier or Courier New, but you need to target user computers to verify this information. Clients may have access to additional fonts; be sure to check your international target audience's font availability. Some designers argue that you have more font options, and with certain audiences and products or on a company intranet, that's true. However, if the font isn't installed on the users' computers, it won't display in their browser. Whether you have the capability to deliver two or 10 fonts, the following principles are valid:

- Don't use more than two fonts on a page/site.

- Don't use one font in multiple colors, sizes, and weights; a couple of variations are okay, but keep it simple.

- Don't bold everything you want noticed; use design elements such as space, shape, and line to grab user attention.

- Clean and clear always works.

One or two fonts, good use of space, supporting design elements, and direct communication to users creates great design results. How you incorporate type is more important than selecting multiple fonts. Typically, you have one font for content readability and a second, emphasis font for design purposes. Incorporate design elements to advance the client's theme.

One of the first decisions you make related to type is whether to use a serif or sans serif font.

Selecting a Font

Serif fonts have a fine line that finish off the main strokes of a letter. Sans serif fonts have no lines. Some designers think Times New Roman (a serif font) works best for paper readability and Arial (a sans serif font) for Web readability. Your consideration is which font works best for communicating the client's story. Times New Roman is used quite a bit for more traditional clients and products. Arial is used quite a bit for high-tech or innovative clients and products. This isn't a rule, though; your choice is to select which works best with the balance of your design.

Other considerations in choosing a serif or sans serif font include the following:

- Matching concepts of existing client assets such as print materials

- Continuing the concept of company identity or branding materials from marketing and media materials

- Penchant of the client for familiar content

- Visual match to an existing company logo and signage

Table 7-1 compares the serif and sans serif fonts Times New Roman and Arial. Times New Roman is a PC font; its Mac counterpart is Times. Arial is a PC font; its Mac counterpart is Helvetica.

TABLE 7-1 *Serif and Sans Serif Fonts*

Times New Roman is a serif font.	Arial is a sans serif font.
London	London
Paris	Paris
Zürich	Zürich
Oslo	Oslo
Praha	Praha
Beograd	Beograd

Text properties in Cascading Style Sheets (CSS) and Scalable Vector Graphics (SVG) allow for some flexibility with fonts. You can make great enhancements with small font adjustments such as adding space between characters (*kerning*) or between lines (*leading*). Watch how your font changes either add or don't add value to the overall design. Don't strut your stuff by making things fancy or complicated. Remember, the design of the type supports site design and text readability—that's all. Type should never compete with the meaning of the content or the intent of the product. Figure 7-17 shows SVG text with a slightly different presentation.

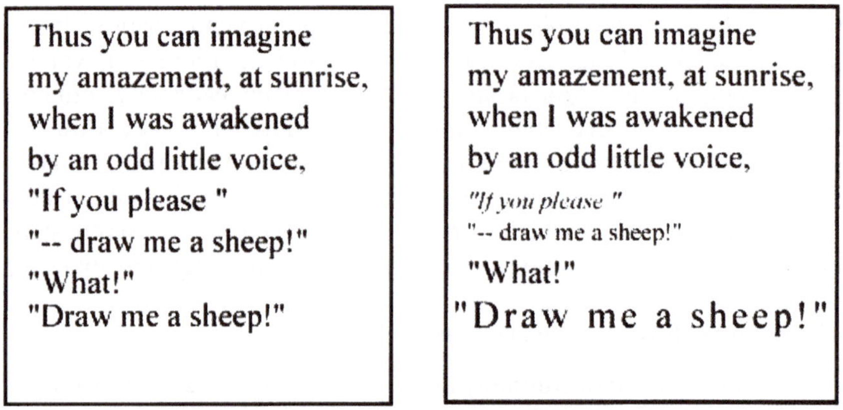

FIGURE 7-17 *Minor changes to the same font for emphasis*

You can make minor adjustments to SVG and CSS to emphasize content. Listing 7-1 generates the Figure 7-17 shape.

LISTING 7-1 *Minor Space and Text Adjustments for Emphasis*

```
<?xml version="1.0"?>
<svg width="300" height="300">
<rect style="fill:none;stroke:black;stroke-width:2;" x="50"
y="50" width="240" height="240" />
<g style="fill:black;font-size:12pt;stroke-width:1;font-family:Times New Roman;">
<text x="63" y= "73" >Thus you can imagine</text>
<text x="63" y= "98">my amazement, at sunrise,</text>
<text x="63" y= "123">when I was awakened</text>
<text x="63" y= "148">by an odd little voice,</text>
<text x="63" y= "173" style="font-size:9pt; font-style:italic;">
"If you please "</text>
<text x="63" y= "192" style="font-size:9pt;">"-- draw me a sheep!"</text>
```

```
<text x="63" y= "218">"What!"</text>
<text x="54" y= "245" style="letter-spacing:2.5px; font-size:14pt;">
"Draw me a sheep!"</text>
</g>
</svg>
```

Although it's not a good idea to bold and italicize each item you want noticed, there are several possible ways to enhance type when font choice is limited, including the following:

- Surround type with whitespace to pull in user attention.

- Place type to the right or left and higher or lower than where the eye expects to see it—not to the point where the design is awkward but enough to shift perception a little.

- Use minor adjustments of font size, weight, or color. Don't overdo it.

- Use italics sparingly and even then only for one or two words.

- Adjust letter spacing when using bold to make words easier to read (a problem with CSS).

- Instead of single line spacing, add 20–50 percent of whitespace between lines (also a problem with CSS).

As your layout evolves, play with type style and placement. Make time to adjust type and ask yourself the following questions after each adjustment: "Does this help the story along? Does it add value to what I want to communicate?" Go back to the language uncovered in your initial discussions. If you see words such as *unique, strong, brusque,* or *innovative,* compare them to what your type is communicating. If there's a match, keep it; if you love the type but it doesn't match the client and users' descriptive language, then get rid of it. If you can't make it come together, can't see it, or can't seem to find a fit, then keep it simple and continue with the project.

In the process of adding content throughout the site, you may discover ideas for changing the type. When this happens, try it; if it works, incorporate it. Making changes to type is much easier than it used to be because of CSS properties. Make good use of classes with Extensible HTML (XHTML) and properties with SVG; they're pretty well supported by browsers and can allow you to change significant amounts of type quickly. Remember to keep changes to type subtle unless you're working on a strong type presence. If you plan to make type the focus of your site, you should bring in a graphics application where outside fonts can be made into images; file size and not font availability then become the issue.

Presenting Content as Meaning

Text on the Web works well when it is the following:

- In active voice

- In present tense (unless past or future tense better fits a specific subject)

- Written directly to the target audience

- Presented in short blocks of paragraphs

- Surrounded with enough whitespace for the eyes to rest

- Presented without the clutter of a lot of ads and active images flashing or moving

- Written as though from one person to another, not from one to a group

As you work with content, think about a conversation. Imagine sitting and talking with one person and telling them the story of the client's products. Encourage them to interact, ask, and begin to rely on the client to meet their product needs. You may envision one example user or make an imaginary composite of four or five users. Be honest, talk with them directly, and give them your attention.

Think of the documentation, requirements, and manuals you've read over the years that do a poor job by explaining things to no one in particular. Think of the times you gave an order at a restaurant, only to repeat yourself several times to get what you thought you asked for the first time. Communication counts. Don't just throw it out there. Connect with the person on the other end. Care about them, listen to them, and show them respect. That's how to interact with friends and family, as well as with customers. Relationships bring results.

Be sure to read the text before you begin working with it. Reading helps you to design from your interpretation and helps you organize your approach, rather than being surprised by the amount or lack of content in the build. Consider the voice, rhythm, quantity, and structure of the text in determining its typographic form. Read and analyze the text, interpret its meaning, and map how it can be designed to communicate its intent. When using XHTML, consider keying all text as <p> elements (no header tags) and setting up class and id attributes to manipulate style. Staying away from header elements allows more flexibility in setting up and refining CSS properties and values. Create headings and subheadings as classes of <p>.

Text is the link between the reader, the design, the purpose, and the intent of the site. You want to invite the reader in, reveal the character of the client, and create a world behind the text between clients and users.

Presenting Content and Type Examples

The following three mini case studies describe the thought process of designing content and type.

Mini Case Study 1: Morgan California House Plans

Dave McMorrine designs house plans for the California market. California's building code differs from most other states because of earthquake restrictions. Dave sells house plans to builders and engineers. He doesn't work directly with homeowners.

Dave describes his company, Morgan California House Plans, as professional, courteous, knowledgeable, flexible, and helpful. He describes the products as high-quality, current, time saving, and efficient.

Exploring the Morgan California House Plans Graphics

Graphics and specifications for each house will be on the Web site. There are approximately 50 plans. Some plans will include sample details. Customers may purchase and download a plan online or request it to be emailed or delivered via courier. Plan books, designed for clients to show to their potential customers, are also available.

Web graphics are in color, show houses of various sizes, and give a better idea of what houses look like on full-sized lots (see Figure 7-18).

FIGURE 7-18 *Plan 15*

Table 7-2 shows the Plan 15 data. (To get square meters, you divide the square feet by 9 approximately.)

TABLE 7-2 *Plan 15 Data*

Area	Description
Upper floor	1,322 square feet
Lower floor	944 square feet
Total finished	2,266 square feet
Garage	736 square feet
Porch unfinished	50 square feet
Bedrooms	4
Full baths	3
Ceiling	9 feet high
Primary roof pitch	5:12
Maximum ridge height	24 feet by 11 inches
Exterior	Stucco
Roof cover	Arch comp
Roof construction type	Truss

The floor plan for each graphic is in black and white, as shown in Figure 7-19. Figures 7-20 and 7-21 show additional examples of styles and sizes of plans.

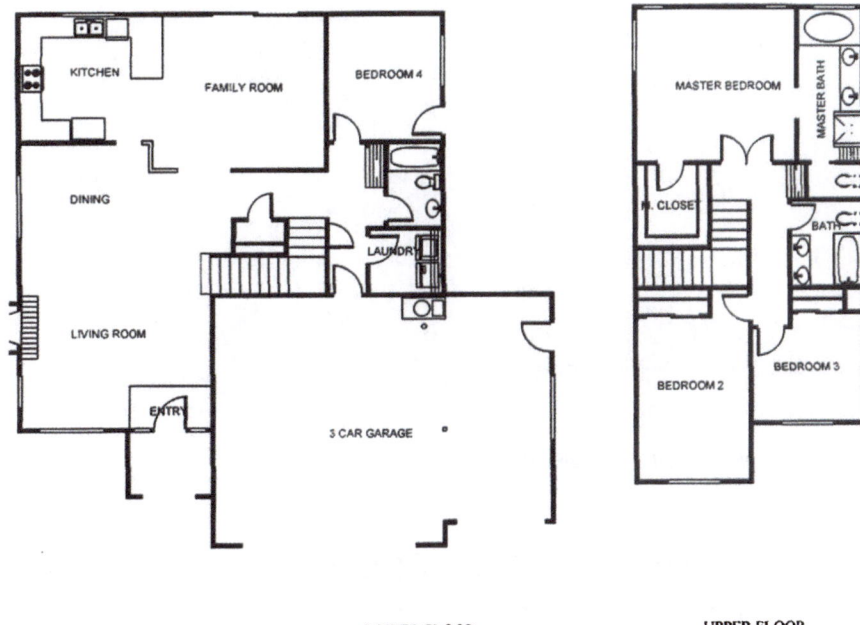

LOWER FLOOR   UPPER FLOOR

FIGURE 7-19 *Plan 15 floor plan*

FIGURE 7-20 *Sample large two-story elevation*

FIGURE 7-21 *Sample medium-sized elevation*

Gathering the Morgan California House Plans Text

The client wrote the following text that will be included on the Web site:

Morgan California House Plans are designed for average-sized lots in most cities. Plans are available by email, FedEx, or other common carriers. Delivery time is a few days. Plans are complete except for energy calculations, engineering, and a site plan. Sheets supplied include the floor plan, foundation plan, foundation details, roof plan, roof details, cross sections, elevations, and electric plan. The current cost for plans is 50 cents per square foot of living area. Most of the houses are designed for ease of construction with truss roof structures. A choice of three foundation types is available: raised floor "T" foundation, slab, and post and grade beam, depending on the soils condition of the site.

Many California cities and counties require different construction standards. Morgan California House Plans are adaptable to most standards, some with minor changes. Plans may also be customized to fit personal requirements at a reasonable additional charge. Delivery time and cost increases depend on the number and magnitude of requested changes.

Nine-foot ceilings for lower floors and eight-foot ceilings in two-story models are common with a few exceptions. Many houses are designed with four bedrooms, two-and-a-half baths, and a three-car garage. Most houses fit on a 60-foot-wide lot, and a few require a 70-foot-wide lot. Several houses are designed for narrower lots.

Quality of design, ease of construction, and service to clients are the standards Morgan California House Plans strives to maintain.

Determining Content Design and Typography for Morgan California House Plans

Your considerations include the following:

- What words does the client and the client's narrative use to describe the company and its products?

- What are the key points you expect to emphasize in the site's content?

- What design elements will help support the site's content? How can line, shape, texture, space, size, and value help convey the content of this site?

- Do you think a serif or a sans serif type best fits the client at this beginning stage?

As you consider these questions, make a list of language, priorities, possible elements, and possible typography for the site. These data translate to how content will be designed and delivered. Determining content design and typography isn't based on a moment of magical inspiration—the results of your considerations determine the content. Sketch a layout with your data, play with it, and see if you can enhance the story with subtle approaches to the design principles and elements you read about in earlier chapters. Delete extraneous information and overdesigned aspects of the site. Prioritize, simplify, and communicate. In this manner, content extends design, and the discourse created between the client and the user will flourish.

So, what's the main purpose of Morgan California House Plans content? The main purpose is to interest builders and engineers in the company and its house plans. The site should support a relationship between the client and the user where quality, trust, timeliness, and support are communicated and delivered.

Responses to the earlier content and typography considerations for Morgan California House Plans could begin with notes such as the following:

What words does the client and the client's narrative use to describe the company and its products? Current, ease of construction, choice, adaptable, customized, fit personal requirements. Quality of design, ease of construction, service to clients.

What are the key points you expect to emphasize in the site's content? Dave described his company as professional, courteous, knowledgeable, flexible, and helpful. He described the products as high quality, current, time saving, and efficient. He works with builders and developers, not directly with homeowners.

Key points include that the company is timely, professional, and knowledgeable with builders and developers and that it's in business to help customers save time and make money. This is a site for professionals that includes accurate information and accurate products.

Check target user familiarity with the Internet and with purchasing products online. What kind of instructional support would this site need? The site could be organized in a similar order to familiar, traditional plans. Check with Dave and a sampling of builders for how they want to access information and present it to the builders' clients. Are sample graphics, data, or floor plans available for builders to put on their own sites? Or is there a place for homeowners to "browse" on Dave's site without bypassing the builder/developer?

What design elements will help support the site's content? How can line, shape, texture, space, size, and value help convey the content of this site? This client probably requires a clean, simple site with enough space and line to denote an organized company with accurate products. The target audience wants to compare plans and clearly present them to their own customers. It should be a simple site to enhance and support the quality of the plans and the availability of information. Don't overdo the site presentation so that it competes with the actual products. Find out if users want to question possible customized changes online.

Buildings and plans typically include geometric shapes, lines, and space. These design elements complement the words *current*, *organized*, and *accurate*.

Do you think a serif or a sans serif type best fits the client at this beginning stage? On the first pass, start with a sans serif font to enhance the words *clean*, *clear*, *accurate*, and *current*. Check the client logo and print assets for previous design considerations. Test all fonts on consumer browsers and check users for versions and platforms.

Mini Case Study 2: Innovative Projects in Socioeconomic Emergence (IPSE)

Anna Quirk founded Innovative Projects in Socioeconomic Emergence (IPSE), a nonprofit organization working in transnational development. Anna leads projects for IPSE and continues to work on her own research interests. The following graphics and text present a slice of one project where Anna conducted a participatory field study and wrote about her observations and interpretation.

Anna describes the article and her studies as interesting to nonprofit practitioners working transnationally in the field and to educators working with students of all ages and ethnic groups. Anna describes IPSE as a caring, responsible, knowledgeable, nonprofit company sensitive to the hopes and needs of the people with which it works. The organization isn't interested in bringing Western ideas to indigenous groups but rather in participatory projects toward socioeconomic emergence.

Exploring the Research Graphics

The graphics interweave through the narrative, both of which are theoretically text, as shown in Figures 7-22 and 7-23. In the research article, Anna shows drawings made by Mlabri students (not included in this chapter).

FIGURE 7-22 *Mlabri children/students*

FIGURE 7-23 *Mlabri village photographs*

Gathering the IPSE Text

The client provided the following text to be included on the site:

Moisture hangs heavily on the green blanket of jungle. The morning sun is dim, straining above low clouds. Nestled deep in the valley, the village's bamboo houses remind me of mobile homes—not quite able to leave without a trace but not so overbuilt that a swift departure isn't possible. The singsong river winds down the mountainside through the village, and though it's stained umber with runoff during the rainy season, today it's clear. As I walk the path on my way to the village school, I gulp deep breaths of cool, moist air infused with the smoke of bamboo and acacia. It smells like exotic incense to me; for the Mlabri it means warmth, hot food, and fewer mosquitoes. The kids are up for hours before school starts and, whether they've eaten or not, are dressed in uniform by 8 A.M., waiting idly for the teachers to come, watching ants, and collecting wild fruit to pass the time.

The teachers have arrived. One Thai, two Hmong, and one American Thai, they call for each grade to line up for the "Thai National Anthem." Because the Mlabri have been added to the list of officially recognized hill tribes of Thailand, their school qualifies for government subsidies. They get boxed milk, hot lunch, uniforms, curriculum materials, and supplies. Whereas 20 years ago most Mlabri lived nomadic lives, children now gather every morning, boys in brown shorts and girls in blue skirts, singing songs that honor Thai royalty. First they sing the "Thai National Anthem," then "Praise to the Great King," and the "King's Anthem" last. Two delegates slowly raise the Thai flag; when they've finished, everyone stands straight and waits to see which line will be chosen first for free milk, perhaps the only breakfast they'll eat that day.

When they've finished their milk, each class disperses to complete their morning chores. Some sweep floors, some pick up trash, some straighten chairs, and some hang out laundry. Mlabri children are used to hard work, and their assigned tasks are as socially interesting as they're practically helpful. When they've finished their jobs, the schoolwork begins.

Baan Boonyuen's curriculum is shaped both by national standards and Mlabri culture. Each week, a new English word or letter is learned, a national requirement of all Thai children in first grade or above. The first-grade students are also learning addition and carrying numbers. There's a clock in every room of the school building, a marker Westerners don't expect to see so deep in the jungle. Until recently, Mlabri didn't measure time except to describe a certain part of the day. So, the clocks mark time, but they also mark a change in the Mlabri way of thinking. Each part of the school day reveals this kind of dual significance.

At noon the children break for one hour during which designated village women serve a hot meal. This is often the only full meal children eat all day. Many parents work in the fields and aren't at home to cook for their children. In the past, mothers have simply brought their kids with them to work in the fields.

Babies were strapped snug to mothers' backs, and older children played alongside their mothers. With the formalization of the new Thai school, however, children not only have a place to go and study during the day, but they eat a hot lunch, provided by the Thai government. The lunch subsidy also provides a small amount of money for the women who help prepare the food. And with more people staying in the village during the day, mothers are able to leave their babies behind for others to watch. Regular and nutritious meals are another way Mlabri life has been imbued by development efforts.

Determining Content Design and Typography for IPSE

Your considerations include the following:

- What words does the client and the client's narrative use to describe the organization and its projects? Narrative plays a key role on this site; it delivers information to the user and forms the actual product. For some clients, text describes available products. For this client, the text is the product.

- How can you tell the story of IPSE and the story IPSE is telling without turning this into an information-only site?

- What design elements support this client? What approach to line, type, shape, texture, space, size, and value communicates this client's personal story?

- Do you think a serif or a sans serif type best fits the client at this beginning stage?

The client's language and the language of the product call for a different design approach than did Morgan California House Plans. Everything about this client is more natural, more humanistic. Both clients want to be understood as professional and knowledgeable. However, the products and the purpose of the two differ and call for a different design, content, and type approach.

So, what's the main purpose of IPSE content? The main purpose is to create relationships and share research with nonprofit agencies, practitioners working in the field, and educators. Also, the purpose is to share ideas and observations with them in such a way that all participants begin to think a little differently. IPSE also needs to portray itself and its content as academically legitimate, not as a journalistic or travel site. Nonprofit organizations depend on grant funding and look for partnerships with other like-minded organizations. In its quest for relationship building, IPSE also wants to communicate a legitimate, ethical, and serious research organization.

Responses to the content and typography considerations for IPSE, presented earlier, may begin with notes such as the following:

What words does the client and the client's narrative use to describe the organization and its projects? Caring, responsible, knowledgeable, non-profit, and sensitive to the hopes and needs of the people with which it works. It's not interested in bringing Western ideas to indigenous groups but rather in participatory projects toward socioeconomic emergence.

Immediate design thoughts are curves, soft shapes, plenty of space, and an interesting use of color. Curves and soft shapes don't have to pair with light, pastel colors. The geometric shapes and lines of the Morgan California House Plans design notes won't work for this site.

Additional words include *commitment*, *serious*, and *legitimate*; the client doesn't want the site to be a personal diary but rather a narrative relationship with indigenous and research-oriented individuals.

How can you tell the story of IPSE and the story IPSE is telling without turning this into an information-only site? Shapes, colors, and space will help the user see the client's interest and commitment to people rather than an attempt at a data-driven site. If, at some time, there were data pages such as economic or health statistics, a simple, complementary data page with more of a linear feel could link to the narrative. The site's simple theme with its interesting text and graphics go a long way toward establishing the desired relationships. The job of the designer will be to enhance and support content rather than to direct or drive the site.

What design elements support this client? What approach to line, type, shape, texture, space, size, and value communicates this client's personal story? A first thought, it may be interesting to adjust space according to the nature of an article. For example, an article about building schools would look great with open space, lines, and shape that signify growth and development. An article about contaminated water or abuse could be presented with tighter spacing and shapes suggesting pressure or lack of freedom. This approach would need to be subtle. Minor changes in color hues, spacing of type, and a separate approach to value and texture could visually support the open lightness of one story and the closed heaviness of another.

You can also incorporate metaphors of land, water, sky, or other traditions and histories of the people studied.

Conversation with the client will help to result in several sketch prototypes. A site such as this has a lot of room for design ideas. Think warm, simple, caring, and unique.

Do you think a serif or a sans serif type best fits the client, at this beginning stage? The first thought is a serif font. Traditional tribes, traditional research industry, and serif fonts also go well with softer shapes and space.

Mini Case Study 3: EyeStockArt

Jeff Rascov teaches Web design, digital audio and video, and several Web applications. On the side, he likes to take photographs. Several of his photographs hang on friends' walls, and several have sold to other designers. Jeff wants to set up his and other designers' photos, graphics, and images for sale.

Jeff envisions the site as simple and easy to operate. He doesn't want to spend a lot of time writing about the images. He wants to offer good navigational tools for searching, viewing, and purchasing products. He's looking for a low-maintenance site where designers know they can find a good selection at fair prices and where they can offer images to other designers. It's a collaborative site, with a little profit to Jeff for the organization and maintenance.

Exploring the EyeStockArt Graphics

Figures 7-24, 7-25, and 7-26 show a small sampling of photographs from a trip to southeastern Europe. Hundreds of other photographs include product, landscape, people, travel, and other stock photography graphics.

FIGURE 7-24 *Slovenian castle*

FIGURE 7-25   Mali Lošinj, Croatia

FIGURE 7-26   Dancers Laško Festival; Laško, Slovenia

Gathering the EyeStockArt Text

The site contains minimal information, most of which is simple instructional sentences such as the following:

- EyeStockArt images are searchable by category, artist, and size.

- To find an image, please go to our search engine.

- The site and layout are clean and simple; their main purpose is to house the images, not to compete with the site's products.

The client likes to take photographs and is only interested in enough text to convey how the site works.

Determining Content Design and Typography for EyeStockArt

Your considerations include the following:

- When minimal narrative is available, what content and type issues should be considered? What about size, color, line, shape, and texture? How can you design these elements to guide and support images of various topics, colors, and sizes?

- Does the audience make a difference? Does type as a design consideration change when the target group works with type, content, and space professionally?

- What kinds of questions might you want to ask the client? Should the site be fun, informative, or entertaining? You know the client is looking for clean and simple, but is there a personality to the project? Is clean and simple enough information to meet the client's expectations?

So, what's the purpose of the EyeStockArt content? To make purchasing images interesting, simple, and affordable and to communicate a relationship of peers working together to save time and enhance work.

Responses to the content and typography considerations for EyeStockArt, presented earlier, could begin with notes such as the following:

When minimal narrative is available, what content and type issues should be considered? What about size, color, line, shape, and texture? How can you design these elements to guide and support images of various topics, colors, and sizes? The site is for Web and graphic designers trying to find photographs and graphics for a specific client and purpose. As such, minimal text works as long as the user priorities are clearly presented. Talking with users before the design process begins will result in conversations about currently available, free and for-purchase photo and graphic sites inundated with advertising and pop-up windows. User analysis is often overlooked on sites where user expectations are assumed. However, user analysis is critical on familiar sites because users have definite opinions on what they want or like, and their needs may be different from the client's current understanding. Simply asking designers how they want to access, pay for, and download images can save a lot of time.

The design for the site should be simple and utilize a minimalist file size; the images should be as enhanced as possible to look good without slowing access to viewing them. At first pass, a diagonal shape and line approach might help to guide the users' focal point to graphics and information. Because many images will be square and rectangular in shape, too much of a straight line and rectangular concept could convey a dull approach to what should be interesting graphics. Simple diagonal background lines, a little color, and a good use of space can showcase the graphics for sale and communicate the site, in parallel, to users.

Does the audience make a difference? Do type and other design considerations change when the target group works with type, content, and space professionally? Yes, the audience always makes a difference. Figure 7-27, for example, shows small boats at the edge of Lake Bled in Slovenia.

The EyeStockArt Web site for this graphic might say something like the following:

Rustic lake, blue water, sky with scattered clouds, blue gray hills in background. Small red rowboat collection, foreground left. Small piece of brown, aged boat dock. Original JPG, saved as TIF for print.

This photo—in a travel piece created by the EyeStockArt customer/designer—might say something about the location, history, and travel possibilities of Lake Bled. In another piece—a mystery book, perhaps—the designer might write of a quiet lake after a night of mayhem and murder. In yet another piece, the designer might write about environmental solutions for tourist regions or fishing rights.

Type and design considerations make a significant difference to any target audience. They support user expectations and priorities every time.

FIGURE 7-27 *Boats on Lake Bled, Slovenia*

What kinds of questions may you want to ask the client? Should the site be fun, informative, or entertaining? You know the client is looking for clean and simple, but is there a personality to the project? Is clean and simple enough information to meet the client's expectations? Sometimes the personality of the client comes through in the design of the product. In the case of EyeStockArt, Jeff's personality is bound to surface in user analysis conversations. He likes projects that are fun, interactive, and simple to manage. He would be more likely to develop a video of instructions than type supporting content. When the client's personality begins to surface as a potential personality for a product, make sure to capture the client's words, gestures, and ideas. The sketches that develop may be a great start toward a relationship with users. Extend the relationship to the users' needs to see if a fit appears. If so, you're halfway to a layout. If not, you'll be in a position to sketch a users' concept, compare it to the client concept, and find a common theme for an overall approach to the project design.

The mini case studies presented in this chapter address significantly different audiences. Their purpose and target audience can be readily defined. Consider content and typography axioms as you transition from concept design to layout.

Content and Typography Axioms

Content and typography considerations focus on the following:

What content looks like, or *content design*: What overall shape does the content take on each page? Text on a screen is tiring to read. How have you organized the text and graphics so that they complement the design and not overwhelm it? Make sketches of various content layouts. Spend as much time organizing how the content looks as you spent on the layout. Content is key.

What type to use, or *typography*: Does the type complement the customer and the layout? Is a serif or a sans serif font a better fit for the client's story? Have you allowed enough space between characters and between lines so that the type is easy to read? Have you used type variations such as bold, color, or italic only when they add value to the communication of the content? Is there anything you can simplify or delete to keep the site as readable as possible?

How content (Web copy and graphics) is interpreted, or *content meaning*: This is critical. Don't simply retype the client's brochure. Determine what the story is. Start collecting assets immediately. Push for clear, clean copy. Use active voice. Be descriptive. Communicate one on one. Think of all the absurd documentation and Web copy you have read. Make this better, and make it personal. Take time to design it. Take time to read it. Can it be better? Does the user interpret the client's intent? Have you done the best job possible with the meaning of the content, or are you in a hurry at this point to finish the job? Content meaning brings customers back. Don't use cheap photos, don't use tacky screenshots without cleaning them up, and don't use jaggy graphics because marketing isn't available to create a better version.

How content is collected, written, edited, and organized, or *managing content*: Don't focus on getting to the build without working on content along the way. Be aware of well-intentioned clients with little time for content delivery. Make sure you know, at prototype approval, what the content will be. Make a checklist of what you're expecting and how to get it. Clients are typically available more at the outset of a project than in the middle, when they're off on other projects. Get the content immediately and save yourself a lot of time and headaches. Encourage them to email you content; then at least it's in an electronic version. Leave enough time to manage content, and don't be shocked by a box of papers, photos, and notes you're expected to type, scan, and edit.

The next chapter incorporates theory and practical ideas for using color to enhance Web-based products.

Using Color

The Mediterranean has the color of mackerel, changeable I mean. You don't always know if it is green or violet, you can't even say it's blue, because the next moment the changing reflection has taken on a tint of rose or gray.

—Vincent van Gogh, painter (1853–1890)

Much has been written about the theory and application of color. Color is an integral part of life. Learning to plan, design, and implement color takes place over several years and numerous projects. This chapter offers a starting point to help you begin with confidence, to experiment, and to work with color.

Developers have a tendency to overdo color. There's a misconception that color enhances a weak design. In fact, a design must first work well in black and white; the addition of color supports and enhances the design concept. Color adds passion, mood, and familiarity to design; it doesn't fix a mediocre product.

The first step for developer consideration in the quest for better color is to simply slow down and think about how the product fits in the world of the client and user. Only then can the color theory and concepts described in this chapter help you to determine the best product color scheme. In the beginning, however, ask yourself questions related to the client's story. Go back to the language the clients and users gave you in the early user analysis phase of the project. Write down keywords that help you describe the product. Visualize those keywords as images and begin to see potential product colors.

For example, imagine you're in a room described as follows:

Nightclub, dancing, drinking, closed space, people, moving, watching, sweating, music, loud, touching, talking, dimly lit, kissing, connecting

Which set of colors best fits this environment?

- Red, white, and blue

- Black, dark blue, accents of yellow and purple, the silver color of chrome and mirrors

- Pastel pink, orange, light blue, light green, and white

Next, imagine you're in a room described as follows:

Classroom, 10 and 11 year olds, laughing, working, talking, listening, desks, student artwork on the walls, science kits, a rabbit, fish in an aquarium, backpacks, books, chalkboards, computers, posters, jeans, and sweatshirts

Would the same colors you selected for the nightclub work for the classroom? How are the colors different? Think of a good nightclub you have been in, then think of a kids' classroom. Which of the following colors are closer to your imagined classroom:

- Neutral colors such as sand, white, beige, and tan

- Dark colors such as black, gray, brown, and burgundy

- Simple, bold colors such as blue, white, green, red, and yellow

Your first decisions with color are based on your understanding of the world. These initial ideas aren't based on color theory; they come from your traditions, experience, and history. Color theory can help you select wonderful color variations and combinations; however, your initial ideas for color often come from your interpretation of the client, users, and the product's purpose.

In the nightclub example, night colors would be the most likely starting place: black, dark blue, accents of yellow and purple, and the silver color of chrome and mirrors. In the classroom, simple, bold colors such as blue, white, green, red, and yellow would probably work best.

So, how do you approach the initial color palette for a specific product? Again, begin with keywords given you by clients and users and then add words that also describe the product. In Table 8-1, keywords differentiate three products.

TABLE 8-1 *Three Columns of Words, Three Moods for Color*

Racetrack Video Game Site	Movie/TV/Music Stars Site	Rare Books Site
Fast	Glitz	Firsts
Cars	Stars	Special
Racetrack	Gossip	Unique
Formula 1	Clothes	Secrets
Loud	Talent	Treasured
Smoke	Creative	Traditional
Maneuver	Ego	Prized
Quick	Fame	Quality

The three products described in Table 8-1 have different purposes. Although they all intend to draw users, the culture and approach of the three aren't the same. You should take two parallel considerations into account: purpose and target audience. Which purpose from the following list best fits the Table 8-1 products?

• Entertainment, baby: Fun, film, television, media

• Excitement: Precision, competition, risk, money

• Adventure: Search, buy, value, pride

You may not be enthralled by any of the three categories of products. Nonetheless, you can talk to users who are. As you do, you'll find that people interested in Formula 1 racing video games have a certain passion that can be put into words. These words form images that in turn suggest colors. The purpose for the Racetrack Video Game site design is excitement.

It's easy to find people who follow stories about movie, television, and music stars. Additionally, there are many examples of successful media projects that cover the entertainment industry. When you speak with movie, television, and music fans, you'll hear keywords and image descriptions that help you better define purpose keywords. The purpose for the Movie/TV/Music Stars site is entertainment, baby!

Rare-book collectors have a keen passion for finding and collecting books. Rare-book stores, book fairs, and the Internet are all sources of information for rare-book collectors. All of these resources help you understand more about the interests and expectations of rare-book collectors. The purpose for the Rare Books site is adventure, the hunt for great deals on treasured books.

With all three product examples, your focus remains on talking to users and researching your target audience, as discussed in Chapter 1. This resource/research approach to color design is no different from your approach of finding and developing a functional requirement.

The target audiences for the three sites, the Racetrack Video Game site, Movie/TV/Music Stars site, and Rare Books site, are diverse. Don't make assumptions about target groups. Remember that individuals see themselves much differently than what stereotypes or cultural assumptions predict.

Understanding Color and Narrative

Once you're comfortable with the purpose and the audience of the site, bring all of your data together in a narrative. This narrative may consist of one or more of the following:

- Graphics

- Keywords

- User analysis conversation text

- Existing client assets such as print products

- Metaphors you or the client think will help to better tell the client's story

- Your own ideas

- Feedback

- Research data

The book *Mainstreams of Modern Art*, Second Edition by John Canaday (International Thomson Publishing, 1981) aptly describes Vincent van Gogh's approach to creating his painting *Sunflowers:*

van Gogh wrote in a letter to Émile Bernard that he was thinking of "decorating my studio with half a dozen paintings of sunflowers, a decoration in which chrome yellow, crude or broken, shall blaze forth against various backgrounds of blue ranging from the very palest emerald up to royal blue and framed with thin strips of wood painted orange. The sort of effect of Gothic stained glass windows." The modeling of the flowers' great coarse central cushions of stamens was done in actual relief, the pigment being built up close to a quarter of an inch in some places, and textured like the rough mass of the stamens themselves. Individual petals are also defined by relief, each one existing as a mass of paint with its edge standing out prominently in front of the petals behind it. The sunflower pictures are large ones, the monstrous blossoms being painted at full size. They have a savage vehemence that is reduced to bright prettiness in the small color prints that are so popular.

Which of the four interpretations of van Gogh's *Sunflowers* in Figure 8-1 best fits with the narrative described by Canaday? Which is most familiar to you?

FIGURE 8-1   *Four interpretations of van Gogh's* Sunflowers

The reproduction of the original is on the bottom left of Figure 8-1. The top-left one does a good job of meeting the narrative of van Gogh's attempt. However, van Gogh conveyed the actual color of the sunflowers, rather than the pink and yellow interpretation of the top-left one. The top-right one is a strange mutation of the original. Distorted colors and images have their purpose and audience, but this version of the image no longer meets van Gogh's intent. The bottom-right one is a grayscale of the original; you get the general idea of texture, but the painting loses its feeling of warmth when it loses its color.

Understanding Color Basics

Once you determine, using your understanding of the client and product, one or more potential key colors, there's a plethora of information available for taking your initial ideas to a product color palette.

The following sections introduce the basic color terms important to understanding and working with color: hue, saturation, and value.

Understanding Hue

Hue is the name of the color: red, yellow, orange, green, blue, or violet. The word *color* is often used, but *hue* is the more exact, technical term describing, for example, the varying degrees of red, reddish orange, reddish yellow, and so on. Although black, white, and gray are colors, they have no hue and are considered *neutral colors*. The color keywords of Cascading Style Sheets (CSS) probably don't need to be referred to as *hues*; however, you do still need to be specific: The hexadecimal color of the Mediterranean Sea on a chart can't be identified simply as *blue*.

Figure 8-2 shows colors as presented using CSS keywords yellow, red, and orange on the left, and it shows different hues of yellow, red, and orange presented on a Web-safe hexadecimal color chart as #ffffcc, #ff6600, and #ffcc99 on the right.

FIGURE 8-2 *CSS keyword colors (left) and hues of the same colors (right)*

Understanding Saturation

Saturation is the degree of purity of a color. A fully saturated color contains no black, white, or gray and contains only one or two of the primary colors but not the third. High intensity, bright colors are more saturated than muted, dull colors. New designers often oversaturate color. Varying degrees of saturation are more or less popular in different countries, according to culture and custom, but the transnational culture of the Web seems to be blurring this distinction.

Figure 8-3 shows saturated color. The blue is CSS keyword blue, hex #0000ff, and Red-Green-Blue (RGB) value 0, 0, 255. The green isn't CSS keyword green; it's hex #33cc00, a different hue. However, it's still saturated at RGB value 48, 207, 0 because it contains two, not three, primary colors. The top yellow button is CSS keyword yellow, hex #ffff00, and RGB value 255, 255, 0. The next three yellows aren't saturated; from top to bottom, they're hex #ffff66 and RGB value 255, 255, 96, hex #ffff99 and RGB value 255, 255, 159, and hex #ffffcc and RGB value 255, 255, 207. All are yellow, one is saturated, and the remaining three are different values of the first without saturation.

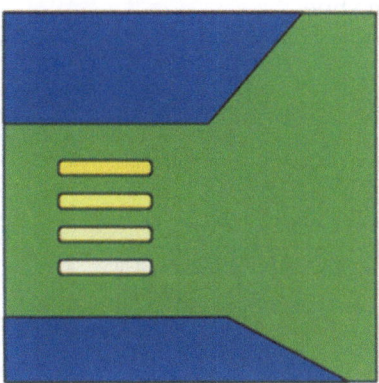

FIGURE 8-3 *Saturated color*

A common mistake is to see a "bright" color and assume it's saturated. Both saturation and brightness can reduce readability and shouldn't dominate a page. Many people like bright, bold colors. Consider using a small amount of these colors for setting the mood and texture of a site and incorporating plenty of white for text readability. Figure 8-4 shows bold, not saturated, color; red, green, and blue are present in each.

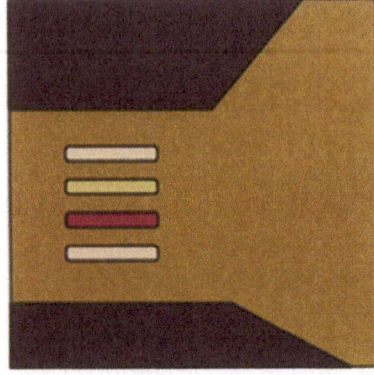

FIGURE 8-4 *Bold, not saturated, color*

Understanding Value

Value is the relative lightness or darkness of a sample, whether or not it contains hue. Lighter values of the same hue contain varying degrees of white. Darker values of the same hue contain varying degrees of black. Both the images shown in Figure 8-5 display lighter and darker values of one hue.

FIGURE 8-5 *Lighter and darker values of one hue per figure*

Following a Simple Approach

This simple approach can help you make good color choices as you learn to work with the nuances of color. Although it isn't intended for all jobs, it's often a good place to start:

1. Determine one or two initial colors from the narrative of the client and user and your own research ideas.

2. Consider additional, descriptive keywords words such as *minimalist, busy, bold, light, heavy, loud, aggressive,* or *simple.*

3. Create a simple Scalable Vector Graphics (SVG) image divided into two, three, or four sections as shown in the color swatches in this chapter (see Figure 8-6 for an example). In each section of your graphic, place hexadecimal or RGB colors that are values of the same hue. Don't bring in additional color at this point.

Print designers have learned that different values of the same hue, created by adding white or black at intermittent levels, convey depth without the cost of printing multiple colors. Web designers often overuse colors—maybe because they're free. In any case, as you bring color into your designs, first consider working with a few values of a single hue (color).

When the design concept is nearly complete, add one complementary color as an accent to guide the user's eye to information you want to convey. Add any subsequent colors only if they enhance the design. Figure 8-6 shows the values of Figure 8-5 with one spot of accent color. Notice that the values don't conflict, and your eye immediately goes to the complementary accent hue. This accent color creates focal points to direct users to important information.

FIGURE 8-6 *A complementary accent to value*

Listing 8-1 shows the simple SVG for the value color swatch shown. You may want to use this or a similar example with different values to see how the colors look on a screen. This approach allows you to quickly adjust hues and see results on a monitor. The simple swatch approach also allows you to take the color of a logo, a favorite piece of client artwork, or a scan of fabric and see how the hue interacts with the complementary accents on a site. After selecting a color palette, create a digital prototype that includes the design, background, and text that represents your expected content. This enables you to preview how everything works from a color and design perspective.

LISTING 8-1 *SVG Color Sample*

```
<?xml version="1.0"?>
<svg width="300" height="300">
<polyline points="250 156, 250 50,150 50, 250 156"
style="fill:rgb(241,255,255); " />
<polyline points="86 50,250 230, 250 156,150 50,86 50"
style="fill:rgb(164,192,213);" />
<polyline points="50 82, 190 250,250 250,250 230,86 50,
50 50, 50 82" style="fill:rgb(51,134,177);" />
<rect style="fill:none;stroke:black;stroke-width:1.5;"
x="50" y="50" width="200" height="200"/>
<polyline points="50 82, 190 250,50 250, 50 82"
style="fill:rgb(19,42,70);" />
<circle cx="200" cy="180" r="10"
style="fill:rgb(255,102,51)" />
<circle cx="200" cy="210" r="10"
style="fill:rgb(204,51,51)" />
</svg>
```

Finding Complementary Colors

Once you know your initial color and its values (you may have two or three options, but don't create a dozen; too many options create confusion), you can determine complementary colors and their subsequent values using a color wheel. Hues directly opposite each other on the color wheel are complementary. Figure 8-7 shows complementary colors on the color wheel. Remember, there are many values of each of these colors.

The six-hue color circle consists of the following:

- Orange = red + yellow

- Green = yellow + blue

- Purple = blue + red

Neutrals/grays will result from combining the three primary colors on the color circle (red, yellow, and blue) or from blending complementary colors.

FIGURE 8-7 *A six-hue color wheel*

The six-hue color circle expands to a 12-hue color circle by adding three additional pairs of complementary colors, as shown in Figure 8-8.

FIGURE 8-8 *A 12-hue color wheel*

The additional complementary pairs include the following colors, clockwise:

- Red-orange and green-blue
- Orange-yellow and blue-purple
- Yellow-green and purple-red

These additional colors complement each other and can complement the color next to a color directly across the circle, depending on the value of each.

Listing 8-2 is an SVG color wheel that you can use to adjust colors for experimental purposes.

LISTING 8-2 *SVG Color Wheel*

```
<svg  onload='dessin(evt)'>
<script><![CDATA[
 function dessin(evt)
{
svgdoc=evt.getTarget().getOwnerDocument();
  root=evt.getTarget();

 color=new Array("green", "#00ccff","blue","#0066cc",
"purple","#cc0066","red","#ff6600","orange","#ffcc33",
"yellow","#33cc33")
rad=3.14/180
r=80
for(i=0;i<12;i++)
{
ax=Math.round(r*Math.sin(30*rad*i))
bx=Math.round(r*Math.cos(30*rad*i))
ax1=Math.round(r*Math.sin(30*rad*i+30*rad))
bx1=Math.round(r*Math.cos(30*rad*i+30*rad))
a=150-ax
b=150+bx
a1=150-ax1
b1=150+bx1
path1="M 150 150 L"+a+" "+b+" "+"A 80 80 0,0,1"+"
"+a1+" "+b1+" L150 150"

  node=svgdoc.createElement('path');
  node.setAttribute('d',path1)
  node.setAttribute('style','fill:'+color[i]);
  root.appendChild(node);
}
```

```
node=svgdoc.createElement('circle');
node.setAttribute('cx',150)
node.setAttribute('cy',150)
node.setAttribute('r',50)
node.setAttribute('style','fill:white;stroke:white');
root.appendChild(node);
}
]]></script>
</svg>
```

The following examples show color possibilities for Web-based products. Some include complementary colors, and others are based on color palettes from artwork and graphic design. Practicing with swatches of colors allows you to visualize how the colors do or do not communicate what you intend. The designs in Figure 8-9 both show diagonal lines, a central white background, and the same accent color in the small circle. The remaining colors, however, communicate differently. Which figure communicates the earth and sky? Which figure seems lighter or heavier in "weight"?

FIGURE 8-9 *Same accent color with different design colors*

The colors in Figure 8-9 show the same white and accent color with different main colors. The right one is obviously more connected to the earth and sky because of its colors. The left one appears lighter in weight. This is in part because of the lighter colors and in part because of the right one's lower brown color. Bold colors don't always appear heavy, however. Adjusting their placement or value and increasing the design whitespace can result in attention-getting bold colors without communicating weight and density.

Colors you may not think of at the outset of a project often work well with a significant amount of whitespace. At the time of this writing, blues and oranges are popular. Not many designers are working with lavender. However, the colors of Figure 8-10 are calming and spring-like. Both designs are crisp and clean. This is because of the large amount of white and the balance of the design rather than the color selection.

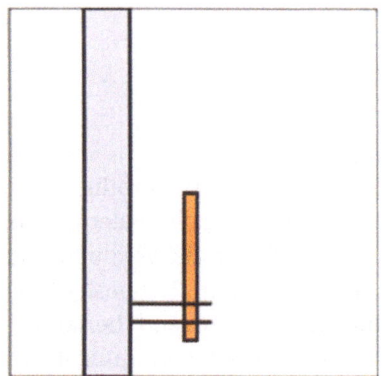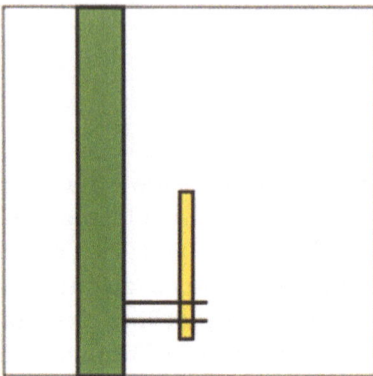

FIGURE 8-10 *Whitespace and atypical colors*

Don't shy away from bold colors if they best tell the client's story. However, readability is an important issue. The colors on the left of Figure 8-11 are popular in strong artist statements from around the world. The exact colors in this swatch are from two disparate sources, a Brazilian brochure and a Picasso painting. The colors on the right show a different viewpoint of the same colors, this time with a significant amount of whitespace. Historically, red was ignored on the Web. In the past year or two, the no-red design standard has lifted. The red and olive in the colors on the right of Figure 8-11 communicate strength. Looking at the colors from both perspectives helps you determine how to approach their use and maintain site readability.

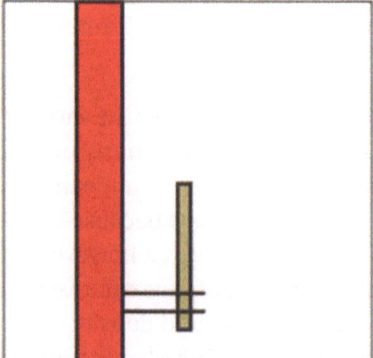

FIGURE 8-11 *Bold colors and readability*

The color design on the left of Figure 8-12 is simple and interesting. At first, your initial color scheme may not appear to be a good candidate for a Web site. If that's the case, bring in whitespace and shapes. As you work with the shapes that the navigation and content demand, keep as much of your original intent as possible. The color design on the right of Figure 8-12 is the start of an icon or shape that may work in a screen layout. Don't simply take your colors and create a traditional top and left bar!

FIGURE 8-12 *Initial idea transitioning toward screen design*

Trying different shapes with color helps to determine what may not work. The design on the left of Figure 8-13 recalls the image of a bull's eye. White background, black text, and icons with the three colors shown or accents with the dark red hue would create a crisp, clean site. The design on the right of Figure 8-13 emerged from an interesting Harrods' advertisement and could provide the basis for a sophisticated color scheme.

FIGURE 8-13 *Crisp, clean designs with black, a light color, and one accent color*

Conservative shapes can take on an interesting flair with subtly contrasting colors. The designs in Figure 8-14 have the same white and blue square. Complementary background colors alter their appearance. You could use these two figures together on a product site where the concept remains consistent but different products display on slightly different pages. Changing colors on a page for a fresh look takes little time when the basic design and content area remain the same and the work involved is graphic or CSS edits.

FIGURE 8-14 *Changing backgrounds with the same foregrounds*

Use shape and line to test colors. Comparing the same color scheme in different compositions allows you to see how it interacts with white and black, its effectiveness at different levels of coverage, and how the hues work together. The design on the left of Figure 8-15 offers the main color palette for a bold site. The design on the right of Figure 8-15 looks at the same colors in lines with the addition of black, white, and yellow.

FIGURE 8-15 *Shapes and lines with a possible color palette*

Colors considered conservative or old-fashioned can make for interesting Web sites. A great detective novel looks more legitimate with a sleuth-like figure and cloak-and-dagger colors. Sometimes clients have existing products in these colors that you want to incorporate; sometimes you want to develop a "retro" look to your site. Consider creating a site based on the colors no one else is using. Figure 8-16 utilizes graphic design colors from an earlier era that could be unique and intriguing today.

FIGURE 8-16 *New colors from the past*

Color combinations you might not initially choose may be the best way to draw users to the client. The designs of Figure 8-17 may not make the cover of a design magazine, but then again, with the right shape and design, they could achieve the desired result. Try an open approach with clients having offbeat sensibilities. A "favorite color" may make you cringe, but think of how you can apply it in places, find a value you can live with, and tell a unique story for the client.

FIGURE 8-17 *Colors with potential?*

Target audience expectations change with colors. The colors in Figure 8-18 came from two award-winning children books. The colors on the left were used to tell the story of a strawberry, and the colors on the right represented an abstract scene with a dog and a cat.

FIGURE 8-18 *Children storybook colors*

Initial color selection of primary and complementary colors along with color ideas from client materials and artwork combine to play a large role in selecting a color palette. The limits of hexadecimal colors can be frustrating, however. For example, you could create a stunning design with black, white, and interesting shades of golds or neutrals. Unfortunately, these colors are rich and sophisticated in print but impossible on the Web. Flexibility in color selection and the limitations of Web-safe colors are issues in Web design in much the same way that tool and code issues are in developing Web applications.

Working with Hexadecimal Color

Much has been written about hexadecimal and Web-safe color. Although many designers believe the need for Web-safe color is significantly lower than it was a few years ago, some tests show that slight to moderate distortion continues between browsers and platforms. Your best bet is to stick with Web-safe color. If your client has a logo or special request, try the main color and test it on browser versions and platforms. Although most browsers support a wide variety of colors, the one or two versions that don't display significantly different results.

Figure 8-19 shows the Web-safe color chart. This color chart was created with SVG. Using screen and printed versions of the color chart can save a lot of time. Consider marking this page for later reference or printing the SVG.

Hexadecimal Color Chart

#FFFFFF	#FFFFCC	#FFFF99	#FFFF66	#FFFF33	#FFFF00
#FFCCFF	#FFCCCC	#FFCC99	#FFCC66	#FFCC33	#FFCC00
#FF99FF	#FF99CC	#FF9999	#FF9966	#FF9933	#FF9900
#FF66FF	#FF66CC	#FF6699	#FF6666	#FF6633	#FF6600
#FF33FF	#FF33CC	#FF3399	#FF3366	#FF3333	#FF3300
#FF00FF	#FF00CC	#FF0099	#FF0066	#FF0033	#FF0000
#CCFFFF	#CCFFCC	#CCFF99	#CCFF66	#CCFF33	#CCFF00
#CCCCFF	#CCCCCC	#CCCC99	#CCCC66	#CCCC33	#CCCC00
#CC99FF	#CC99CC	#CC9999	#CC9966	#CC9933	#CC9900

FIGURE 8-19 *Hexidecimal Web-safe color chart*   *(continues)*

FIGURE 8-19 *Hexidecimal Web-safe color chart*   *(continues)*

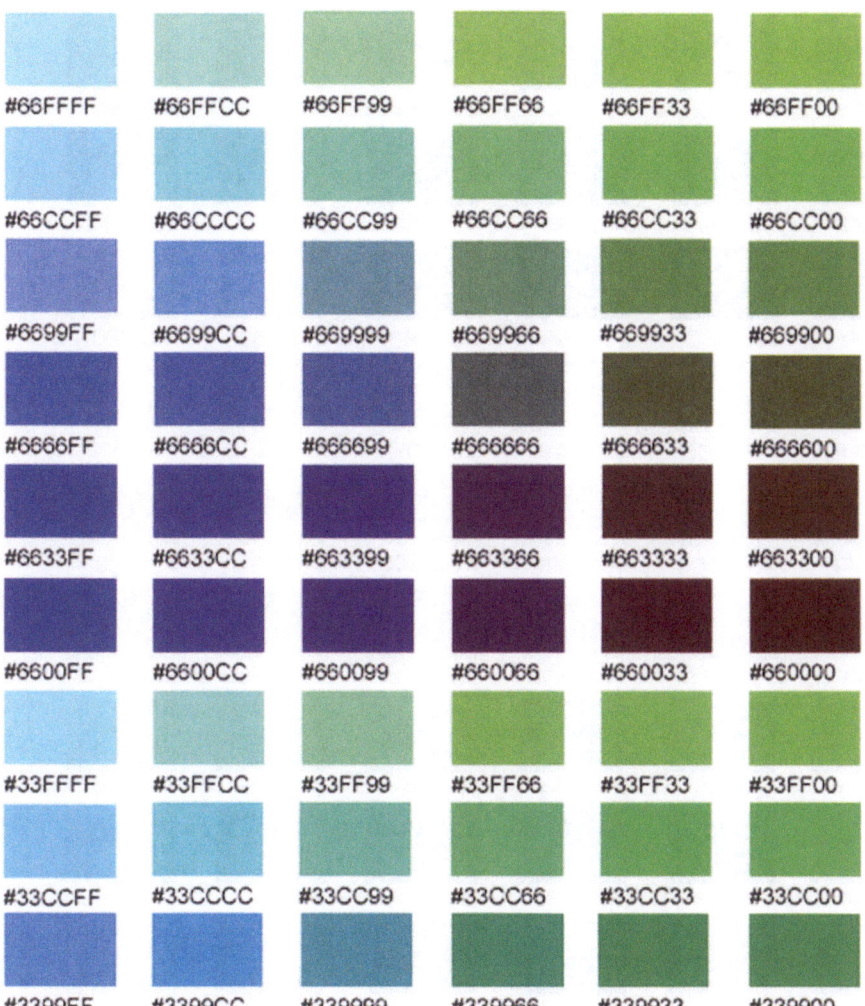

Hexidecimal Web-safe color chart   *(continues)*

FIGURE 8-19 *Hexidecimal Web-safe color chart (continued)*

Listing 8-3 shows the SVG that generates the hexadecimal color chart.

LISTING 8-3 *Hexidecimal Web-Safe Color Chart*

```
<svg  onload='dessin(evt)'>
<script><![CDATA[
 function dessin(evt)
{
  var x=-1, y=0;
  var svgdoc,root,color;
  var hexarray= new Array(256);
  hexarray[0]="00";
  for( index=1; index<256; index++) {
    hexarray[index]=getHex(index);
  }
  svgdoc=evt.getTarget().getOwnerDocument();
  root=evt.getTarget();
 for (red=255;red>=0;red=red-51)
 {
   for (green=255;green>=0;green=green-51)
   {
     for (blue=255;blue>=0;blue=blue-51)
     {
      if(x==5) {
        x=-1;
        y++;
      }
      x++;
    hexcode = "#" + hexarray[red] + hexarray[green] +
hexarray[blue];
   node=svgdoc.createElement('rect');
   node.setAttribute('x',220+x*80);node.setAttribute('y',30+y*60);

node.setAttribute('width','60');node.setAttribute('height','40');
   node.setAttribute('style','fill:'+ hexcode);
   root.appendChild(node);

   node=svgdoc.createElement('rect');
   node.setAttribute('x',220+x*80);node.setAttribute('y',60+y*30);
```

```
node.setAttribute('width','60');node.setAttribute('height','40');
  node.setAttribute('style','fill:none');
  root.appendChild(node);
  nodet=svgdoc.createElement('text');
  nodet.setAttribute('x',220+x*80);
  nodet.setAttribute('y',85+y*60);
  nodet.setAttribute('style','font-size:12');
  texte=svgdoc.createTextNode(hexcode);
  nodet.appendChild(texte);
  root.appendChild(nodet);

 }//blue
}//green
}//red
}//function
function getHex(num){
   hexStr = "0123456789ABCDEF";
   hex="";
   if (num>=16) {
      hex = hexStr.substr(parseInt(num/16),1);
      num = num%16;
   }
   hex += hexStr.substr(num,1);
   if (hex=="0") her="00";
   return hex;
}
]]></script>
<text x='220' y='20' style='font-size:20'>Hexadecimal Color Chart</text>
</svg>
```

Having a printed and a screen version of the Web-safe color chart allows you to compare client printed materials to printed Web-safe colors for a primary match and to the screen for a secondary match. Keep both print and screen swatches of color large enough that you don't need to squint and guess. In addition, invest in a Web color wheel (available online and in art stores). A Web color wheel is a paper product with separate movable layers designed to show hue values and complementary colors. The combination of a printed Web-safe color chart, a screen view of the same, and a Web color wheel saves an enormous amount of time and helps you make reliable color decisions with confidence.

Coloring Images

Photographs of landmarks, people, and products often help identify the location and purpose of the client's organization. If a client wants to show the actual color of the image, you must manage its file size. If you want to subtly incorporate the image as a part of your design, consider using an application such as Adobe Photoshop to tint or duotone (a grayscale image with one color added) the images for placement as quiet points of interest that blend into the design. Figure 8-20 shows the same bicycle scene muted with different colors. The original has nice coloring, but if the yellow clashes with the site design or draws focus from the content, muting the colors with tint or converting to duotone may provide the solution by allowing the graphic to blend into the design and provide a subliminal communication tool.

FIGURE 8-20 *Color blended with images*

Clients sometimes want small graphics of landmarks that communicate the location of the company without the varied colors of the actual landmark photographs. Not all of the graphics would be recognizable by every user, but the collection would suggest the company is located in Moscow, Paris, San Francisco, Silicon Valley, Tokyo, London, and so on. Make sure you don't overdo the images to the point of looking like a tourism Web site. This approach works best when it's subtle; the central focus of the user remains on content and purpose. Figure 8-21 depicts the focal point of a historic landmark, a hallway from the California Mission at San Juan Bautista, in different hues.

FIGURE 8-21 *Color blends and landmarks*

Updating a Site with Color and Content

Keeping a site looking fresh by changing the color of the graphics is easy and effective. Sometimes a client has a successful, existing site design but wants something a little different. A color change combined with updated content is one way to draw user attention without the time and expense of a major site rebuild. The design on the top of Figure 8-22 shows a graphic from Chapter 3, and the design on the bottom shows the same image with a different color scheme. The effect is substantial without redesign time and expense.

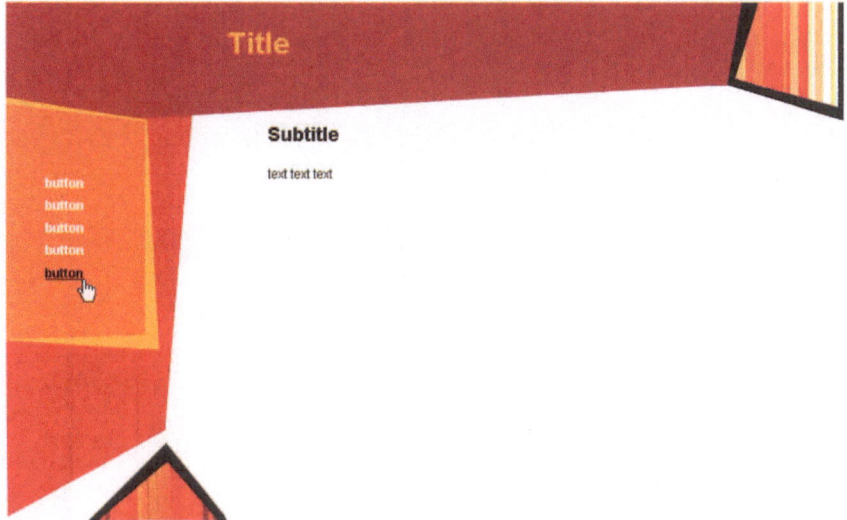

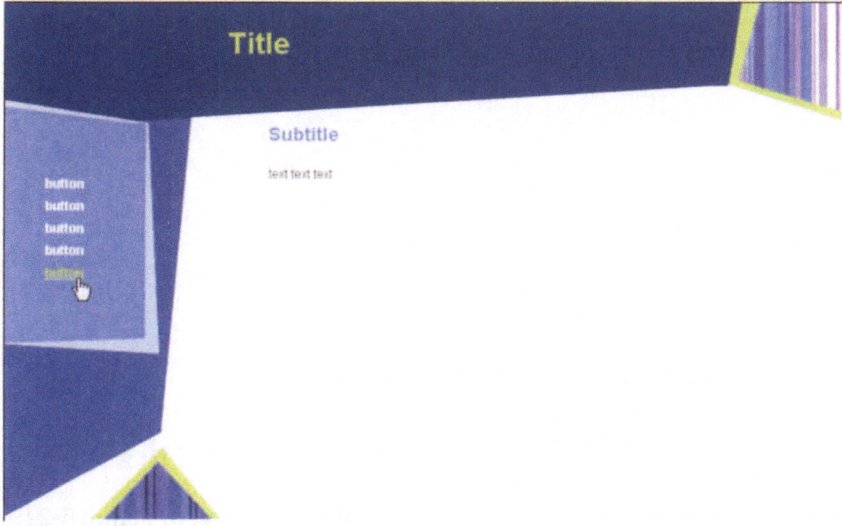

FIGURE 8-22 *Original open-source portal entry page (top) and with a new color palette (bottom)*

Additional design prototypes developed for the open-source portal allow teachers/professors to apply a different look to a course. Varying the color and shape changes the mood, as shown in Figure 8-23.

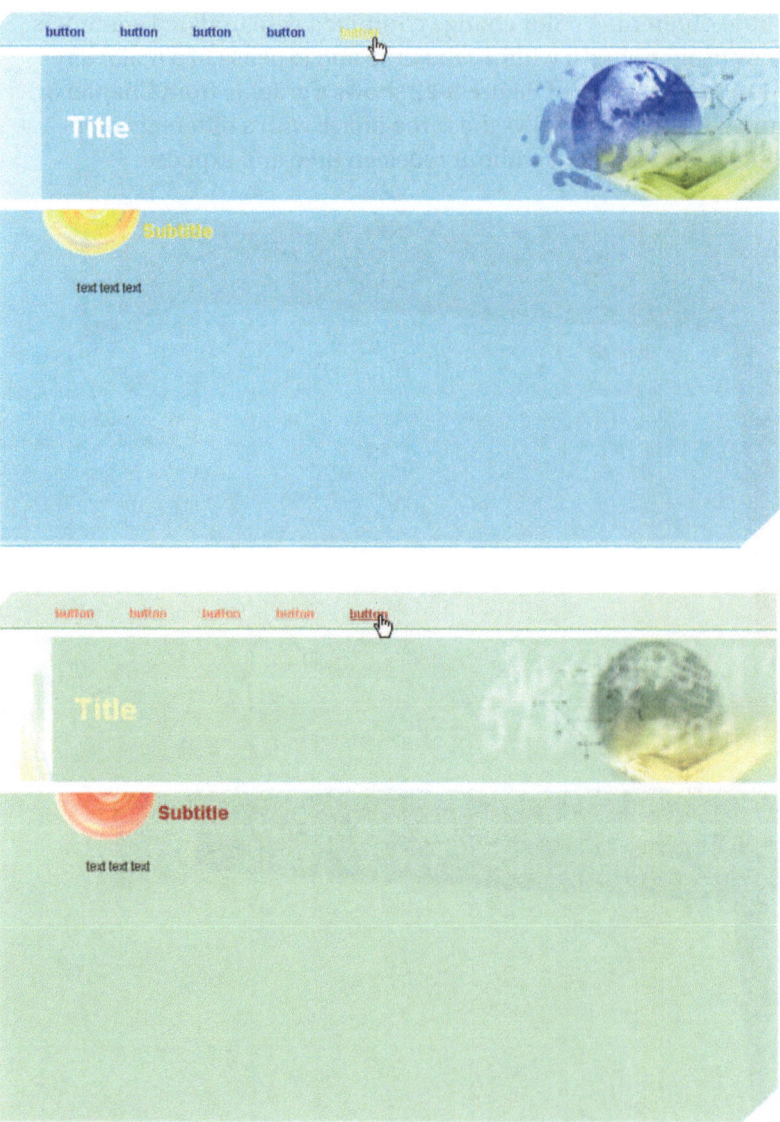

FIGURE 8-23 *Different colors for the second open-source prototype*

The colors selected for Figures 8-23 combine with rectangular shapes to convey a more solid and traditional layout.

Color works well with designs that contain significant space. In Figure 8-24, the color enhances the graphics while maintaining the openness of the design.

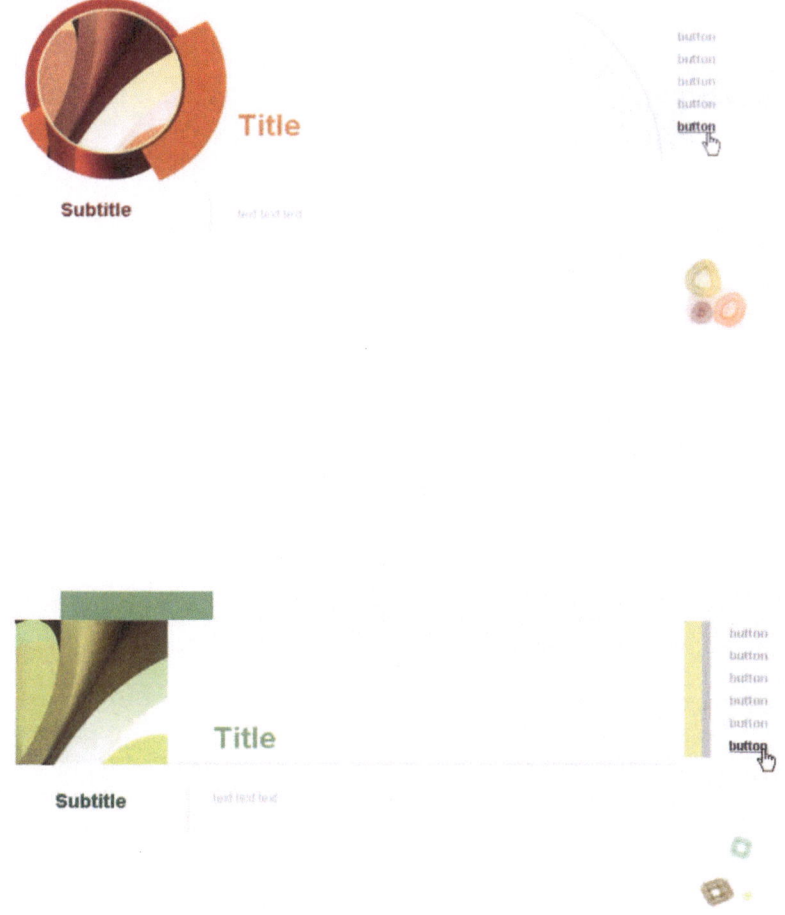

FIGURE 8-24 *Open-source portal prototypes, with significant space*

Unusual combinations of color can suggest unique courses, as shown in Figure 8-25.

FIGURE 8-25 *Open-source portal prototypes, with significant space*

The open-source portal layouts demonstrate the simple shapes, colors, and graphics you can create with SVG. Color, shape, line, and space interact to communicate to the user. Remember, whether the site is simple or complex, the best sites always support the users' quest for information, excitement, or adventure.

Color Axioms

It takes time to become proficient at choosing color. However, it's possible to understand and work with color by taking into account a few basic color principles:

Color adds passion, mood, and familiarity to design; it doesn't fix a mediocre layout.

Go back to the language that clients and users gave you in the early user analysis phase of the project. Write down keywords and other data that help you describe the product.

Basic color terms important to working with color include hue, saturation, and value. Hue is the name of the color: red, yellow, orange, green, blue, or violet. Saturation is the degree of purity of a color (color without white, black, or gray). High intensity, bright quality colors are more saturated. Muted, dull colors are less saturated. Value is the relative lightness or darkness of a sample.

Your first decisions with color are based on your understanding of the world. These initial ideas don't need to be based on color theory; they come from your traditions, experience, and history. Determine one or two separate possible colors. Play with their values. Keep it simple. After you determine the hues and possible values to tell the client's story, begin incorporating text and graphics. Test the color and design with content.

Add color only if it adds value to the design. Begin by selecting a complementary hue from the color wheel. Place color sparingly on your layout. Add additional colors only if needed to communicate the intent of the design.

Consider tinting photographs to match the hues in your site as one approach to adding texture to a site.

Consider color and content updates for clients who want something fresh without the time and expense of a site redesign.

The next chapter incorporates the concepts of Chapter 7 and Chapter 8 (content, typography, and color) into a commercial project.

Project 3:
Building a Webzine

Simplicity is at the core of things wabi-sabi. Nothingness, of course, is the ultimate simplicity. But before and after nothingness, simplicity is not so simple.

—Leonard Koren, artist[1]

In her webzine, `SItalk.info`, Jean McIntosh presents innovative ideas on digital culture. Jean wanted to do something different and stay away from the common blue and red colors of journalistic publications. She thought it would be challenging to work with green, a color that symbolizes things fresh and new and a color with which Web designers aren't clamoring to work. She wanted her green webzine to be eye-catching and nontraditional. Thus, SItalk uses an adventurous palette, red and green, and looks elegant, simple, fresh, and attractive. SItalk communicates understated elegance and simplicity.

In this chapter, you'll help Jean redesign her green webzine using Scalable Vector Graphics (SVG) and Extensible Markup Language (XML). The chapter starts by looking at a mini-requirements document based on the Volere Requirements Specification Template, and then the chapter presents the underlying code.

Creating a Mini-Requirements Specification for the Webzine

Just like in Chapters 3 and 6, you first must create a mini-requirements specification before you can dive into any project. The following sections cover the webzine's purpose and its clients and users.

---

1. Wabi-Sabi: for Artists, Designers, Poets & Philosophers (Stone Bridge Press, 1994)

The Purpose of the Product

The purpose of the product is as follows:

The user problem or background to the project effort: SItalk is an online magazine, a webzine that combines graphics and text to explore stories about life in Silicon Valley. The client wants a site that looks different from typical print magazines and newspapers adapted for the Web. The tone is artistic, personal, and entertaining, and the site explores the positive and negative aspects of living in Silicon Valley. The client designed an earlier version of the site and a Hypertext Markup Language (HTML) version of the current site.

The client, Jean McIntosh, is a Canadian who lives and works in Silicon Valley. She appreciates the positive aspects of life in the valley and sees its underbelly as well. As a result of her family's journalism background and her own art education, Jean loves to tell stories that mesh narrative, visual communication, and all aspects of the Silicon Valley environment.

The goal of the project: The goal of the webzine is to cultivate relationships with its visitors. The client and the webzine's users aren't interested in a basic information site. The client wants to create an online community of artists, writers, and designers who contribute, comment, and critique the site and its content. Jean wants readers to interact online and talk offline about ideas presented on SItalk.

Jean McIntosh created the previous version of the site using Macromedia Dreamweaver. There have been some browser problems involving Cascading Style Sheets (CSS) and stability. Additionally, the client wants an SVG/XML site that's smaller and more consistent than the current version.

Client, Customer, and Other Stakeholders

The clients, customers, and other stakeholders are as follows:

The client (the people paying for the development and the owners of the delivered system): The client is Jean McIntosh, a freelance print and Web designer and a full-time instructor at a California community college. Jean grew up in a family that owned a community newspaper in Canada and worked at the paper for most of her early life. Her love of text, news, and the community aspect of the paper led Jean to study the combination of traditional printmaking and electronic art. This background has led her to seek a better, more contemporary way to deliver text and graphics. Jean is most interested in telling stories, and she views good code with clean style as the ultimate technology goal.

The customer (the people who will buy the product from the client):
The customer is interested in exploring, learning, and being exposed to thoughts/ideas on the site beyond what one might find in a traditional newspaper or magazine. Customers expect SItalk to be somewhat risky and to offer visual images that intrigue and inform. Customers, for the most part, are technically savvy; Jean wants the code of the site to be as current as its content.

 NOTE Jean defines *customers* as the community of users interested in exchanging ideas about art, technology, culture, creativity, and other aspects of living in Silicon Valley. Customers will participate and contribute; the site offers no fee-based products.

Examining the Code

The SItalk splash page, shown in Figure 9-1, utilizes different values of the same color and uses text for both information and design accents.

The SVG in Listing 9-1 outputs the Figure 9-1 SItalk splash page.

FIGURE 9-1 *The* SItalk.info *index page*

LISTING 9-1 *SItalk Splash Page SVG*

```xml
<?xml version='1.0'?>
<svg>
<rect x="0" y="0" width="1024" height="900"
style="fill:#666633;" />
<a xlink:href="sitalk.xml"><image xlink:href="cover_02.gif"
x="0" y="20" width="490" height="392" /></a>
<rect x="0" y="20" width="277" height="60"
style="fill:rgb(153,0,0)" />
<a xlink:href="sitalk.xml"><text x="168" y="75"
style="word-spacing:2; font-family:courier, mono, courier new;
font-size:10pt; fill:rgb(231,222,212);">SItalk.info</text></a>
<text x="37" y="92" style="word-spacing:2;
font-family:courier, mono, courier new;
font-size:10pt; fill:rgb(0,0,0);">
digital culture magazine</text>
<text x="280" y="92" style="word-spacing:2;
font-family:courier, mono, courier new; font-size:10pt;
fill:rgb(231,222,212);"> Volume 3 No 1</text>
<text x="150" y="440" style="word-spacing:2;
font-family:courier, mono, courier new; font-size:10pt;
fill:white;">culture at your fingertips and just out of the
door...</text>
<text x="120" y="470" style="word-spacing:1pt;
font-family:courier, mono, courier new; font-size:8pt;
stroke:#999933;">technology art living in SI kulture</text>
<g style="word-spacing:-2pt;font-family:courier, mono,
courier new;;font-size:7pt;stroke:#999933;">
<text x="380" y="470">technology art living in SI
kulture</text>
<text x="95" y="474">technology art living in SI
kulture</text>
<text x="305" y="474">technology art living in SI
kulture</text>
<text x="545" y="474">technology art living in SI
kulture</text>
<text x="130" y="478">art living in SI kulture</text>
<text x="300" y="478">technology art living in SI
kulture</text>
<text x="330" y="482">kulturetechnology art living in SI
kulture</text>
</g></svg>
```

Creating the Navigation Page

The SVG for the splash page links to an XML document, which is the SItalk navigation page. The navigation page, shown in Figure 9-2, offers short blocks of text next to simple navigational icons and contains a generous use of space. The result is a distinctive site that offers effortless reading and navigation. Jean photographs street text (placards, images, murals, and posters) and explores communicating street messages (notices, flyers, graffiti, and bulletins) within the site's color palette using a clean approach to content presentation. As a result, users see site articles introduced with clean navigation.

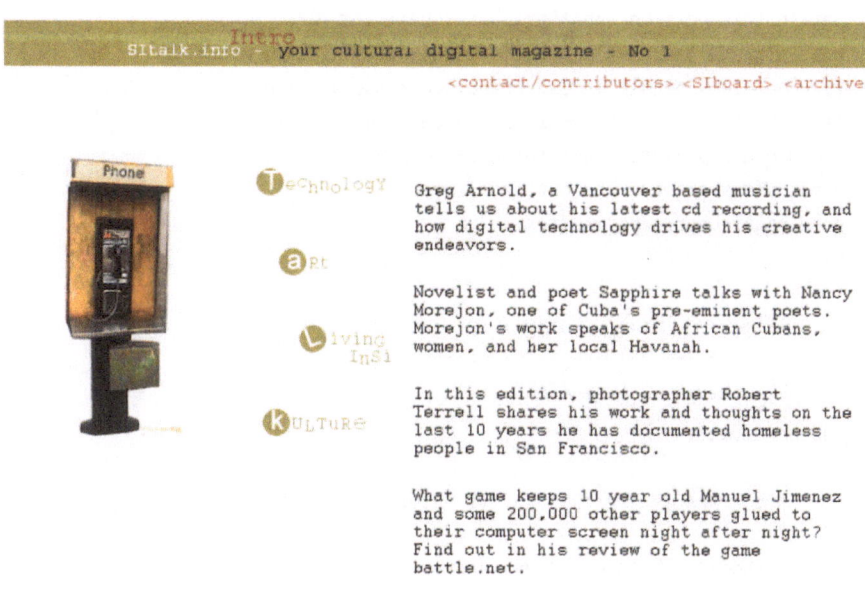

FIGURE 9-2 *SItalk navigation page with content*

Listing 9-2 shows the XML document for the site's navigation page. This navigation page transforms to Extensible HTML (XHTML) using XSL Transformations (XSLT) for broader version support. The XHTML links to two SVG images. One additional image, a GIF file, is embedded in the second SVG image.

LISTING 9-2 *SItalk Navigation Page XML*

```xml
<?xml version="1.0"?>
<?xml-stylesheet type="text/xsl" href="sitalk.xsl"?>
<sitalk>
<item><par>Greg Arnold, a Vancouver based musician tells us
about his latest cd recording, and how digital technology
drives his creative endeavors.</par></item>
<item><par>Novelist and poet Sapphire talks with Nancy
Morejon, one of Cuba's pre-eminent poets. Morejon's work
speaks of African Cubans, women, and her local Havanah.
</par></item>
<item><par>In this edition, photographer Robert Terrell
shares his work and thoughts on the last 10 years he spent
documenting homeless people in San Francisco.</par></item>
<item><par>What game keeps 10 year old Manuel Jimenez and
some 200,000 other players glued to their computer
screen night after night? Find out in his review
of the game battle.net.</par></item>
</sitalk>
```

Listing 9-3 shows the XSLT page.

LISTING 9-3 *SItalk Navigation Page XSLT*

```xml
<?xml version='1.0'?>
<xsl:stylesheet
xmlns:xsl="http://www.w3.org/1999/XSL/Transform"
version="1.0">
<xsl:output method="xml" indent="yes" doctype-
system="http://www.w3.org/TR/xhtml1/DTD/xhtml1-strict.dtd"
doctype-public="-//W3C//DTD XHTML 1.0 strict//EN" />
<xsl:template match="/">
<html xmlns="http://www.w3.org/1999/xhtml" xml:lang="en"
lang="en">
<head>
<title>SItalk</title>
<link rel="stylesheet" type="text/css" href="sitalkNav.css" />
</head>
<body>
<p class="svg1"><embed src="sitalk.svg" type="image/svg+xml"
width="800" height="120" /></p>
<p class="svg2"><embed src="sitalkA.svg" type="image/svg+xml"
width="360" height="330" /></p>
```

```
<table class="text1" border="0" width="400">
<xsl:for-each select="sitalk/item">
<tr><td ><br />
<p class="text"><xsl:value-of select="par" /></p>
</td></tr>
</xsl:for-each>
</table>
</body>
</html>
</xsl:template>
</xsl:stylesheet>
```

Listing 9-4 shows the CSS file for the SItalk navigation page.

LISTING 9-4 *SItalk Navigation Page CSS*

```
.svg1 {position:absolute; top:0 px; left:0;}
.svg2 {position:absolute; top:120 px; left:0;}
.text1 {position:absolute; left:360px;
top:120px; right:170px;}
.text {font:13px courier, mono, courier new; color:#000000;}
```

Doubling selectors and using a hierarchical approach to CSS properties can organize the CSS file more compactly. However, these examples keep the rules separate so the client can easily edit and maintain the site.

As mentioned, the navigation page consists of two SVG images embedded in the XSLT that contain the contents of the page. The first image, Figure 9-3, creates the top bar and the page's secondary navigation links.

FIGURE 9-3 *Navigation page's top bar*

Listing 9-5 generates the top bar shown in Figure 9-3.

LISTING 9-5 *SItalk Navigation Page Top Bar SVG*

```
<?xml version='1.0'?>
<svg width="800" height="120">
<rect x="12" y="12" width="760" height="40"
style="fill:rgb(145,129,43);" />
```

```
<text x="120" y="42" style="word-spacing:2;
font-family:courier, mono, courier new; font-size:9pt;
fill:white;">SItalk.info    -</text>
<text x="252" y="42" style="word-spacing:2;
font-family:courier, mono, courier new; font-size:9pt;
fill:black;">your cultural digital magazine - No 1 </text>
<a xlink:href="contact.xml"><text x="401" y="70"
style="word-spacing:2; font-family:courier, mono, courier new;
font-size:9pt;
fill:rgb(153,0,0);">&lt;contact/contributors&gt;</text></a>
<a xlink:href="siboard.xml"><text x="606" y="70"
style="word-spacing:2; font-family:courier, mono, courier new;
font-size:9pt; fill:rgb(153,0,0);">&lt;SIboard&gt;</text></a>
<a xlink:href="archive.xml"><text x="697" y="70"
style="word-spacing:2; font-family:courier, mono, courier new;
font-size:9pt; fill:rgb(153,0,0);">&lt;archive&gt;</text></a>
<g id="txline" style="font-family:courier, mono, courier new;
font-size:4pt; stroke:#999933;">
<text x="12" y="28">iving tuzla kueculIkulture artin
SIkultureturehap</text>
<text x="12" y="29">eartkulturkung sd woodstockulture living
tuzla </text>
<text x="120" y="31">iving tuzla kueculIkujkwlture artin
SIkultureturehap eartkultjhurekung sd iving tuzla
kueculIkulture artin SIkultureturehapwoodwerty stocultckulture
living tuzla </text>
<text x="120" y="32">iving twtguzla kueculIkulgfgture artin
SIkultureroleturehdghhgjhgfpeartkulturekung sd iving tuzla
kueculIkulture artin SIkultureturehapwoodstockulture living
tuzla </text>
</g>
<text x="207" y="32" style="word-spacing:1;
font-family:courier, mono, courier new; font-size:12pt;
fill:rgb(149,10,1);">Intro</text>
</svg>
```

The navigation page's left bar, shown in Figure 9-4, links to the telephone booth GIF file and generates the category links.

FIGURE 9-4 *Navigation page's left bar*

Listing 9-6 generates the left bar shown in Figure 9-4.

LISTING 9-6 *Sltalk Navigation Page Left Bar SVG*

```
<?xml version='1.0'?>
<svg width="360" height="330">
<image xlink:href="home_03.gif" x="0" y="0" width="160"
height="260" />
<circle cx="236" cy="26" r="12"
style="fill:rgb(145,129,43);" />
<circle cx="256" cy="97" r="12"
style="fill:rgb(145,129,43);" />
<circle cx="274" cy="165" r="12"
style="fill:rgb(145,129,43);" />
<circle cx="242" cy="239" r="12"
style="fill:rgb(145,129,43);" />
<a xlink:href="kulture.xml"><text x="237" y="245"
style="font-family:arial, helvetica, sans-serif;
font-size:14pt; fill:white;">k</text>
<text x="255" y="245" style="font-family:courier,
mono, courier new; font-size:10pt; letter-spacing:1;
fill:rgb(145,129,43);">U<tspan y="247">L</tspan>
<tspan y="245">TuR</tspan><tspan
font-size="13pt">e</tspan></text></a>

<a xlink:href="living.xml"><text x="270" y="173"
style="font-family:arial, helvetica, sans-serif;
font-size:14pt; fill:white;"
transform="rotate(-20,270,173)">L</text>
```

```
<text x="288" y="170" style="font-family:courier, mono,
courier new; font-size:10pt; fill:rgb(145,129,43);">ivin
<tspan y="172">G</tspan><tspan x="305" y="185">I</tspan>
<tspan y="187">n</tspan><tspan y="185">Si</tspan></text></a>

<a xlink:href="technology.xml"><text x="230" y="33"
style="font-family:arial, helvetica, sans-serif;
font-size:14pt; fill:white;">T</text>
<text x="249" y="33" style="font-family:courier, mono,
courier new; font-size:10pt; fill:rgb(145,129,43)">e
<tspan y="31" >c</tspan><tspan y="36" >h</tspan>
<tspan y="33" >n</tspan><tspan y="36">o</tspan>
<tspan y="33">log</tspan><tspan y="33" >Y</tspan></text></a>

<a xlink:href="art.xml"><text x="251" y="103"
style="font-family:arial, helvetica, sans-serif;
font-size:14pt; fill:white;" >a</text>
<text x="270" y="103" style="font-family:courier,
mono, courier new; font-size:10pt;
fill:rgb(145,129,43);" >Rt</text></a>
</svg>
```

Creating the Content Pages

The content category pages of Technology, Art, Living, and Kulture include an SVG header graphic, links, and page content, as shown in the Living page (see Figure 9-5). Content layout can vary to emphasize text or graphics.

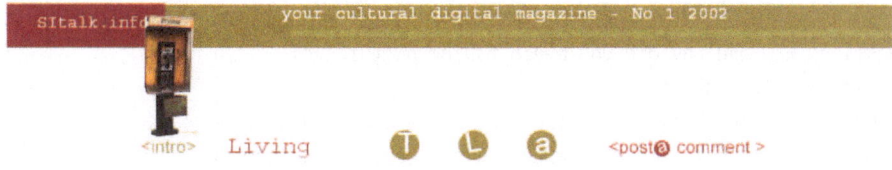

TEN YEARS PHOTOGRAPHING SAN FRANCISCO'S HOMELESS
An Interview with Robert L. Terrell by Jean McIntosh

jm:Describe your photographs.

rt: I photograph those who reside at the bottom of society. Thus,
I try to document the plight of the poor, the homeless, the
addicted, the hopeless, and those whose minds and bodies no longer
function in a normal manner. Frantz Fanon referred to such people
as "the Wretched of the Earth." Those I photograph aren't
wretched, but the conditions in which they subsist are. I have
been taking such photographs in San Francisco for the past 10
years.

FIGURE 9-5 *Header graphic and content for the Living category*

Listing 9-7 shows the content page's XML file.

LISTING 9-7 *SItalk Content Page XML*

```
<?xml version="1.0"?>
<?xml-stylesheet type="text/xsl" href="living.xsl"?>
<document>
<title>TEN YEARS PHOTOGRAPHING SAN FRANCISCO'S
HOMELESS</title>
<author>An Interview with Robert L. Terrell
by Jean
McIntosh</author>
<item>
<question>Describe your photographs.</question>
<answer><p>I photograph those who reside at the bottom of
society. Thus, I try to document the plight of the poor, the
homeless, the addicted, the hopeless, and those whose minds
and bodies no longer function in a normal manner. Frantz Fanon
referred to such people as "the Wretched of the Earth." Those
I photograph aren't wretched, but the conditions in which they
subsist are. I have been taking such photographs in
San Francisco for the past 10 years.</p></answer>
</item>
```

```
<item>
<question> How and why did you begin taking pictures of
homeless people?</question>
<answer><p>Looking back, I realize that I was always attracted
to this task. It began in 1968 when I was a general assignment
reporter for the New York Post covering the Northeast
contingent of "The Poor People's Campaign." The last one led
by Martin Luther King, Jr. before he was assassinated. Each
day along the route between New York City and Washington,
D.C., I filed stories about the ragtag band of drifters and
dreamers caught in the drama of the campaign.</p>
<p>After the first few days, I began to photograph what I was
witnessing. Some of my photos were printed in the New York
Post, and from that point I began to critically address public
poverty from the perspective of a journalist/photographer. I
got the idea of shooting a single subject over an extended
period during 1980-1981 while living in Beijing, where I was
an Editor/Consultant for the Beijing Review.</p>
<p>Beijing is an excellent city for walkers and bicyclists,and
I spent as much time as I possibly could doing each. Most
important, I carried a camera with me everywhere I went,
photographing street scenes as they unfolded before me. I was
primarily interested in documenting the passing of the last
vestiges of traditional urban life in Beijing. And those who
lived in the most traditional ways were desperately poor.
Given my inexperience, many of the shots I took in Beijing
were poor. But little by little, my photographs began to
capture what I was seeing. Most important, I replicated the
project during 1984-85 in Nairobi, Kenya, a period during
which I was a Fulbright Fellow in the School of Journalism at
the University of Nairobi.</p></answer>
</item>
<!--more content here, taken out to shorten the Listing-->
</document>
```

XSLT transforms the XML to XHTML for universal browser presentation, as shown in Listing 9-8.

LISTING 9-8 *SItalk Content Page XSLT*

```
<?xml version='1.0'?>
<xsl:stylesheet
xmlns:xsl=http://www.w3.org/1999/XSL/Transform version="1.0">
```

```xml
<xsl:output method="xml" indent="yes" doctype-
system="http://www.w3.org/TR/xhtml1/DTD/xhtml1
strict.dtd"
doctype-public="-//W3C//DTD XHTML 1.0 strict//EN" />
<xsl:template match="/">
<html xmlns="http://www.w3.org/1999/xhtml" xml:lang="en"
lang="en">
<head>
<title>SItalk Living</title>
<link rel="stylesheet" type="text/css" href="sitalk.css" />
</head>
<body>
<p class="svg1"><embed src="living.svg"
type="image/svg+xml" width="900" height="200" />
</p>
<table class="text1" border="0" width="600">
<tr>
<td vAlign="top" align="left">
<p><span class="red"><xsl:apply-templates
select="document/title" /></span><span class="text">
<br /><xsl:apply-templates
select="document/author" /></span></p>
</td></tr>
<xsl:for-each select="document/item">
<tr>
<td><br /><br />
<p><span class="green"><br />jm:</span><span
class="text">
<xsl:value-of select="question" /></span></p>
<p><span class="red"><br />rt:</span><span
class="text">
<xsl:for-each select="answer//p">
<span class="text"><xsl:value-of select="." /></span>
<br/><br />
</xsl:for-each></span></p>
</td>
</tr>
</xsl:for-each>
</table>
</body>
</html>
</xsl:template>
</xsl:stylesheet>
```

Listing 9-9 shows the CSS file for all the SItalk pages, except for the navigation page.

LISTING 9-9 *SItalk Site CSS*

```css
.svg1 {position:absolute; top:0 px; left:0;}
.text1 {position:absolute; left:170px; top:250px; right:170px;}
.text {font:13px courier, mono, courier new; color:#000000;}
.green {font:13px courier, mono, courier new;
text-transform:none; color:#666600; text-decoration:none;}
.red {font-weight:normal; font-size:14px; color:#990000;
font-family:courier, mono, courier new;}
.regred {font-weight:normal; font-size:13px;
color:#990000; font-family:courier, mono, courier new;}
```

Listing 9-10 generates the content page shown in Figure 9-5.

LISTING 9-10 *SItalk Content Page SVG*

```xml
<?xml version='1.0'?>
<svg width="800" height="250">
<rect x="10" y="20" width="780" height="38"
style="fill:rgb(145,129,43);" />
<rect x="10" y="19" width="140" height="38"
style="fill:rgb(153,0,0)" />
<image xlink:href="home_03.gif" x="105" y="27"
width="74" height="113" />
<text x="252" y="32" style="word-spacing:2;
font-family:courier, mono, courier new; font-size:9pt;
fill:white;">your cultural digital magazine - No 1 2002</text>
<text x="37" y="40" style="word-spacing:2;
font-family:courier, mono, courier new; font-size:9pt;
fill:rgb(231,222,212);">SItalk.info</text>
<circle cx="479" cy="144" r="13"
style="fill:rgb(145,129,43);" />
<circle cx="419" cy="144" r="13"
style="fill:rgb(145,129,43);" />
<circle cx="359" cy="144" r="13"
style="fill:rgb(145,129,43);" />
<circle cx="585" cy="147" r="7"
style="fill:rgb(153,0,0);" />
<a xlink:href="art.xml"><text x="473" y="151"
style="font-family:arial, helvetica, sans-serif;
font-size:15pt; fill:white;">a</text></a>
```

```
<a xlink:href="living.xml"><text x="413" y="151"
style="font-family:arial, helvetica, sans-serif;
font-size:15pt; fill:white;"
transform="rotate(-10,413,147)">L</text></a>
<a xlink:href="technology.xml"><text x="353" y="151"
style="font-family:arial, helvetica, sans-serif;
font-size:15pt; fill:white;">T</text></a>
<a xlink:href="sitalk.xml"><text x="128" y="151"
style="font-family:arial, helvetica, sans-serif;
font-size:9.5pt; fill:rgb(145,129,43);">&lt;intro&gt;</text></a>
<a xlink:href="living.xml"><text x="205" y="151"
style="font-family:courier, mono, courier new;
font-size:13pt; fill:rgb(153,0,0);">Living</text></a>
<a xlink:href="contact.xml"><text x="538" y="151"
style="font-family:arial, helvetica, sans-serif;
font-size:9.5pt; fill:rgb(153,0,0);">&lt;post</text>
<text x="582" y="151" style="font-family:arial, helvetica,
sans-serif; font-size:9.5pt; fill:white;"
transform="rotate(-15,582,151)">a</text>
<text x="598" y="151" style="font-family:arial, helvetica,
sans-serif; font-size:9.5pt; fill:rgb(153,0,0);">
comment &gt;</text>
</a>
<g id="txline" style="font-family:courier, mono, courier new;
font-size:4pt; stroke:#999933;">
<text x="260" y="46">technology art SI kulture
kulturetechnology art living tuzla kulture art living in SI
kulture artin SI kultureivinginSIkulturehap</text>
<text x="262" y="47">artliving
kulturetechnologyartlivinginSIsarajevokultureartkultureartkult
ureartlivinginSIkulturehappeningwoodstockulture living tuzla
</text>
</g>
</svg>
```

SVG can fine-tune design with detailed accents. For example, the Figure 9-6 graphic is made with SVG text. The graphic is enlarged for a clear presentation of text that appears to the user as a blurred, eraser-like line.

FIGURE 9-6 *Close-up example of text as a blurred line, implemented on the top bar and as a shadow on the telephone stand*

Listing 9-11 generates the blurred line.

LISTING 9-11 *SItalk Text Blurred SVG*

```
<g id="txline" style="font-family:courier, mono, courier new;
font-size:4pt; stroke:#999933;">
<text x="260" y="46">technology art SI kulture
kulturetechnology art living tuzla kulture art living in SI
kulture artin SI kultureivinginSIkulturehap</text>
<text x="262" y="47">artliving
kulturetechnologyartlivinginSIsarajevokultureartkultureartkult
ureartlivinginSIkulturehappeningwoodstockulture living tuzla
</text>
</g>
```

Because SItalk's design is optimal for large screen resolutions and because users may want to print articles, we decided to develop Portable Document Format (PDF) documents using Apache FOP. Starting with an XML document that contains the content of the article, we developed an Extensible Stylesheet Language: Formatting Objects (XSL-FO) document that Apache FOP transformed to PDF. Because the XML documents are small, we didn't use XSLT to transform the XML to XSL-FO. Instead, we wrote it directly in the same time it would take to write the XSLT.

Figure 9-7 shows the resulting PDF file.

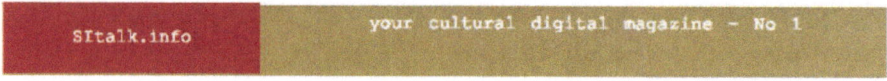

THE STRATEGY OF DISTRACTION - STARCRAFT THE GAME

An interview with Manuel Jimenez By Jean McIntosh

The MANUEL is my neighbor, and his mom is my colleague. Last summer the three of us were part of a group of educators who traveled to Slovenia for a month. It's been a while since I've been in the company of a ten-year old, and I learned a lot. For example, I learned that 10 year olds learn things fast and can be very good travelers. Being a seasoned traveler myself, I was quite impressed with how he ordered meals in restaurants, and got along with Slovenian kids in a game of scrub or soccer. I also learned that Manuel's favorite game is StarCraft. StarCraft caught my attention because it's a computer game that can be played on line with hundreds of thousands of other players. The following is my interview with Manuel about his favorite computer game.

s So Manuel, what's the name of the computer game I always see you playing?
mn StarCraft and StarCraft Brood War. StarCraft is the game that you learn when you are a beginner. StarCraft Brood War is more difficult. The game has three races: the Terren (humans), Zerg (aliens created by the xel'naga temple) and the protoss, my favorite high tech guys, who are also created by

FIGURE 9-7 *SItalk interview converted to PDF*

Listing 9-12 generates the PDF file.

LISTING 9-12 *SItalk XSLF Transformed to PDF with Apache FOP*

```
<?xml version="1.0" encoding="utf-8"?>
<fo:root xmlns:fo="http://www.w3.org/1999/XSL/Format">
<fo:layout-master-set>
<fo:simple-page-master master-name="first"
page-height="29.7cm" page-width="21cm" margin-top="1cm"
margin-bottom="2cm" margin-left="2.5cm" margin-right="2.5cm">
<fo:region-body margin-top="3cm" margin-bottom="1.5cm" />
<fo:region-before extent="3cm" />
<fo:region-after extent="1.5cm" />
</fo:simple-page-master>
<fo:simple-page-master master-name="rest" page-height="29.7cm"
page-width="21cm" margin-top="1cm" margin-bottom="2cm"
margin-left="2.5cm" margin-right="2.5cm">
<fo:region-body margin-top="2.5cm" margin-bottom="1.5cm" />
<fo:region-before extent="3cm" />
<fo:region-after extent="1.5cm" />
</fo:simple-page-master>
<fo:page-sequence-master master-name="siArt" >
<fo:repeatable-page-master-alternatives>
<fo:conditional-page-master-reference master-reference="first"
page-position="first" />
<fo:conditional-page-master-reference master-reference="rest"
page-position="rest" />
<fo:conditional-page-master-reference master-reference="rest" />
</fo:repeatable-page-master-alternatives>
</fo:page-sequence-master>
</fo:layout-master-set>
<fo:page-sequence master-reference="siArt">
<fo:static-content flow-name="xsl-region-before">
<fo:block><fo:external-graphic src="file:art.svg" />
</fo:block>
</fo:static-content>
<fo:flow flow-name="xsl-region-body" font-size="10pt"
font-family="arial, helvetica, sans-serif" line-height="14pt"
space-after.optimum="3pt" text-align="start">
<fo:block font-size="16pt" font-family="courier, mono"
line-height="22pt" space-after.optimum="15pt"
color="rgb(153,0,0)" text-align="center"
padding-top="3pt" font-variant="small-caps">
```

THE STRATEGY OF DISTRACTION - STARCRAFT THE GAME
</fo:block> <fo:block font-size="12pt"
font-family="sans-serif" line-height="18pt"
space-before.optimum="10pt"
space-after.optimum="10pt" text-align="start"
padding-top="3pt">
An interview with Manuel Jimenez By Jean McIntosh
</fo:block><fo:block>
<fo:inline font-variant="small-caps">Manuel</fo:inline> is my
neighbor, and his mom is my colleague. Last summer the three
of us were part of a group of educators who traveled to
Slovenia for a month. It's been a while since I've been in the
company of a ten-year old, and I learned a lot. For example, I
learned that 10 year olds learn things fast and can be very
good travelers. Being a seasoned traveler myself, I was quite
impressed with how he ordered meals in restaurants, and got
along with Slovenian kids in a game of scrub or soccer.
</fo:block>
<fo:block>I also learned that Manuel's favorite game is
StarCraft. StarCraft caught my attention because it's a
computer game that can be played online with hundreds of
thousands of other players. The following is my interview with
Manuel about his favorite computer game.</fo:block>
<fo:block><fo:inline color="rgb(145,129,43)">s:</fo:inline> So
Manuel, what's the name of the computer game I always see you
playing?</fo:block>
<fo:block><fo:inline color="rgb(153,0,0)">mn:</fo:inline>
StarCraft and StarCraft Brood War. StarCraft is the game that
you learn when you are a beginner. StarCraft Brood War is more
difficult. The game has three races; the Terren (humans), Zerg
(aliens created by the xel'naga temple) and the protoss, my
favorite high tech guys, who are also created by the xel'naga
temple.</fo:block>
<fo:block><fo:inline color="rgb(145,129,43)">s:</fo:inline>
What kind of game is it?</fo:block>
<fo:block><fo:inline color="rgb(153,0,0)">mn:</fo:inline> Why
it's a strategy game, Jean. Basically you build up an army and
defense just like in real life war, and you attack the enemy
with all you've got.</fo:block>
<fo:block><fo:inline color="rgb(145,129,43)">s:</fo:inline>
Why do you like this game?</fo:block>

```
<fo:block><fo:inline color="rgb(153,0,0)">mn:</fo:inline>I
like it because it is fully designed for strategy and there
are no levels except on one player so you can't really beat
the game. I also like it because you can play it online with
other players.</fo:block>
<fo:inline color="rgb(145,129,43)">s:</fo:inline> How does
that work?</fo:block>
<fo:block><fo:inline color="rgb(153,0,0)">mn:</fo:inline>
StarCraft and some other games like WarCraft and the Diablo
Series are made by Blizzard Entertainment. They also have a
website called battle.net that you can go to and play all
their games online. Battle.net is an online play system where
you may chat, battle, have tournaments, make your own clans,
and do whatever you want. You can play on a public channel,
where a lot of people play or a private channel, where you can
meet up with your friends and battle or chat.</fo:block>
<fo:block>At this point the interview started to become a
little stilted. It was Friday afternoon and I sensed that this
fifth grader had endured enough of trying to explain his game
to an adult who had never played it. I decided that if I
really wanted to know more about this game I should go buy it,
get online, and play. The only problem is what if I got into
it, and it took up 10-30 hours a week? In the end, I decided
that some things are just better left never understood.
</fo:block>
</fo:flow></fo:page-sequence></fo:root>
```

Creating the Forum Page

To enhance and encourage user participation, Jean requested a guest book/forum for message posts. Rather than uploading a previously developed product, we created a simple XML version so that, in the future, a simple search mechanism could be developed to use XML and the Document Object Model (DOM). Figure 9-8 shows the SIboard.

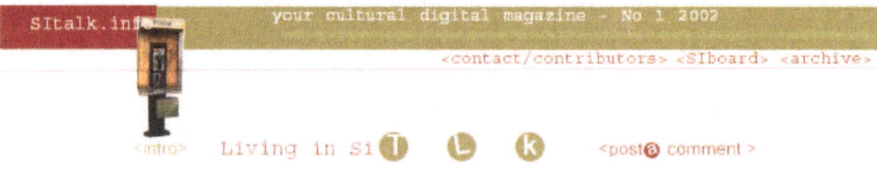

Queen Jean! What a wonderful addition to the web, a magazine that
deals intelligently with all lifes cerebral pleasures technology,
art, kulture. Congrats and looking onward and forward to the next
issue. sr

Ruadh Reed

- Tuesday, 30 July at 23:36:10 (CDT)

The graphics/colors/layout/fonts are really cool. Very good design
elements and form. Easy to navigate, easy on the eyes. Good work.
Would like to see other web pages you may do in the future!

Greg Arnold

- Monday, 10 June at 19:30:16 (CDT)

FIGURE 9-8 *SIboard*

Listing 9-13 shows the XML file for the SIboard.

LISTING 9-13 *SItalk SIboard XML*

```
<?xml version='1.0'?>
<?xml-stylesheet type="text/xsl" href="siboard.xsl"?>
<document>
<item>
<content>Queen Jean! What a wonderful addition to the web, a
magazine that deals intelligently with all lifes cerebral
pleasures technology, art, kulture. Congrats and looking
onward and forward to the next issue. sr</content>
<mail>Ruadh Reed</mail><ref>mailto:shona@yyyy.com</ref>
<date>- Tuesday, 30 July at 23:36:10 (CDT)</date></item>
<item>
<content>The graphics/colors/layout/fonts are really cool.
Very good design elements and form. Easy to navigate, easy on
the eyes. Good work. Would like to see other web pages you may
do in the future!</content>
```

```
<mail>Greg Arnold</mail>
<ref>mailto:gregarnold32@yyyy.com</ref>
<date>- Monday, 10 June at 19:30:16
(CDT)</date></item>
<item>
<content>Wow, that Greg Arnold guy sounds fascinating! Any
chance you could hook us up? Great website, simple, clear,
easy to get around. Lots of good info. I think I might have a
story for you (digital maps) but will give it more thought .
.</content>
<mail>PeBell</mail>
<ref>mailto:Pbell@yyyy.com</ref>
<date>- Monday, 10 June at 16:15:24(CDT)</date></item>
<item>
<content>Jean MCIntosh has done an excellent job of presenting
my photographs, Moreover, the excellent questions she posed
during her interview with me moved me to put into words my
thoughts, feelings and objectives regarding the photos.
Good job, Jean.</content>
<mail>Bob Terrell</mail>
<ref>mailto:bobterrell@yyyy.com</ref>
<date>- Friday, 07 June at 22:04:25(CDT)</date></item>
</document>
```

The SIboard XML file transforms to XHTML for universal browser support using XSLT. Listing 9-14 shows the XSLT that generates the transformation.

LISTING 9-14 *SItalk SIboard XSLT*

```
<?xml version='1.0'?>
<xsl:stylesheet xmlns:xsl=http://www.w3.org/1999/XSL/Transform
version="1.0">
<xsl:output method="xml" indent="yes" doctype
system="http://www.w3.org/TR/xhtml1/DTD/xhtml1
strict.dtd"
doctype-public="-//W3C//DTD XHTML 1.0 strict//EN" />
<xsl:template match="/">
<html xmlns="http://www.w3.org/1999/xhtml" xml:lang="en"
lang="en">
<head>
<title>SIboard</title>
<link rel="stylesheet" type="text/css" href="sitalk.css" />
</head>
```

```
<body>
<p class="svg1"><embed src="siboard.svg"
type="image/svg+xml" width="900" height="200" />
</p>

<table class="text1" border="0" width="600">
<tr>
<td vAlign="top" align="left">
          <p><span class="red"><xsl:apply-templates
select="document/title" /></span><span
          class="text"><br /><xsl:apply-templates
select="document/author" /></span></p>

</td></tr>
<xsl:for-each select="document/item">
 <tr>

  <td><br />
  <p class="text">
     <xsl:value-of select="content"/></p>
 <p><a class="regred">
      <xsl:attribute name="href">
          <xsl:value-of select="ref"/>
      </xsl:attribute>
      <xsl:value-of select="mail"/></a></p>
   <p class="text">
  <xsl:value-of select="date"/></p>
 <p class="red">_____

_____</p>
    </td>
 </tr>

    </xsl:for-each>
</table>
</body>
</html>
</xsl:template>
</xsl:stylesheet>
```

Listing 9-15 generates the SIboard SVG.

LISTING 9-15 *SItalk SIboard SVG*

```xml
<?xml version='1.0'?>
<svg width="800" height="250">
<rect x="10" y="20" width="780" height="38"
style="fill:rgb(145,129,43);" />
<rect x="10" y="19" width="140" height="38"
style="fill:rgb(153,0,0)" />
<image xlink:href="home_03.gif" x="105" y="27"
width="74" height="113" />
<text x="252" y="32" style="word-spacing:2;
font-family:courier, mono, courier new; font-size:9pt;
fill:white;">your cultural digital magazine - No 1 2002</text>
<text x="37" y="40" style="word-spacing:2;
font-family:courier, mono, courier new; font-size:9pt;
fill:rgb(231,222,212);">SItalk.info</text>
<a xlink:href="contact.xml"><text x="401" y="70"
style="word-spacing:2; font-family:courier, mono,
courier new; font-size:9pt;
fill:rgb(153,0,0);">&lt;contact/contributors&gt;</text></a>
<a xlink:href="siboard.xml"><text x="606" y="70"
style="word-spacing:2; font-family:courier, mono, courier new;
font-size:9pt; fill:rgb(153,0,0);">&lt;SIboard&gt;</text></a>
<a xlink:href="archive.xml"><text x="697" y="70"
style="word-spacing:2; font-family:courier, mono, courier new;
font-size:9pt; fill:rgb(153,0,0);">&lt;archive&gt;</text></a>
<circle cx="479" cy="144" r="13"
style="fill:rgb(145,129,43);" />
<circle cx="419" cy="144" r="13"
style="fill:rgb(145,129,43);" />
<circle cx="359" cy="144" r="13"
style="fill:rgb(145,129,43);" />
<circle cx="585" cy="147" r="7"
style="fill:rgb(153,0,0);" />
<a xlink:href="kulture.xml"><text x="473" y="151"
style="font-family:arial, helvetica, sans-serif;
font-size:15pt; fill:white;">k</text></a>
<a xlink:href="living.xml"><text x="413" y="151"
style="font-family:arial, helvetica, sans-serif;
font-size:15pt; fill:white;"
transform="rotate(-10,413,147)">L</text></a>
```

```
<a xlink:href="technology.xml"><text x="353" y="151"
style="font-family:arial, helvetica, sans-serif;
font-size:15pt; fill:white;">T</text></a>
<a xlink:href="sitalk.xml"><text x="128" y="151"
style="font-family:arial, helvetica, sans-serif;
font-size:9.5pt; fill:rgb(145,129,43);">&lt;intro&gt;</text></a>
<a xlink:href="art.xml"><text x="205" y="151"
style="font-family:courier, mono, courier new;
font-size:13pt; fill:rgb(153,0,0);">Living in Si</text></a>
<a xlink:href="contact.xml"><text x="538" y="151"
style="font-family:arial, helvetica, sans-serif;
font-size:9.5pt; fill:rgb(153,0,0);">&lt;post</text>
<text x="582" y="151" style="font-family:arial, helvetica,
sans-serif; font-size:9.5pt; fill:white;"
transform="rotate(-15,582,151)">a</text>
<text x="598" y="151" style="font-family:arial, helvetica,
sans-serif; font-size:9.5pt; fill:rgb(153,0,0);">
comment &gt;</text>
</a>
<g id="txline" style="font-family:courier, mono, courier new;
font-size:4pt; stroke:#999933;">
<text x="260" y="46">technology art SI kulture
kulturetechnology art living tuzla kulture art living in SI
kulture artin SI kultureivinginSIkulturehap</text>
<text x="262" y="47">artliving
kulturetechnologyartlivinginSIsarajevokultureartkultureartkult
ureartlivinginSIkulturehappeningwoodstockulture living tuzla
</text>
</g>
</svg>
```

Creating the Archive Page

The client requested an archive page for past articles, discussions, and ideas. Figure 9-9 shows the SItalk archive page.

FIGURE 9-9 *SItalk archive page*

Listing 9-16 shows the XML file for the archive section of the site.

LISTING 9-16 *SItalk Archive Page XML*

```
<?xml version='1.0'?>
<?xml-stylesheet type="text/xsl" href="archive.xsl"?>
<document>
<title>SItalk - Volume 1 Number 1</title>
<item>
<field>Technology</field>
<ref>technology.xml</ref>
<name>Practice Makes Praxis</name>
<content>Kelly Carey discusses her company Praxis Development,
an international non profit co-operative that makes IT
educational products.</content>
</item>
<item>
<field>Art</field>
<ref>art.xml</ref>
<name>Breeding New Life Into Digital Video</name>
```

```
<content>This interview features Shona Reed, a digital media
artist who has her roots in photography and film-making. She
discusses the overlapping of science and art which has led her
to make a desktop video breeding system which questions how we
view digital video.</content>
</item>
<item>
<field>Living In SI</field>
<ref>living.xml</ref>
<name>The Unspoken Words of Street Text</name>
<content>The first in a series of Jean McIntosh's street text,
features photographs from Venice, Italy.</content>
</item>
<item>
<field>Kulture</field>
<ref>kulture.xml</ref>
<name>Where the Cool Ones Are</name>
<content>An article reviewing the site www.coolgirlsjapan.com.
Web master Sayuri Kosugi, has created a trendy web world for
the fashion-minded, world curious Japanese teen.</content>
</item>
</document>
```

Listing 9-17 shows the XSLT file for the archive section's transformation from XML to XHTML for universal browser support.

LISTING 9-17　*SItalk Archive Page XSLT*

```
<?xml version='1.0'?>
<xsl:stylesheet xmlns:xsl="http://www.w3.org/1999/XSL/Transform"
version="1.0">
<xsl:output method="xml" indent="yes" doctype-
system="http://www.w3.org/TR/xhtml1/DTD/xhtml1-strict.dtd"
doctype-public="-//W3C//DTD XHTML 1.0 strict//EN" />
<xsl:template match="/">
<html xmlns="http://www.w3.org/1999/xhtml" xml:lang="en"
lang="en">
<head>
<title>SItalk Archive</title>
<link rel="stylesheet" type="text/css" href="sitalk.css" />
</head>
<body>
<p class="svg1"><embed src="archive.svg" type="image/svg+xml"
width="900" height="200" />
</p>
```

```
<table class="text1" border="0" width="600">
<tr>
<td vAlign="top" align="left">
<p><span class="green"><xsl:apply-templates
select="document/title" /></span></p>
</td></tr>
<xsl:for-each select="document/item">
<tr>
<td><br /><br />
<p><a class="regred">
<xsl:attribute name="href">
<xsl:value-of select="ref" />
</xsl:attribute>
<xsl:value-of select="field" />
</a>
<span class="green">:
<xsl:value-of select="name" /></span></p>
<p class="text">
<xsl:value-of select="content" /></p>
</td>
</tr>
</xsl:for-each>
</table>
</body>
</html>
</xsl:template>
</xsl:stylesheet>
```

Listing 9-18 shows the SVG file for the archive section of SItalk.

LISTING 9-18 *SItalk Archive Page SVG*

```
<?xml version='1.0'?>
<svg width="800" height="250">
<rect x="10" y="20" width="780" height="38"
style="fill:rgb(145,129,43);" />
<rect x="10" y="19" width="140" height="38"
style="fill:rgb(153,0,0)" />
<image xlink:href="home_03.gif" x="105" y="27" width="74"
height="113" />
<text x="252" y="32" style="word-spacing:2;
font-family:courier, mono, courier new; font-size:9pt;
fill:white;">your cultural digital magazine - No 1 2002</text>
```

```
<text x="37" y="40" style="word-spacing:2;
font-family:courier, mono, courier new; font-size:9pt;
fill:rgb(231,222,212);">SItalk.info</text>
<a xlink:href="contact.xml"><text x="401" y="70"
style="word-spacing:2; font-family:courier, mono, courier new;
font-size:9pt; fill:rgb(153,0,0);">&lt;contact/contributors&gt;</text></a>
<a xlink:href="siboard.xml"><text x="606" y="70"
style="word-spacing:2; font-family:courier, mono, courier new;
font-size:9pt; fill:rgb(153,0,0);">&lt;SIboard&gt;</text></a>
<a xlink:href="archive.xml"><text x="697" y="70"
style="word-spacing:2; font-family:courier, mono, courier new;
font-size:9pt; fill:rgb(153,0,0);">&lt;archive&gt;</text></a>
<g id="txline" style="font-family:courier, mono, courier new;
font-size:4pt; stroke:#999933;">
<text x="260" y="46">technology art SI kulture
kulturetechnology art living tuzla kulture art living in SI
kulture artin SI kultureivinginSIkulturehap</text>
<text x="262" y="47">artliving
kulturetechnologyartlivinginSIsarajevokultureartkultureartkult
ureartlivinginSIkulturehappeningwoodstockulture tuzla </text>
</g>
<circle cx="479" cy="144" r="13"
style="fill:rgb(145,129,43);" />
<circle cx="419" cy="144" r="13"
style="fill:rgb(145,129,43);" />
<circle cx="359" cy="144" r="13"
style="fill:rgb(145,129,43);" />
<circle cx="585" cy="147" r="7"
style="fill:rgb(153,0,0);" />
<a xlink:href="kulture.xml">
<text x="473" y="151" style="font-family:arial, helvetica,
sans-serif; font-size:15pt; fill:white;">k</text></a>
<a xlink:href="living.xml"><text x="413" y="151"
style="font-family:arial, helvetica, sans-serif;
font-size:15pt; fill:white;"
transform="rotate(-10,413,147)">L</text></a>
<a xlink:href="technology.xml"><text x="353" y="151"
style="font-family:arial, helvetica, sans-serif;
font-size:15pt; fill:white;">T</text></a>
<a xlink:href="sitalk.xml"><text x="128" y="151"
style="font-family:arial, helvetica, sans-serif;
font-size:9.5pt;
fill:rgb(145,129,43);">&lt;intro&gt;</text></a>
```

```
<a xlink:href="archive.xml"><text x="205" y="151"
style="font-family:courier, mono, courier new;
font-size:12pt; fill:rgb(153,0,0);">Archive</text></a>
<a xlink:href="contact.xml"><text x="538" y="151"
style="font-family:arial, helvetica, sans-serif;
font-size:9.5pt; fill:rgb(153,0,0);">&lt;post</text>
<text x="582" y="151" style="font-family:arial, helvetica,
sans-serif; font-size:9.5pt; fill:white;"
transform="rotate(-15,582,151)">a</text>
<text x="598" y="151" style="font-family:arial, helvetica,
sans-serif; font-size:9.5pt; fill:rgb(153,0,0);">
comment &gt;</text></a>
</svg>
```

Creating the Contact Page

For one-on-one interaction with readers, Jean requested a contact/contributor area, as shown in Figure 9-10.

FIGURE 9-10 *SItalk contact/contributor page*

Listing 9-19 shows the XML file for the SItalk contact/contributor page.

LISTING 9-19 *SItalk Contact/Contributor Page XML*

```
<?xml version='1.0'?>
<?xml-stylesheet type="text/xsl" href="contact.xsl"?>
<document>
<par>With this edition of SItalk I have archived the first
issue and added a bulletin board where you can post comments,
information, or thoughts. Contact me if you would like to have
your work featured on SItalk. I am interested in featuring
your writing, photography, art or whatever it is you do.</par>
<par1>The first SIboard was made possible with the help of
Jasmine Cai. I am grateful for her effort in getting SIboard
going. Thanks Jasmine!!</par1>
<par2>Special thanks to Sapphire for her interview with
Nancy Morejon. I look forward to gathering more stories,
and finding more art to showcase on SItalk.</par2>
<name>jean</name><ref>mailto:jean@sitalk.info</ref>
<mail>jean@sitalk.info </mail>
</document>
```

Listing 9-20 shows the XSLT file for the SItalk contact/contributor page's transformation from XML to XHTML for wider browser support.

LISTING 9-20 *SItalk Contact/Contributor Page XSLT*

```
<?xml version='1.0'?>
<xsl:stylesheet
xmlns:xsl="http://www.w3.org/1999/XSL/Transform"
version="1.0">
<xsl:output method="xml" indent="yes" doctype-
system="http://www.w3.org/TR/xhtml1/DTD/xhtml1-strict.dtd"
doctype-public="-//W3C//DTD XHTML 1.0 strict//EN" />
<xsl:template match="/">
<html xmlns="http://www.w3.org/1999/xhtml" xml:lang="en"
lang="en">
<head>
<title>SItalk Contact/Contributors</title>
<link rel="stylesheet" type="text/css" href="sitalk.css" />
</head>
<body>
<p class="svg1"><embed src="contact.svg" type="image/svg+xml"
width="900" height="200" /></p>
<table class="text1" border="0" width="600">
```

```
<tr>
<td vAlign="top" align="left">
<p class="text"><br /><br /><xsl:apply-templates
select="document/intro" />
<br /><br /><xsl:apply-templates select="document/par" />
<br /><br /><xsl:apply-templates select="document/par1" />
<br /><br /><xsl:apply-templates select="document/par2" />
<br /><br /><br /><br /><xsl:apply-templates
select="document/name" />
<br /><p><a class="regred">
<xsl:attribute name="href">
<xsl:value-of select="document/ref" />
</xsl:attribute>
<xsl:value-of select="document/mail" />
</a></p></p>
</td></tr></table>
</body>
</html>
</xsl:template>
</xsl:stylesheet>
```

Listing 9-21 shows the SVG file for the SItalk contact/contributor page.

LISTING 9-21 *SItalk Contact/Contributor Page SVG*

```
<?xml version='1.0'?>
<svg width="800" height="250">
<rect x="10" y="20" width="780" height="38"
style="fill:rgb(145,129,43);" />
<rect x="10" y="19" width="140" height="38"
style="fill:rgb(153,0,0)" />
<image xlink:href="home_03.gif" x="105" y="27"
width="74" height="113" />
<text x="252" y="32" style="word-spacing:2;
font-family:courier, mono, courier new; font-size:10pt;
fill:white;">your cultural digital magazine - No 1 2002</text>
<text x="37" y="40" style="word-spacing:2;
font-family:courier, mono, courier new; font-size:9pt;
fill:rgb(231,222,212);">SItalk.info</text>
<a xlink:href="siboard.xml"><text x="606" y="70"
style="word-spacing:2; font-family:courier, mono, courier new;
font-size:9pt; fill:rgb(153,0,0);">&lt;archives&gt;</text></a>
<a xlink:href="archive.xml"><text x="697" y="70"
style="word-spacing:2; font-family:courier, mono, courier new;
font-size:9pt; fill:rgb(153,0,0);">&lt;SIboard&gt;</text></a>
```

```
<circle cx="585" cy="147" r="7" style="fill:rgb(153,0,0);" />
<a xlink:href="sitalk.xml"><text x="128" y="151"
style="font-family:arial, helvetica, sans-serif;
font-size:9.5pt; fill:rgb(145,129,43);">&lt;intro&gt;</text></a>
<a xlink:href="art.xml"><text x="205" y="151"
style="font-family:courier, mono, courier new; font-size:13pt;
fill:rgb(153,0,0);">contact/contributors</text></a>
<a xlink:href="contact.xml"><text x="538" y="151"
style="font-family:arial, helvetica, sans-serif;
font-size:9.5pt; fill:rgb(153,0,0);">&lt;post</text>
<text x="582" y="151" style="font-family:arial,
helvetica, sans-serif; font-size:9.5pt; fill:white;"
transform="rotate(-15,582,151)">a</text>
<text x="598" y="151" style="font-family:arial, helvetica,
sans-serif; font-size:9.5pt; fill:rgb(153,0,0);">
comment &gt;</text>
</a>
<g id="txline" style="font-family:courier, mono, courier new;
font-size:4pt; stroke:#999933;">
<text x="260" y="46">technology art SI kulture
kulturetechnology art living tuzla kulture art living in SI
kulture artin SI kultureivinginSIkulturehap</text>
<text x="262" y="47">artliving
kulturetechnologyartlivinginSIsarajevokultureartkultureartkult
ureartlivinginSIkulturehappeningwoodstockulture living tuzla
</text>
</g>
</svg>
```

Realizing the client's intent and fulfilling the users' expectations by combining content, type, and color with a sound design philosophy makes SItalk a fun, unique Web site. Jean notes that the site will change and evolve—not because it should, but because it can.

Project 3 Axioms

Content and typography present the client's story from both a meaningful and visual perspective. Color brings the story to life as it creates a mood, reminds users of something familiar, or enhances the purpose of a site. Look separately at content, typography, and color to determine if you have selected narrative, font, and hues that meet the language of the client. Create a word list and hold it next to the screen to compare your language to your results. Think of antonyms or synonyms for comparative purposes. Think of exaggerated or muted words to determine if you've selected the right size font or color value to express your intent. A simple paper with about a dozen words can support your type and color decisions. For example, a "cooking outdoor BBQ" store might see itself as innovative and fun, and yet a word list that intrigues users and sells products could be as follows:

- Friends and family, kids playing
- Warm, sunny weather, light breeze
- Ice-cold beer and soda
- Chicken, steak, and sausage smells from the grill
- Fresh corn on the cob
- Laughing, joking, relaxing

Finding the color, type, and content to communicate this list will sell the client's products.

As a designer/developer, plan to refine and adjust your sites over the months and years as they're read and used. Revising layout, color, and content is as much a part of the design process as updating is a part of the code process. Successful sites evolve to meet the changing needs of clients and users and to take advantage of emerging technology options.

The next chapter considers issues related to the design and development of commercial sites.

Exploring Site Issues and Accessibility

Design in art, is a recognition of the relation between various things, various elements in the creative flux. You can't invent a design. You recognise it, in the fourth dimension. That is, with your blood and your bones, as well as with your eyes.

—D.H. Lawrence, author (1885–1930)

Creating a Web site or Web-based application encompasses all of the design ideas and axioms of the previous nine chapters. However, as many additional issues seem to arise as there are clients looking to build Web sites. A well-planned approach to design concepts, layout, and content limits the bulk of the surprises; this chapter presents a few ways to go through the process of working on different projects and presents additional site and accessibility issues.

Outsourcing Work to a Designer

After having been hired to design, build, and test a client's Web site, you may determine that an outsourced designer is necessary. This type of job typically evolves in several ways; one example is as follows:

1. You meet with a contact person for a Web site. In the past, you may have generated or contracted out for code. For this job, you decide to also participate in the design process.

2. You initiate and implement the user analysis process, develop a narrative, and determine several rough ideas for the site. You develop sketch prototypes that have merit. You develop a requirements specification that clearly defines the project from client, user, and technical perspectives.

3. When you complete the user analysis and sketch prototypes, you should pause and ask some critical questions: Can you create the site you envision with the code you know? Do the browsers used by the target audience support your code? If your answer to both is "yes," proceed with your design as outlined in this book. If your answer to either is "no," proceed to the next step.

4. Don't scale back, rework, or throw out the sketch prototypes you've developed as a result of the user analysis and your original ideas. It's important you build the site as it needs to be built. Never constrain a design to your current level of understanding of either code or an application. There are times when you need to hire a designer to work up your ideas in Adobe Photoshop or another graphics application. This doesn't mean you need to be a Photoshop guru. Trust your ideas; outsource your graphics to someone who can implement them just as designers might outsource server-side code to you. Once the initial graphic is complete and the images are sliced (cut into separate GIF or JPG images so they load faster), you're back in control. You implement the design, add content, perform the build, and test the site.

5. You know the client's expectations, the users' expectations, and how the product should present to users. Don't get sidetracked by designers who want to show you how artistic they are or how much more they know about graphics applications than you. Most designers are interested in working with developers who can clearly describe their design needs. Furthermore, most designers are happy to produce the graphics you describe and often offer subtle suggestions that strengthen your concept. Most designers are creative and charge fair prices for their work. Be sure to find a designer with these qualities rather than a big talker.

 NOTE In fact, many designers are eager to find a developer who will be a code resource for their design gigs.

This approach increases your flexibility—it's bad business to turn down a job because you're unable to create the application graphics you've visualized. Running the user analysis, initial design phase, site build, and testing for a good client is a rewarding project whether or not you create the final graphics. As Scalable Vector Graphics (SVG) become readable by browsers, more and more of your design work will make it to the Web. In the meantime, SVG remains a good option for some target audiences and some intranet applications.

For example, we wrote a grant proposal to the European Commission's EU Programme Minerva to develop online case study–based learning for industrial process control.

NOTE Stanko taught physics at the University of Tuzla in Bosnia and Herzegovina before the war. After the war, industry was crippled for the most part. At that time, Stanko started teaching online for the University of Sarajevo.

The purpose of the online course was to teach process control when there wasn't any existing industry to serve as a model. The target audience consisted of fourth-year and post-graduate university students. The user analysis and narrative for the project resulted in keywords such as *different, interesting, graphical, transnational,* and *timely.* We knew we needed an interface that was welcoming and inviting and that wouldn't intimidate students or professors skeptical about an online approach to process control and engineering. Because of the limitations of browsers that support SVG and the older equipment available in the target countries, we decided we needed application graphics to best tell the story. As such, we developed the product, code, content, and asked designer Hye Park to create graphics that were soft and welcoming as a contrast to the industrial content. Figure 10-1 shows the site's splash page.

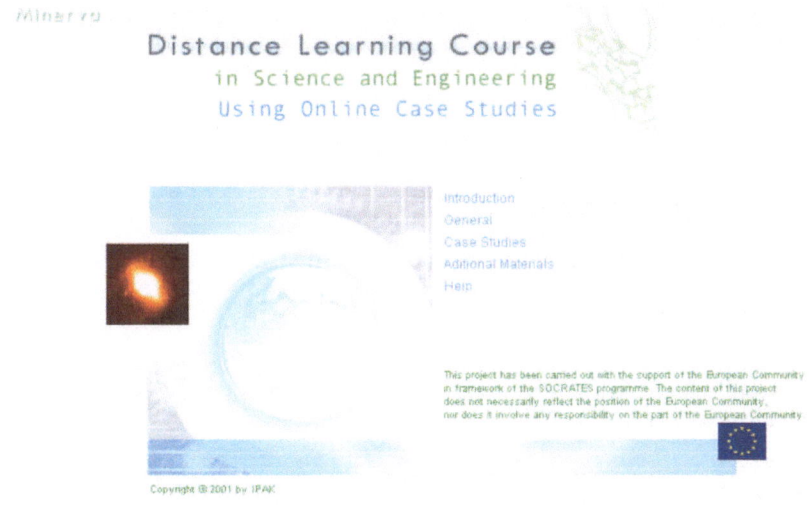

FIGURE 10-1 *Process control splash page*

The color and style of the site graphics will change from year to year; these graphics suggest that this product is technical but creative. If the graphics were strictly geometric, scientific, technical, or mathematical, the user would expect to approach the case studies in a traditional manner. These graphics support technical information but ask the right side of the user's brain to register the course as nontraditional. Figure 10-2 shows the start of an introduction to students.

FIGURE 10-2 *Case study introductory page*

Figure 10-3 shows the simple navigation links to the CD-ROM or Web site case studies.

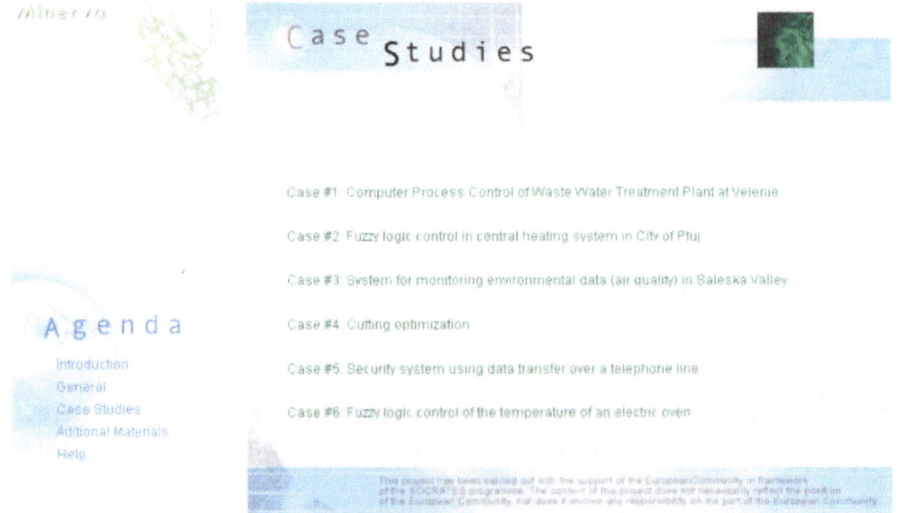

FIGURE 10-3 *Case study navigation page*

The case studies incorporate video, audio, images, and text. A simple drop-down menu offers navigation within each case study. Figure 10-4 shows the start of a case study on a self-contained wastewater treatment plant powered by methanol derived from waste products.

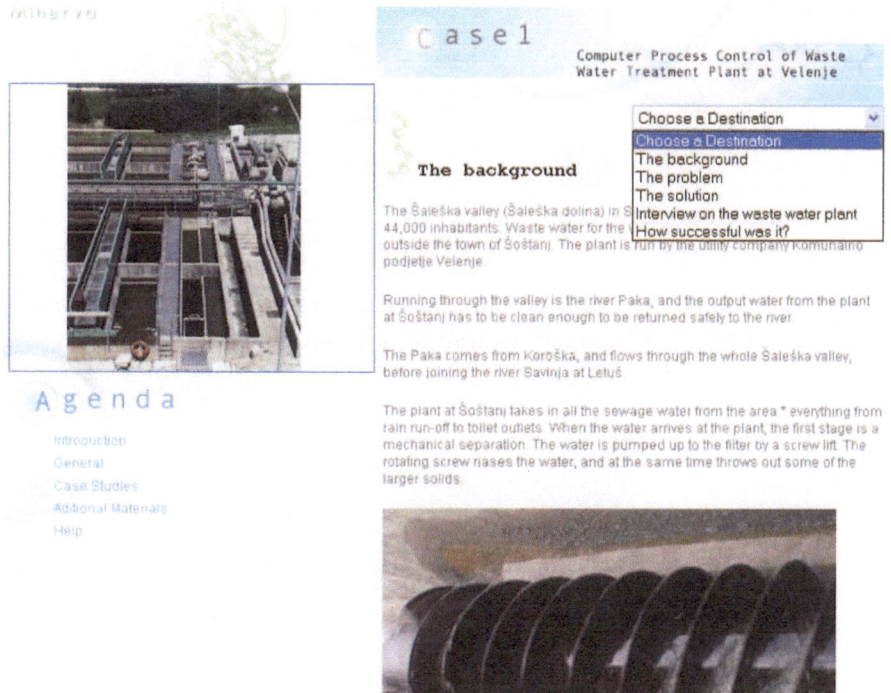

FIGURE 10-4 *Case study navigation*

The user analysis data determined that professors/facilitators expect a separate site that offers and supports teaching and evaluation materials. This support site needed to be separate but visually connected to the case study product. Figure 10-5 shows the support site's splash page.

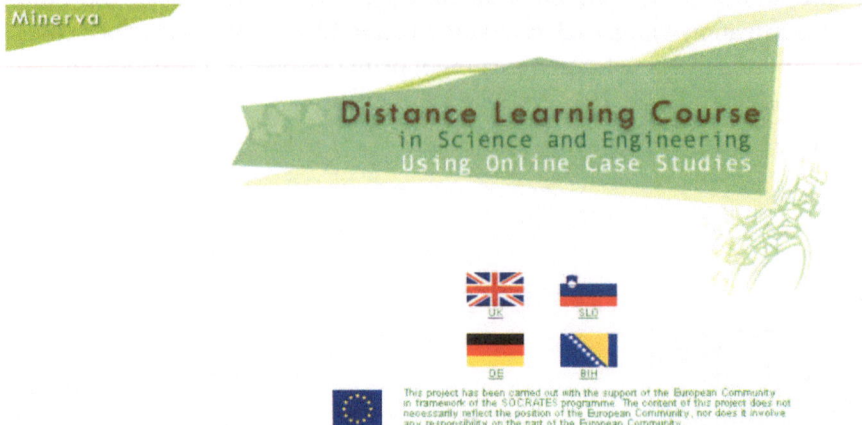

FIGURE 10-5 *Support site splash page*

The presentation of the support materials suggests a different approach to deliver the learning process. Figure 10-6 shows a support site content page.

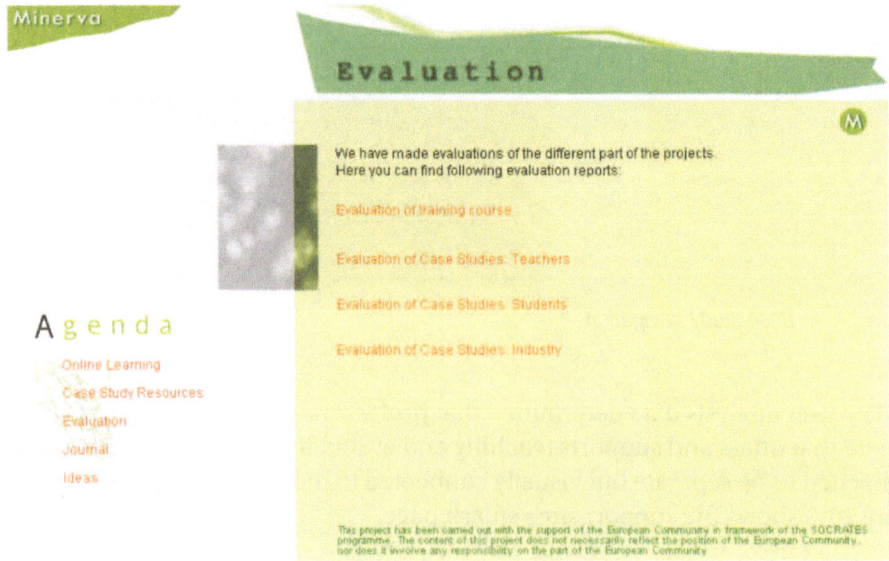

FIGURE 10-6 *Support site content page*

Developers involved in the design process, especially freelance developers, save time and money by being directly involved with a job. Designers become expensive when they need to do the client/user research to determine what kind of site graphic you require. Your knowledge of shape, space, color, line, user priorities for navigation images, browsers, and other design considerations greatly enhances an outsourced graphic designer's ability to support your vision.

Updating or Reworking a Site's Design

You may enter a project as a designer/developer hired or contracted to update or rework an existing site. Your decision to design the graphics yourself or to outsource to a designer will be based on the extent of the graphic changes. Because of rapidly changing styles on the Web, many clients prefer to completely change the site design during an update. This type of job typically evolves in several ways; one example is as follows:

1. The client wants something new. Typically, the existing site is described as *amateur, clunky, boring, bland, has too much text,* and *too slow.* Sometimes the client likes certain aspects of the site but wants users to be able to interact with it, rather than simply read it.

2. Sometimes a few minor layout changes and new content are what's really needed. Listen carefully to the client's description. A lot of people don't like to write or update content. In some cases, the site just looks bad by today's standards. First-generation and second-generation sites often have a certain period look to them or an outdated style. The important thing to grasp is what the client likes about the existing site and how the client wants to present it to new users. Some clients are open to new ideas; some are constantly comparing your work to their old product.

3. Sketch and digital prototypes help the client envision how the "new look" translates to the screen. Upload your digital prototypes to the Web for the client to evaluate. Your decision to design the site yourself or bring in a designer will be determined by the criteria described in the previous example. Clients with existing sites that you update or re-create come to the job with a different perspective than clients building a new site. They have definite opinions on what they like, and they've heard from coworkers and customers about the perceived strengths and weaknesses of the old site. They often have a "we're going to get it right this time" attitude. Having uploaded prototypes available to the client expedites the design approval process.

4. Be clear with the client about content. Clients in a hurry typically want to carry over the old content. Clients with large investments in content from the previous version of the site also like to carry over old content. After you add the content to the new site, allow a couple of days for the client to see the new design and the content together. There's a moment when many clients "see" their content differently with the new design and often decide on some changes.

5. Consider the browser limitations of the client's customer. There's only so much you can do if customers use old equipment and outdated browsers.

6. Finally, be a little leery of clients who talk about a long string of designers and developers who did terrible jobs. The same holds true for clients with really bad existing sites. Only occasionally is the designer or developer to blame.

For example, Greg Mainis owns Simplified Software, a small software company specializing in applications for produce brokers, flower brokers, and shippers. Greg's existing site, developed by students, now appears amateurish in contrast to the sophisticated functionality of his products. In this case, there were no problems with the client. The process started with the old site, as shown in Figure 10-7.

FIGURE 10-7   *Original Simplified Software entry page*

Figure 10-8 shows a content page from the original Simplified Software site.

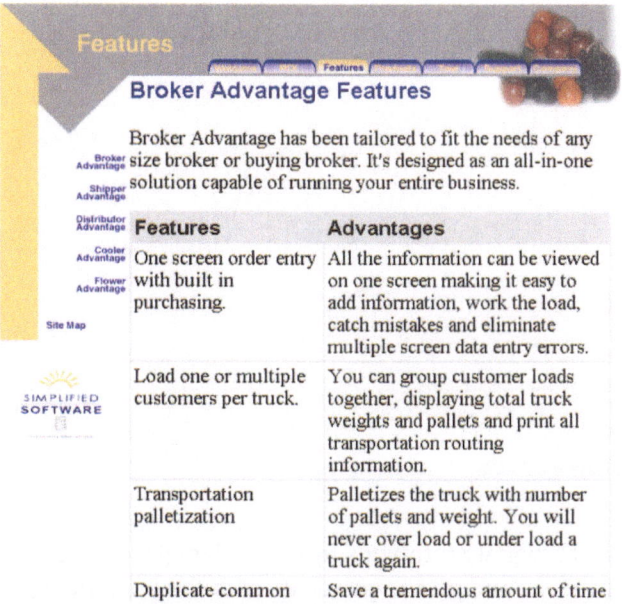

Simplified Software users aren't interested in downloading an SVG reader. The client wants users to have straightforward access to the site. We talked with the client about the story he wanted to convey and outsourced the design, again to designer Hye Park, for a clean, fresh, outdoor look to communicate the high-end applications Simplified Software offers. The first set of digital prototypes was on track for the client, but he requested they suggest a more masculine than feminine interpretation of produce, flowers, and commercial farms. Flowers and vegetables worked as icons because of the nature of his customers' products; however, men working as produce brokers may not connect with a feminine layout. Figure 10-9 shows the first prototype set. The top row shows potential splash page layouts, and the second shows accompanying content page layouts.

A_simp_splash1.jpg   B_simp_splash2.jpg   C_simp_splash3.jpg

D_simp_layout1.jpg   E_simp_layout2.jpg   F_simp_layout3.jpg

FIGURE 10-9 *First new digital prototype options*

We submitted a second set of digital prototypes, and the client gave his design approval. Figure 10-10 shows the second prototype set. As with the first, the top row shows potential splash page layouts, and the second shows accompanying content page layouts.

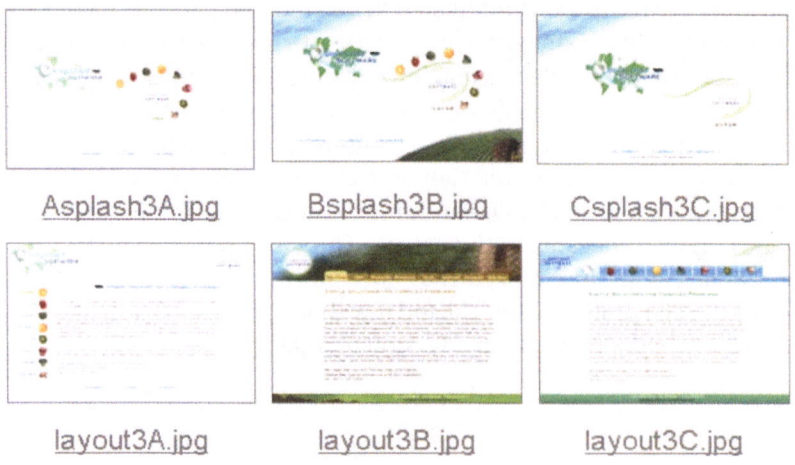

Asplash3A.jpg   Bsplash3B.jpg   Csplash3C.jpg

layout3A.jpg   layout3B.jpg   layout3C.jpg

FIGURE 10-10 *Second set of digital prototype options*

The client liked the farm ground on one prototype and the world on another, as shown in Figure 10-11. He specified that the world graphic appear slightly more dominant than the ground graphic.

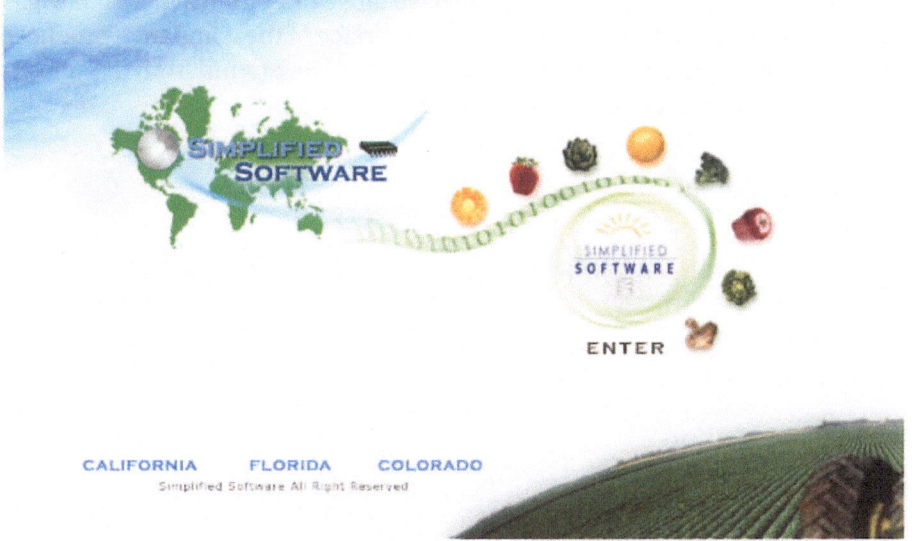

FIGURE 10-11 *Second prototype option, closer to what the client wants to convey*

The lightness and colors of produce, a larger version of the world (one of the product's strengths is the business of shipping produce transnationally), and a small piece of farmland result in the final splash page shown in Figure 10-12.

FIGURE 10-12 *Final splash page*

The client preferred the content page have tabs rather than icons for navigational purposes; tabs define the navigational interface of the company's products. He preferred the design of Figure 10-13, but he liked the ground from the splash page and from the content page shown in Figure 10-14.

FIGURE 10-13 *Preferred design*

FIGURE 10-14 *The client requested the ground image on the lower right.*

The preferred content page combined with the ground aspect of the second option resulted in the site's final content page layout shown in Figure 10-15.

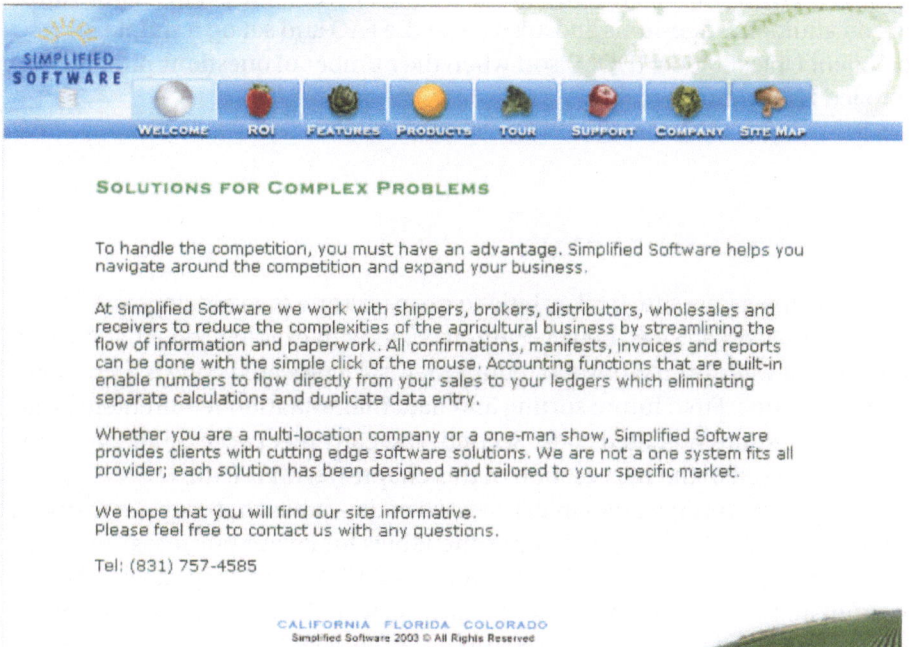

FIGURE 10-15 *Content page final layouts*

The nature of the graphics, more like photographic representations than digital illustrations, limits the options for hand-coding SVG. Some applications (Adobe Illustrator 10, for example) create SVG a little more realistically; however, the code is composed of paths and loses some of its simplicity. For this design, we decided to stay with the graphics and had the designer slice the images and import them to Macromedia Dreamweaver, the Hypertext Markup Language (HTML) editor the client will use to maintain the site.

Finally, we transferred the content from the previous site into the new site, working with the code generated by Dreamweaver. We adjusted the Cascading Style Sheets (CSS) to better fit the content style with the new layout. The Simplified Software site includes information about its products, a Return on Investment calculator, and a FAQ. The code tested well on browsers, but we would have preferred the code be well-formed for future Extensible HTML (XHTML) and Extensible Markup Language (XML) compatibility. The Dreamweaver-generated HTML opened the door to discussions regarding what we might do with the deprecated code. We wanted the site to be clean in Dreamweaver for client updates, and yet we decided to transition a portion of the site to XML and use XSL Transformations (XSLT) for HTML output. This way, the client (in this case, the client knows XML) can add additional questions and answers to the FAQ and set up a simple Document Object Model (DOM) sort when the number of questions prohibits a scrolled HTML interface.

Editing Deprecated Code

When building a new site, it takes little to no extra time to avoid deprecated tags. Updated or reworked sites, however, often begin with existing code that doesn't meet current well-formed or valid requirements. Deprecated code is a problem for a few reasons. First, future sorting and data manipulation requirements will, most likely, require validated code. Second, you can't meet accessibility requirements (discussed in the next section of this chapter) with HTML.

There are some gray areas in deprecated code—areas that may not insist on validation, such as CSS for positioning and tables for layout purposes. That said, some deprecated tags such as HTML frames and HTML style tags do need to be taken out and replaced with linked CSS files. As with the SVG decisions from the site rework, code decisions are based on user browser support. Your ability to produce clean, well-formed code easily modified for future interfaces will result in recommendations and increased business for you as a designer/developer.

On the Simplified Software site, the code generated with Dreamweaver can be "cleaned up" to a certain extent with closed tags, proper nesting, current attributes, and well-planned CSS classes. Because the client will most likely maintain the site with Dreamweaver, trying to work with XML or an XHTML Strict Document Type Definition (DTD) won't work. Therefore, we simplified the code, without Dreamweaver, indicating errors in its design mode.

Setting up the FAQ XML file and outputting it to HTML using XSLT took little time because we were already in the site's code. Figure 10-16 shows the FAQ page.

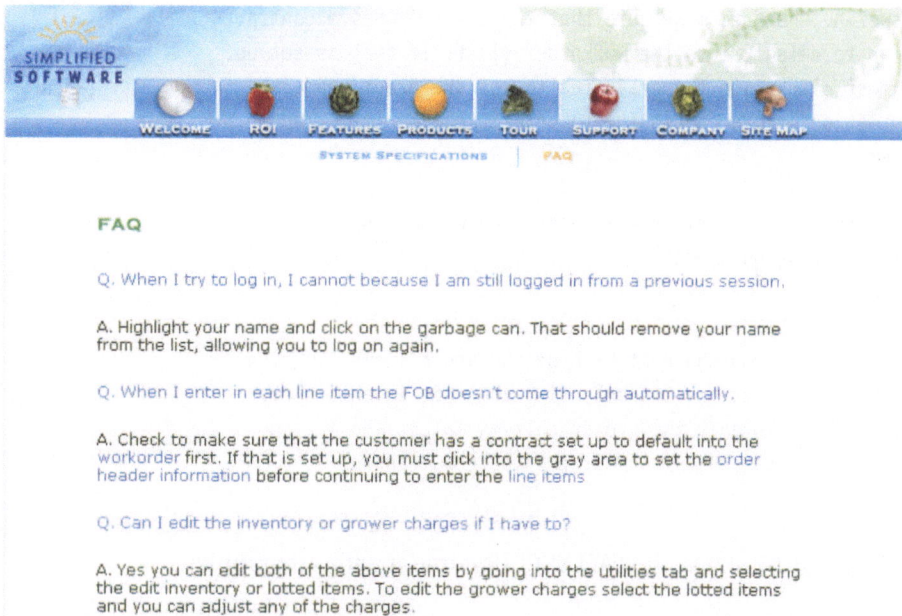

FIGURE 10-16 *Simplied Software FAQ page*

Listing 10-1 shows a small piece of the FAQ's XML document.

LISTING 10-1 *Simplified Software FAQ XML*

```
<?xml version="1.0"?>
<?xml-stylesheet type="text/xsl" href="faq.xsl"?>
<faq>
<title>FAQ</title>
<item>
<question>Q. When I try to log in, I cannot because I am
still logged in from a previous session.</question>
</item>
<item>
<answer>A. Highlight your name and click on the garbage can.
That should remove your name from the list, allowing you to
log on again.</answer>
</item>
<item>
<question>Q. When I enter in each line item the FOB
doesn&apos;t come through automatically.</question>
```

```
<answer>A. Check to make sure that the customer has a contract
set up to default into the workorder first. If that is set up,
you must click into the gray area to set the order header
information before continuing to enter the line items</answer>
</item>
<item>
<question>Q. Can I edit the inventory or grower charges
if I have to?</question>
</item>
<item>
<answer>A. Yes you can edit both of the above items by going
into the utilities tab and selecting the edit inventory or
lotted items. To edit the grower charges select the lotted
items and you can adjust any of the charges.</answer>
</item>
```

Listing 10-2 shows the FAQ XSLT document without graphics.

LISTING 10-2 *Simplified Software FAQ XSLT*

```
<?xml version='1.0'?>
<xsl:stylesheet
xmlns:xsl="http://www.w3.org/1999/XSL/Transform"
version="1.0">
<xsl:output method="xml" indent="yes" doctype-
system="http://www.w3.org/TR/xhtml1/DTD/xhtml1-
transitional.dtd"
doctype-public="-//W3C//DTD XHTML 1.0 strict//EN" />
<xsl:template match="/">

<html xmlns="http://www.w3.org/1999/xhtml" xml:lang="en"
lang="en">
<head>
<title>FAQ</title>
<link rel="stylesheet" type="text/css" href="simplified.css"/>
</head>
<body>
<xsl:for-each select="faq/item">

  <p class="tex2">
    <xsl:value-of select="question"/></p>
  <p class="text1">
  <xsl:value-of select="answer"/></p>
```

```
</xsl:for-each>
</body>
</html>
</xsl:template>
</xsl:stylesheet>
```

The FAQ page style is in the XSL document. The transformation to an XHTML document is on the server side using Active Server Pages (ASP) for a Microsoft server or JavaServer Pages (JSP) for a Java-based server. Transforming the XML document to XHTML on the server provides broader browser support, regardless of browser XSLT capability. Listing 10-3 shows the example with ASP server-side code.

LISTING 10-3 *Simplified Software FAQ ASP*

```
<%@Language="JavaScript"%>
<%
yourXml = Server.CreateObject("Microsoft.XMLDOM")
yourXml.async = false
yourXml.load(Server.MapPath("faq.xml"))
yourXsl = Server.CreateObject("Microsoft.XMLDOM")
yourXsl.async = false
yourXsl.load(Server.MapPath("faq.xsl"))
Response.Write(yourXml.transformNode(yourXsl))
%>
```

Listing 10-4 shows the same example with JSP server-side code.

LISTING 10-4 *Simplified Software FAQ JSP*

```
<%@taglib uri="http://jakarta.apache.org/taglibs/xsl-1.0"
prefix="xsl" %>
<html><body bgcolor="white">
<xsl:apply xml="jsp/fag.xml" xsl="jsp/faq.xsl"/>
</body>
</html>
```

Creating Technical Designs

The design for Simplified Software required an entirely different approach from some technical sites. It's important to distinguish the technical aspect of a product from the story it communicates. In other words, although the Simplified

Software products are technical, the client wants to convey that they're simple, usable, and greatly enhance the tracking capabilities of user companies. Simplified Software is a company that's open, helpful, and understands the complex needs of its customers. The technical nature of the product didn't need to be conveyed in the design. The content speaks to the market niche and the product capabilities. Don't assume technology companies want a site from the 25th century.

Products that are very technical tend to be developed by people not very interested in design. Problems arise if users aren't of the same mind as the developers/programmers who built the Web-based application or software product. As an example, the Artes company—located in Velenje, Slovenia—developed an air pollution monitoring system for air quality control at a Tuzla canton in Bosnia-Herzegovina. The monitoring system collects data about air pollution from different locations. Data travel over phone lines or wireless Ethernet to a central computer and are saved in a database (mySQL).

The user, the Environmental Protection Agency, can access the data online. The Web application extracts the data to an XML document that is transformed, by XSLT, to an SVG document for display. There are three main elements to the application:

- Extracting data from a database as XML documents

- Converting XML documents to SVG using XSLT

- Using Java to display SVG documents with Batic

  The application consists of five layers:

- Presentation layer

- Application layer

- Service layer

- Business layer

- Persistence layer

  Figure 10-17 shows data for the region, resulting from code.

  Listing 10-5 shows a section of the XML that contains data from the mySQL database.

FIGURE 10-17 *SVG with region results*

LISTING 10-5 *Air Pollution Monitoring System XML Sample*

```
<?xml version="1.0" encoding="iso-8859-2"?>
<display-data name="MAP">
    <tag name="SO2.MP1">2</tag>
    <tag name="SO2.MP2">3</tag>
    <tag name="SO2.MP3">4</tag>
    <tag name="SO2.MP4">3,4</tag>
    <tag name="SO2.MP5">2,5</tag>
    <tag name="SO2.MP6">2,5</tag>
    <tag name="DOOR.MP6">1</tag>
    <tag name="DOOR.MP5">345</tag>
    <tag name="DOOR.MP4">1</tag>
    <tag name="DOOR.MP3">0</tag>
    <tag name="DOOR.MP2">1</tag>
    <tag name="DOOR.MP1">0</tag>
</display-data>
```

Listing 10-6 shows a sample of the XSLT that transforms the XML document from Listing 10-5 to SVG.

LISTING 10-6 *Air Pollution Monitoring System XSLT Sample*

```xml
<?xml version="1.0" encoding="iso-8859-2"?>
<xsl:stylesheet version="1.0"
    xmlns:xsl="http://www.w3.org/1999/XSL/Transform"
    xmlns="http://www.w3.org/2000/svg"
    xmlns:xlink="http://www.w3.org/1999/xlink">
<xsl:output method="xml" version="1.0" indent="no"
encoding="windows-1250"
    cdata-section-elements="script" />
<xsl:strip-space elements="*" />
<xsl:template match="display-data">
<!--selection of data which to be displayed-->
<xsl:variable name="SO2.MP1">
<xsl:value-of select="tag[@name='test1']" /></xsl:variable>
<xsl:variable name="SO2.MP2"><xsl:value-of
select="tag[@name='test2']" /></xsl:variable>
<xsl:variable name="SO2.MP3"><xsl:value-of
select="tag[@name='test3']" /></xsl:variable>
<xsl:variable name="SO2.MP4"><xsl:value-of
select="tag[@name='test4']" /></xsl:variable>
<xsl:variable name="SO2.MP5"><xsl:value-of
select="tag[@name='test5']" /></xsl:variable>
<xsl:variable name="SO2.MP6"><xsl:value-of
select="tag[@name='test6']" /></xsl:variable>
<xsl:variable name="DOOR.MP1"><xsl:value-of
select="tag[@name='test1_DI']"/></xsl:variable>
<xsl:variable name="DOOR.MP2"><xsl:value-of
select="tag[@name='test2_DI']"/></xsl:variable>
<xsl:variable name="DOOR.MP3"><xsl:value-of
select="tag[@name='test3_DI']"/></xsl:variable>
<xsl:variable name="DOOR.MP4"><xsl:value-of
select="tag[@name='test4_DI']" /></xsl:variable>
<xsl:variable name="DOOR.MP5"><xsl:value-of
select="tag[@name='test5_DI']"/></xsl:variable>
<xsl:variable name="DOOR.MP6"><xsl:value-of
select="tag[@name='test6_DI']"/></xsl:variable>

<svg viewBox="0 0 800 600" width="100%" height="100%">
<g id="station">
<g class="measurement">
<xsl:choose>
```

```
<xsl:when test="$DOOR.MP1>0"><ellipse id="L1" cx="22" cy="306"
rx="5" ry="5"  style="fill:rgb(255,0,0); stroke:rgb(0,0,0);
stroke-width:1" />
</xsl:when>
<xsl:when test="$DOOR.MP1='????'"><ellipse id="L1"
cx="22" cy="306" rx="5" ry="5" style="fill:rgb(0,0,0);
stroke:rgb(0,0,0); stroke-width:1" />
</xsl:when>
<xsl:otherwise><ellipse id="L1" cx="22" cy="306" rx="5" ry="5"
style="fill:rgb(0,192,0); stroke:rgb(0,0,0); stroke-width:1"
/>
</xsl:otherwise>
</xsl:choose>
</g>
<g class="location_data" transform="translate(-13 152)">
<a xlink:type="simple" xlink:href="map1b.svg">
<rect x="30" y="100" width="120" height="43"
style="fill:none; stroke:rgb(0,102,204); stroke-width:2" />
<rect x="30" y="100" width="120" height="43"
style="fill:rgb(0,102,204); fill-opacity:0.8" />
<rect x="35" y="120" width="110" height="17"
style="fill:rgb(179,218,255); fill-opacity:0.5" />
<text x="35px" y="115px" style="fill:rgb(255,255,255);
font-size:12;font-family:arial">ML</text></a>
<text x="40px" y="133px" style="fill:rgb(0,0,0);
font-size:12;font-family:arial">NO</text>
<text x="105px" y="133px" style="fill:rgb(0,0,0);
font-size:12;font-family:arial;text-anchor:end">
<xsl:value-of select="$SO2.MP1" /></text>
</g>
.....
```

The SVG displays in real time using Batic.

Using the same procedure, with different XML and XSLT documents, more detailed information for each location returns in real time. Figure 10-18 shows data for a specific location.

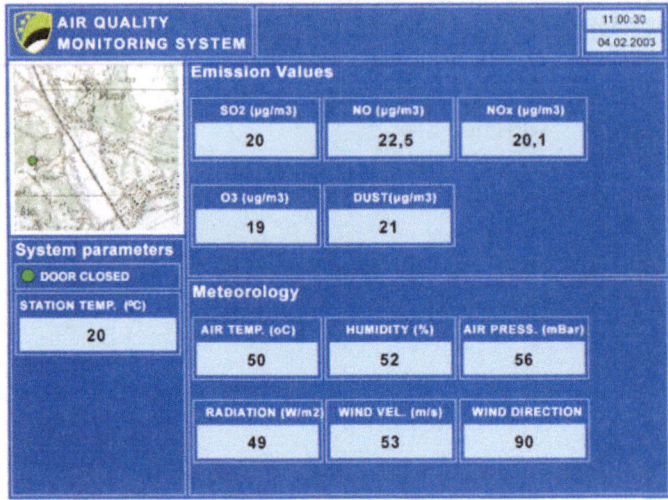

FIGURE 10-18 *SVG with location results*

Detailed data reports can return for a specific location, as shown in Figure 10-19.

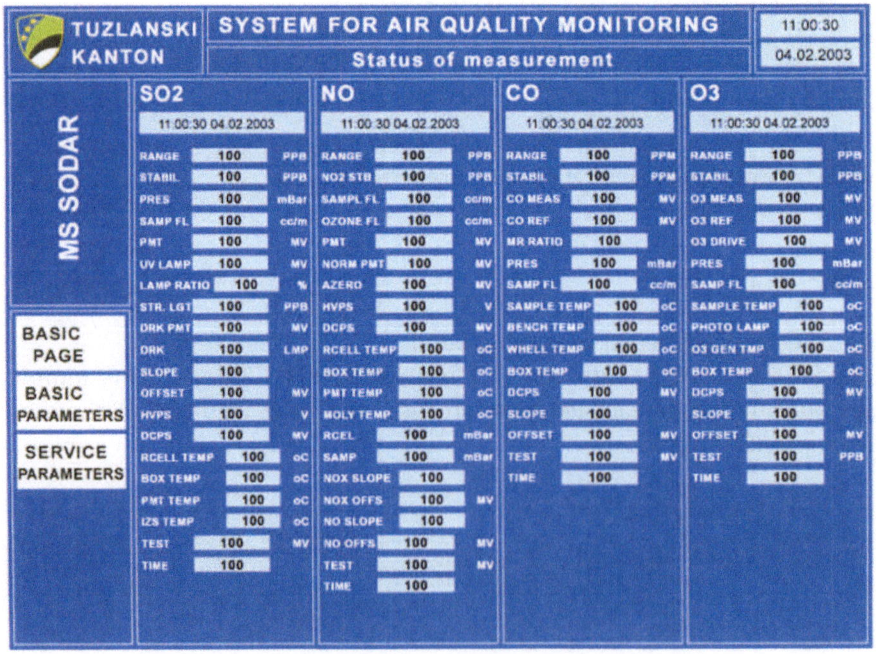

FIGURE 10-19 *SVG with detailed data for a specific location*

Additional XML and XSLT documents generate reports for data specific dates, times, and locations. Additional project information includes the following:

The project's presentation layer uses flat XSLT files with other XML documents dynamically created by the application layer. Then, depending on the querying data, an XSLT file converts an XML document to SVG for user graphic presentation. The SVG document is displayed with Java using Batic.

The project's application layer retrieves current data from the service layer and creates XML documents for the presentation layer.

The service layer contains session beans representing controllers in the J2EE layer architecture. In the session bean Facade design pattern, session beans always mask entity beans. Session beans represent use cases and can therefore delimit transactional boundaries. Session beans are an extension of the client on the server side.

The business layer of the Enterprise JavaBean (EJB) application contains business objects shared by multiple clients. Entity beans represent a row in a database and a Java object. Entity beans are two types, Container Managed Persistent (CMP) entity beans and Bean Managed Persistent (BMP) entity beans. The TagCMP bean has eight persistent fields: Date, Description, Group, Id, Rules, SourceAddress, Value, and ValueType.

The persistence layer uses a mySQL open-source database bundled with JBoss.

Because the project is more of a technical Web-based application than a typical Web site, developers tend to limit their involvement with design. In this case, however, Figure 10-20 can be more easily read with better alignment and a white background. You can change SVG text that blurs on the screen can from Arial to Courier, which results in a less than perfect style but for a crisper screen readability. Better alignment enhances readability as well. Figure 10-20 shows an original section, and Figure 10-21 shows the start of simple design improvements on the right. You can easily adjust SVG font, color, size, and space.

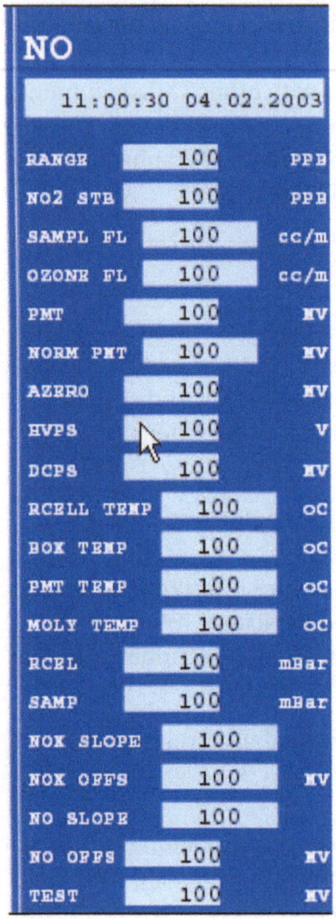

NO		
11:00:30 04.02.2003		
RANGE	100	PPB
NO2 STB	100	PPB
SAMPL FL	100	cc/m
OZONE FL	100	cc/m
PMT	100	MV
NORM PMT	100	MV
AZERO	100	MV
HVPS	100	V
DCPS	100	MV
RCELL TEMP	100	oC
BOX TEMP	100	oC
PMT TEMP	100	oC
MOLY TEMP	100	oC
RCEL	100	mBar
SAMP	100	mBar
NOX SLOPE	100	
NOX OFFS	100	MV
NO SLOPE	100	
NO OFFS	100	MV
TEST	100	MV

FIGURE 10-20 *Original screenshot section*

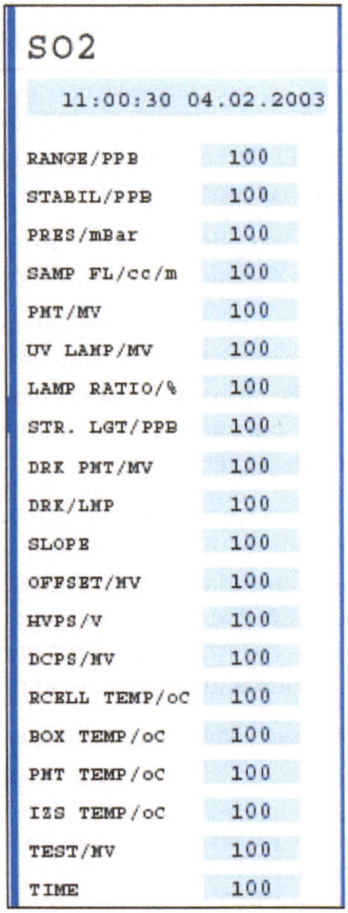

SO2	
11:00:30 04.02.2003	
RANGE/PPB	100
STABIL/PPB	100
PRES/mBar	100
SAMP FL/cc/m	100
PMT/MV	100
UV LAMP/MV	100
LAMP RATIO/%	100
STR. LGT/PPB	100
DRK PMT/MV	100
DRK/LMP	100
SLOPE	100
OFFSET/MV	100
HVPS/V	100
DCPS/MV	100
RCELL TEMP/oC	100
BOX TEMP/oC	100
PMT TEMP/oC	100
IZS TEMP/oC	100
TEST/MV	100
TIME	100

FIGURE 10-21 *Modifications for improved readability*

Once a project is in place for 90 days, a user analysis follow-up session can provide valuable new feedback. During this user analysis, developers often focus on functionality when simple style modifications such as readability changes can greatly enhance usability.

Implementing Usability

Readability is only the beginning of usability. Browsers currently support many aspects of accessibility, yet the majority of companies, organizations, and individuals don't develop for the significant audience of people with disabilities. By law (in the United States), federal Web sites and the Web sites of organizations or individuals the government does business with must be accessible to people with disabilities. Unfortunately, the private sector, in many cases, isn't adopting technologies and designs for people with visual, hearing, or mobility impairments. There are many resources on the Web for learning about accessibility. Information found from 25 sites includes the following information:

An estimated 20 percent of people living in the United States (40.8 million individuals) have some kind of disability.

An estimated 10 percent (27.3 million individuals) have a severe disability and limited Internet access.

Approximately 4 percent (10.4 million individuals) are visually impaired or blind. Approximately .5 percent (1.3 million individuals) are legally blind. Approximately 2 percent (5.7 million individuals) of elderly people are blind or visually impaired. Approximately .2 percent (57,300 individuals) of children are legally blind.

Approximately 10 percent of male individuals and .5 percent of female individuals experience some form of color deficiency such as color blindness.

The World Wide Web Consortium (W3C) and federal guidelines state there are five types of disabilities that affect Internet usage:

- Visual impairments
- Hearing impairments
- Mobility impairments
- Cognitive impairments
- Seizure disorders

Disabilities also include long-term or short-term access issues such as an eye or hand injury or recovery from illness. No final set of international guidelines for accessibility has been established to cover all needs. It's important, however, to learn how you can adjust code to increase access to the sites you develop. The following quick explanations offer a starting point; however, you'll need more comprehensive information to design and develop sites that truly serve the public.

Users with visual disabilities often rely on screen readers, which are software programs that read text on the screen and output the content to either a speech synthesizer or a Braille display. Some people who are blind use text-based browsers or voice browsers. The following steps, according to the W3C, help eliminate barriers for this group:

- Use `alt` text for all images.

- Describe data images such as charts; don't just label them.

- Describe videos in text and in audio.

- Organize tables and forms so that tabbing through data coincides with the logical progression of how the table or form reads.

- Eliminate frames; if that's not possible, offer a no-frame alternative.

- Provide keyboard support for all commands.

- Use standard document formats.

Users with impaired vision may access the Web with a large monitor with these provisions:

- They can change font sizes with author style sheets (no absolute font sizes).

- The layout supports size increases of pages without increased difficulty in navigation.

- Author style sheets can override images for more contrast.

- They can view text and images, when enlarged, on a monitor without extensive horizontal scrolling.

Users with color blindness can access the Web when designer and developer considerations include the following:

- Color used as a unique marker, such as a link with `text-decoration:none`, should have some other indication that it's unique, such as italic or bold italic. If possible, keep links underlined; individuals who are color blind can't see the emphasis of color alone.

- Text and background needs enough color contrast that the two can be easily differentiated.

- The site contains the ability to override author style sheets.

Users who are deaf or hard of hearing have better access to the Web when designers and developers offer the following:

- Captions or transcripts of audio files

- Images in the context of text for individuals without a history of written/spoken language

- Options other than voice input on Web and mobile output devices

- The ability to adjust volume for users with limited hearing capability

- The ability to easily toggle between audio files and their supporting text

In addition, users with physical disabilities need more time to respond to Web data requests. In many cases, these users can't operate a mouse, so keyboard options should be available for navigating and interacting with a site. Forms need to be organized logically and accessible with keyboard options.

Users with speech disabilities need alternate modes of communication when voice-based interaction is required.

Users with dyslexia need alternative modalities such as video or audio and supplementary images to minimize difficulties in reading a narrative.

Furthermore, users with Attention Deficit Disorder (ADD) may experience difficulty in focusing on information. Sites with clear and consistent organization and no distracting visual or audio elements, such as blinking moving banners, enhance user interaction for this group.

Users with impaired intelligence, memory impairments, or mental health disabilities may learn slowly or have difficulty in learning and retaining complex concepts. They may rely more on graphics to facilitate understanding. Graphical support and clear, consistent navigation helps this group of users access, understand, and retain the contents of a Web site.

Much more information is available about this important topic. All considerations you make as a designer and developer toward increased access play a significant role in the usability of the products you develop. The following section offers a few ideas that demonstrate some of the accessibility issues described.

Considering Accessibility: Geometry and SVG

SVG has tremendous potential for creating educational materials because it's free, open source, and can run on any fifth-generation and above browser with an SVG reader. The product in this section provides a learning style not possible with a textbook. The main idea is to use SVG to make interesting graphics and animation that help students understand basic geometry.

Text graphics, for this example, include the traditional approach of drawn triangles, an explanation on finding the area of a triangle, and exercises for the student to perform. The SVG is an animated sequence of images and text designed to teach how to find the area of a triangle. The following figures present the basic idea of the SVG exercise. Figure 10-22 shows the initial image on the left and the beginning iteration of the animation on the right.

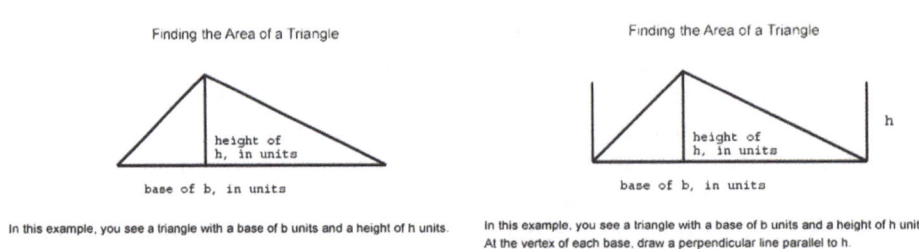

FIGURE 10-22 *Initial and transition images for the triangle sequence*

Figure 10-23 represents the next frames of the triangle animation.

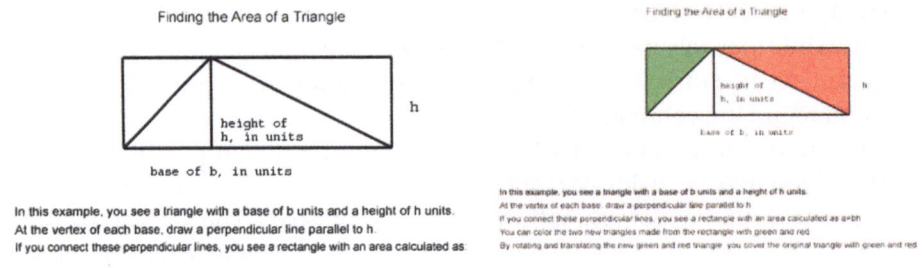

FIGURE 10-23 *Completed rectangle (left) and filled rectangle (right)*

Figure 10-24 slowly rotates around as additional explanatory text appears.

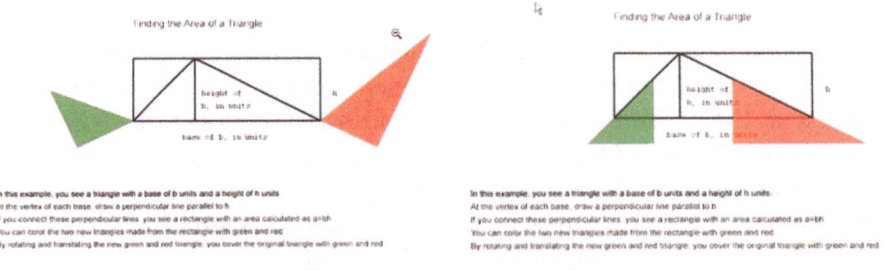

FIGURE 10-24 *Movement and text for concept*

Figure 10-25 shows how the site looks with the color and final text in place.

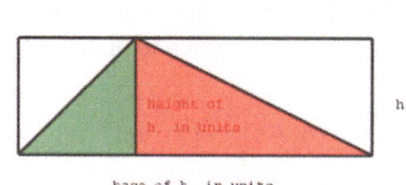

Finding the Area of a Triangle

height of
h, in units

h

base of b, in units

In this example, you see a triangle with a base of b units and a height of h units.

At the vertex of each base, draw a perpendicular line parallel to h.

If you connect these perpendicular lines, you see a rectangle with an area calculated as a=bh

You can color the two new triangles made from the rectangle with green and red.

By rotating and translating the new green and red triangle, you cover the original triangle with green and red.

As you see, the area of the original triangle is half of the area of the rectangle.

The area of a triangle is one half of the product of its base and height.

In algebra $\qquad a = \dfrac{1}{2}\, bh$

FIGURE 10-25 *Movement of color*

The animated triangle with its color and evolving text appears to enhance the learning process. Action, color, and text can help students with different learning styles form a clearer idea of a concept. A sixth-year student or an older student returning to the classroom after a decade or two might find this a nice addition to the text. That said, there are serious accessibility problems with the exercise.

Incorporating Accessibility

First, most people who are color blind (about one in 12) can't distinguish between shades of red and green. Shades of these colors appear lighter or darker to people who are color blind. The two most common forms of color blindness leave users unable to perceive red (protanopia) or green (deuteranopia). A much rarer form leaves users unable to perceive blue (tritanopia).

You can easily change the red and green to yellow and blue, greatly increasing accessibility for users with color blindness. Yellow allows more transparency for the right triangle, and few users aren't able to distinguish the blue triangle. The few who can't see blue will be able to see the yellow one as a guideline.

Second, students with reading disabilities can't follow animation easily. In a short time, you can create graphics at different points in the animation and link to the next graphic for students struggling with animation movement, taking color and font size into account, as shown in Figure 10-26.

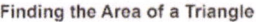

Finding the Area of a Triangle

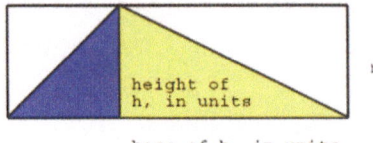

height of h, in units

base of b, in units

1. In this example, you see a triangle with a base of b units and a height of h units.
2. At the vertex of each base, draw a perpendicular line parallel to h.
3. You can color the two new triangles made from the rectangle with blue and yellow.
4. By rotating and translating the new blue and yellow triangle, you cover the original triangle with blue and yellow.
5. As you see, the area of the original triangle is half of the area of the rectangle.
6. The area of a triangle is one half of the product of its base and height.
7. In algebra $a = \frac{1}{2} bh$

Begin

FIGURE 10-26 *Quick changes for enhanced accessibility*

One approach to accessibility for this product is to use the original animation with accessible support options. For example, an entry page with text, audio, and icons representing possible viewing options for the project might include a graphic with an L representing larger visualization, an A representing an audio presentation, a V representing a video presentation, and a G representing a graphical presentation. On each page of the site, these icons would be large, consistently positioned, clearly visible, and return audio as well. Figure 10-27 shows a quick sketch, over a graphic, noting changes that would result in better usability. An explanation of the purpose of the icons would introduce the graphics and include clear text, graphic, and audio definitions of the navigation.

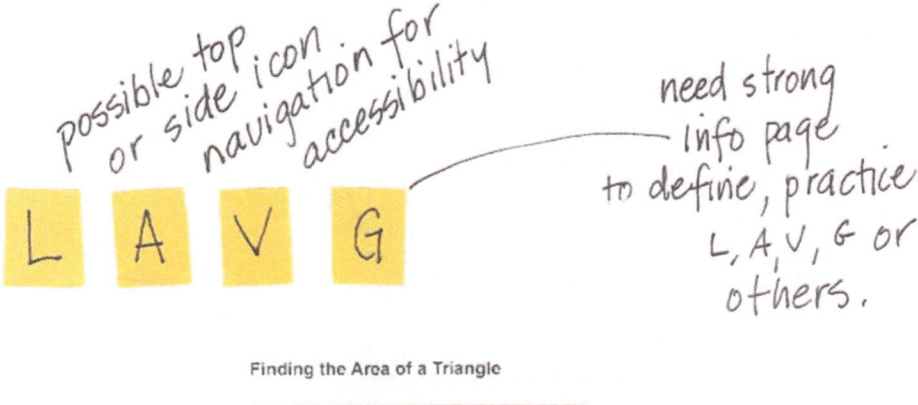

possible top icon
or side icon for
navigation for
accessibility

need strong
info page
to define, practice
L, A, V, G or
others.

Finding the Area of a Triangle

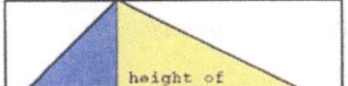

height of
h, in units

h

base of b, in units

1. In this example, you see a triangle with a base of b units and a height of h units.

2. At the vertex of each base, draw a perpendicular line parallel to h.

3. You can color the two new triangles made from the rectangle with blue and yellow.

4. By rotating and translating the new blue and yellow triangle, you cover the original triangle with blue and yellow.

5. As you see, the area of the original triangle is half of the area of the rectangle.

6. The area of a triangle is one half of the product of its base and height.

7. In algebra $a = \frac{1}{2}bh$

Begin

FIGURE 10-27 *Possible navigation additions for enhanced accessibility*

The SVG triangle exercise, in this case, evolved to a prototype for a math textbook and companion Web site. The prototype incorporated accessibility variations from the Figure 10-27 concept. Buttons added were V for Video, A for Audio/Large, and G for Graphic. Video for the prototype became a combination of SVG and QuickTime videos for instructor demonstrations of problems. Initial user analysis suggested that students weren't accessing QuickTime on previous products because of slow download times. Thus, the publisher determined SVG be used in most cases for video and QuickTime be used intermittently.

A for Audio/Large incorporated large-sized graphics and a clear audio presentation of the problem. The emphasis with Large is to show oversized images without distorting overall understanding of the problem. In this case, zooming in on one portion of the triangle problem can't cut off another portion, or students will miss the overall concept. Figure 10-28 shows the rotating triangle as a large graphic.

Example 1   Fifth Graphic   in-depth   the big picture   technical help Note: Large top links are not activated on prototype

Link to: Next Graphic or Previous Graphic

Finding the Area of a Triangle

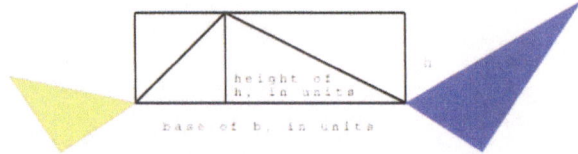

By rotating and translating the new yellow and blue rectangle, you cover the original triangle with yellow and blue.

FIGURE 10-28 *Large graphic example, rotating shape*

The prototypes also incorporate large graphic instructions and links. Figure 10-29 shows an additional frame from the triangle exercise.

Example 1   Sixth Graphic   in-depth   the big picture   technical help Note: Large top links are not activated on prototype

Link to: Next Graphic or Previous Graphic

Finding the Area of a Triangle

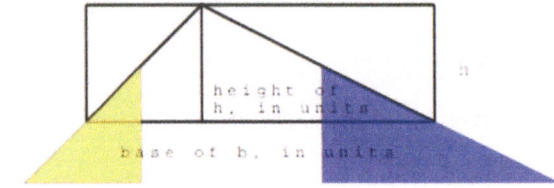

Rotating toward center.

FIGURE 10-29 *Large graphic example, second example*

G for Graphic incorporates a standard-sized graphic. Moving images are difficult for some learners. Audio was added to G as well, in a different fashion from in the Audio/Large section. Students lose one-on-one contact with teachers in an online learning environment. The G section incorporates the audio of a teacher communicating with students in a more informal manner than with A. In G, the audio explains the problem and supports student learning. G may include additional explanations or commentary by the teacher. In A, the audio is a clear, simple presentation of the problem. G graphics are standard sized, as shown in Figure 10-30.

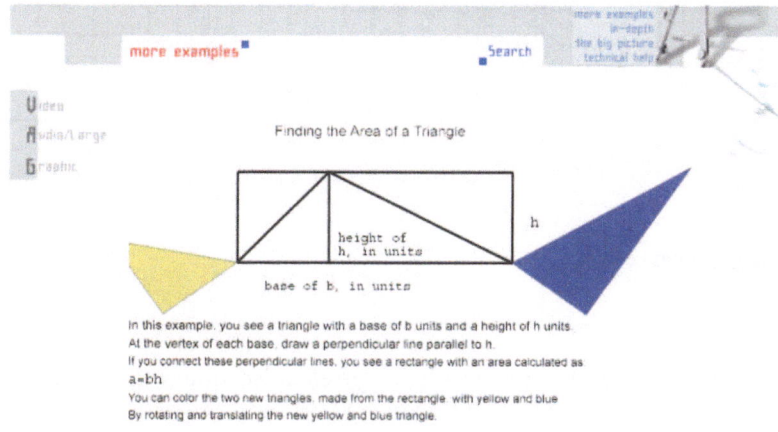

FIGURE 10-30 *Rotating triangles*

The triangle rotation and fill must not deter from the basic understanding of the math exercise. Sometimes incorporating accessibility distorts the meaning of the original author intent. Figure 10-31 suggests movement and supports the exercise, even though it's a static image.

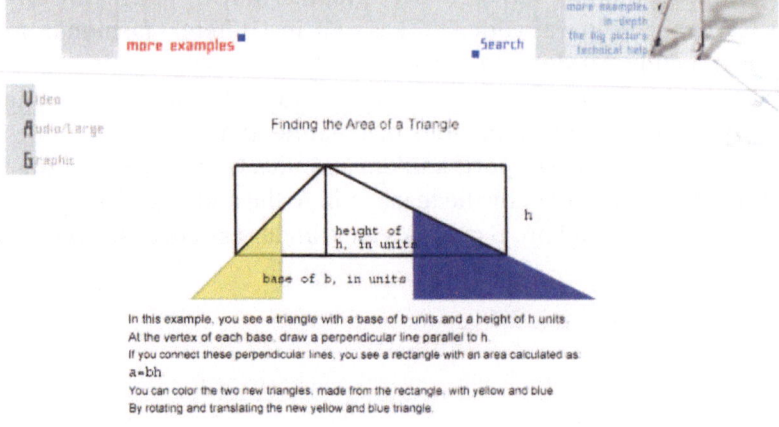

FIGURE 10-31 *Triangle sliding into place*

Figure 10-32 shows the last image of the triangle exercise, under the G button.

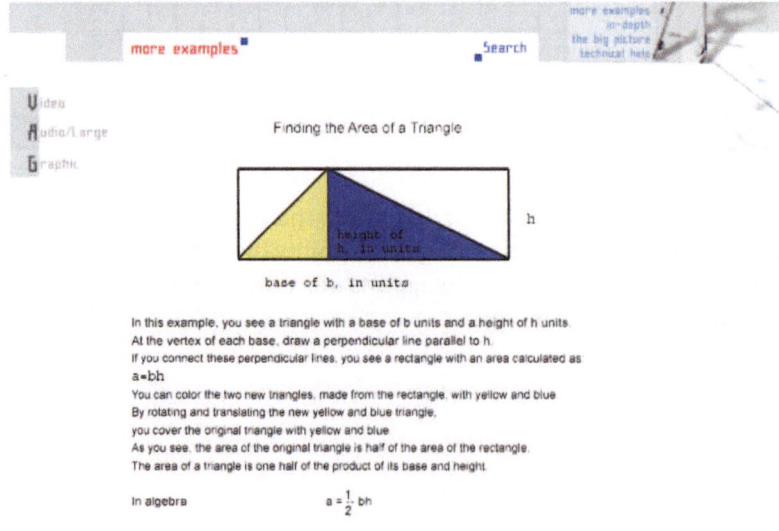

FIGURE 10-32 *Final triangle image under the G button*

Listing 10-7 shows the SVG that creates the triangle animation.

LISTING 10-7 *Triangle Animation SVG*

```
<svg width="500" height="500">

<g transform= "scale(0.94) translate(-180,-10)" >

<line x1="400" y1="100" x2="400" y2="200" style="stroke:black;
stroke-width:3; fill:none;" />
<polyline points="300 200,400 100, 600 200, 300 200"
style="stroke:black; stroke-width:3; fill:none; " />
<line x1="300" y1="200" x2="300" y="100" style="stroke:black;
stroke-width:3; fill:none; visibility:hidden;">
<animate attributeName="y2" begin="2s" dur="1s" from="200"
to="100" fill="freeze" />
<set attributeName="visibility" attributeType="CSS"
to="visible" begin="2s" dur="1s" fill="freeze" />
</line>
<line x1="600" y1="200" x2="600" y="100" style="stroke:black;
stroke-width:3; fill:none; visibility:hidden;">
<animate attributeName="y2" begin="2s" dur="1s" from="200"
to="100" fill="freeze" />
<set attributeName="visibility" attributeType="CSS"
to="visible" begin="2s" dur="1s" fill="freeze" />
</line>
<line x1="300" y1="100" x2="600" y2="100" style="stroke:black;
stroke-width:3; fill:none; visibility:hidden;">
<animate attributeName="x2" begin="5s" dur="1s" from="300"
to="600" fill="freeze" />
<set attributeName="visibility" attributeType="CSS"
to="visible" begin="5s" dur="1s" fill="freeze" />
</line>
<polyline points="300 200,300 100, 400 100, 300 200"
style="stroke:black; fill:yellow; opacity:0.6;
visibility:hidden; ">
<set attributeName="visibility" attributeType="CSS"
to="visible" begin="9s" dur="1s" fill="freeze" />
<animateTransform attributeName="transform" additive="sum"
type="rotate" from="0 300 200;" to="-180,300,200" begin="11s"
dur="4s" fill="freeze"/>
<animateTransform attributeName="transform" additive="sum"
type="translate" from="0 0;" to="-100 100" begin="15s"
dur="4s" fill="freeze" />
</polyline>
```

```
<polyline points="400 100,600 100, 600 200, 400 100"
style="stroke:black; fill:blue; opacity:0.6;
visibility:hidden;">
<set attributeName="visibility" attributeType="CSS"
to="visible" begin="9s" dur="1s" fill="freeze" />
<animateTransform attributeName="transform" additive="sum"
type="rotate" from="0 600 200;" to="180,600,200" begin="11s"
dur="4s" fill="freeze"/>
<animateTransform attributeName="transform" additive="sum"
type="translate" from="0 0;" to="200 100" begin="15s" dur="4s"
fill="freeze" />
</polyline>
<text x="340" y="60" style="font-family:arial, helvetica,
sans-serif; font-size:16; fill:black;">Finding the Area of a Triangle</text>
<text x="410" y="177" style="font-family:courier, 'courier
new', mono; font-size:14; fill:black;">height of</text>
<text x="410" y="192" style="font-family:courier, 'courier
new', mono; font-size:14; fill:black;">h, in units</text>
<text x="330" y="230" style="font-family:courier, 'courier
new', mono; font-size:14; fill:black;">base of b, in
units</text>
<text x="620" y="160" style="font-family:courier, 'courier
new', mono;font-size:16; fill:black; visibility:hidden;">h
<set attributeName="visibility" attributeType="CSS"
to="visible" begin="2s" dur="1s" fill="freeze" /></text>
</g>
<g transform= " scale(0.93)translate(-80,-2)" >
<text x="80" y="270" style="font-family:arial, helvetica,
sans-serif; font-size:14; fill:black;">In this example, you
see a triangle with a base of b units and a height of
h units.</text>
<text x="80" y="290" style="font-family:arial, helvetica,
sans-serif; font-size:14;fill:black; visibility:hidden;">At
the vertex of each base, draw a perpendicular line
parallel to h.
<set attributeName="visibility" attributeType="CSS" to="visible"
begin="2s" dur="1s" fill="freeze" /></text>
<text x="80" y="310" style="font-family:arial, helvetica,
sans-serif;font-size:13; fill:black; visibility:hidden;">
If you connect these perpendicular lines, you see a
rectangle with an area calculated as:
<set attributeName="visibility" attributeType="CSS"
to="visible" begin="4s" dur="1s" fill="freeze" /></text>
```

```
<text x="80" y="330" style="font-family:courier, 'courier
new', mono; font-size:16; fill:black; visibility:hidden;">a=bh
<set attributeName="visibility" attributeType="CSS"
to="visible" begin="6s" dur="1s" fill="freeze" /></text>
<text x="80" y="350" style="font-family:arial, helvetica,
sans-serif; font-size:13; fill:black; visibility:hidden;">
You can color the two new triangles, made from the rectangle,
with yellow and blue.
<set attributeName="visibility" attributeType="CSS"
to="visible" begin="8s" dur="1s" fill="freeze" /></text>
<text x="80" y="370" style="font-family:arial, helvetica,
sans-serif; font-size:13; fill:black; visibility:hidden;">
By rotating and translating the new yellow and blue triangle,
<set attributeName="visibility" attributeType="CSS"
to="visible" begin="8s" dur="1s" fill="freeze" /></text>
<text x="80" y="390" style="font-family:arial, helvetica,
sans-serif; font-size:13; fill:black; visibility:hidden;">
you cover the original triangle with yellow and blue.
<set attributeName="visibility" attributeType="CSS"
to="visible" begin="18s" dur="1s" fill="freeze" /></text>
<text x="80" y="410" style="font-family:arial, helvetica,
sans-serif; font-size:13; fill:black; visibility:hidden;">
As you see, the area of the original triangle is half of the
area of the rectangle.
<set attributeName="visibility" attributeType="CSS"
to="visible" begin="22s" dur="1s" fill="freeze" /></text>
<text x="80" y="430" style="font-family:arial, helvetica,
sans-serif; font-size:13;fill:black; visibility:hidden;">
The area of a triangle is one half of the product of its
base and height.
<set attributeName="visibility" attributeType="CSS"
to="visible" begin="24s" dur="1s" fill="freeze" /></text>
<text x="80" y="470" style="font-family:arial, helvetica,
sans-serif;;font-size:14; fill:black; visibility:hidden;">
In algebra<tspan x="298">a = --</tspan><tspan x="320"
y="462">1</tspan><tspan x="320" y="480">2</tspan>
<tspan x="335" y="470">bh</tspan>
<set attributeName="visibility" attributeType="CSS"
to="visible" begin="26s" dur="1s" fill="freeze" /></text>
</g>

</svg>
```

Presenting Accessible Products

Multiple versions of the same product harkens back to the early browser days with different sites for Apple and Windows products. Creating one simple site that meets usability requirements results in primarily text-based sites or content so large that users without visual impairment find it difficult to read the screen. Text-based sites are popular for certain audiences, but consumers prefer graphics, some text, and simple-to-navigate Web sites that react quickly.

Users determine final decisions regarding accessibility and navigation. Design and development time may become costly with accessibility site enhancements, but the increase in target market size surpasses initial expense. Consider users, markets, client relationships, and sales when determining whether to create a site that meets accessibility guidelines. Then vote your conscience; the Web is about access, and disabled users benefit as much or more from the opportunities that the Internet offers.

When conversations with potential users who are disabled aren't possible, defer to the W3C and federal guidelines. Additional quality research comes from speaking with members of organizations who advocate for people with disabilities.

For additional ideas and resources, please see the Web site http://www.praxis.ws.

Accessibility Axioms

The power of design and accessibility is in creating a shared world for a transnational audience. By incorporating design concepts with usability requirements, you significantly expand the perception, understanding, and appreciation of your work. You don't need to memorize all of the ideas offered in this chapter or categorize them as though they're a group of Java classes. The key to creating successful relationships between clients and users on the Web is in your understanding of the language, priorities, and passions of your client and the needs, expectations, and hopes of the user. As a designer and developer, you have the privilege of connecting people through language and images—two of the most powerful and significant assets we have.

Considering the design concepts and design elements presented in these chapters will help you satisfy clients with the style of Web sites you develop as well as with their functionality.

Index